Researching Leisure, Sport and Tourism

Researching Leisure, Sport and Tourism

The Essential Guide

Jonathan Long

SAGE Publications
Los Angeles • London • New Delhi • Singapore

© Jonathan Long 2007

First published 2007

SAGE Publications Ltd
1 Oliver's Yard
55 City Road
London EC1Y 1SP

SAGE Publications Inc.
2455 Teller Road
Thousand Oaks, California 91320

SAGE Publications India Pvt Ltd
B 1/I 1 Mohan Cooperative Industrial Area
Mathura Road, New Delhi 110 044

SAGE Publications Asia-Pacific Pte Ltd
33 Pekin Street #02-01
Far East Square
Singapore 048763

Library of Congress Control Number: 2006935865

British Library Cataloguing in Publication data

A catalogue record for this book is available from the British Library

✓ISBN 978-0-7619-4453-9
ISBN 978-0-7619-4454-6 (pbk)

Typeset by C&M Digitals Pvt Ltd., Chennai, India
Printed in Great Britain by The Cromwell Press Ltd, Trowbridge, Wiltshire
Printed on paper from sustainable resources

Contents

List of Figures

List of Tables

Foreword

Over the years I have had the privilege of working with some very talented researchers. I have tried to learn something from each of them, so if the people concerned think they see some of their ideas in this book I hope they will at least be able to satisfy themselves that I was listening. I also have to thank a number of my present colleagues as well as the publisher's reviewers for providing comments on draft chapters.

A special thanks, though, should go to Brian Duffield, who gave me my first job in research (a three-month contract that became 11 years).

My research into methods took me into wider areas than I'd originally envisaged. If readers are interested in exploring these areas, I would direct them to my website: www.leedsmet.ac.uk/carnegie/default/jalong.htm (look for 'Research Methods Resources').

Firstly, there are two substantive chapters on Personal Histories and Action Research.

There then follow some case studies/exemplars edited out of the book:

- different forms of dissertation challenge (associated with Chapter 2 on research design and the research process)
- a short section dealing with systematic review and meta analysis and a summary of some of the key data sets for people researching leisure, sport and tourism (associated with Chapter 3)
- a case study associated with Chapter 7 on interviewing
- a personal experience of participant observation (associated with Chapter 8)
- an exemplar associated with Chapter 9 on interpreting texts
- an exercise in coding qualitative data associated with Chapter 12
- an example of a 'mock' research proposal associated with Chapter 16 on ways of writing and communicating
- some guidelines for those having to write a research brief for others.

1

Wanting to Know

> Whatever you can do or dream you can do, begin it. Boldness has genius, magic and power in it. Begin it now. (Popularly attributed to Johann Wolfgang von Goethe)

Research should be exciting because, quite simply, it is about discovery, finding out. It provides challenges that people resolve in different ways. This chapter introduces that challenge and tries to reinforce the desire to do research. People should not be deterred if they have an image of research involving extremely complex procedures. A thoughtful and careful person can soon acquire the necessary knowledge and skills, but slapdash, casual research should certainly be discouraged. Just as we should not be prepared to accept a simplistic understanding of the subjects under study so we should be critical of simplistic (mis)understandings of what is meant by research. Hence the task of this book is to offer guidance on making appropriate decisions in reaching towards better research.

The Appeal of Research

For me research is the natural activity of an inquiring mind; it is simply what humans do. I enjoy the detective story that is research, the challenge of acquiring evidence and resolving problems. Others see research as being difficult, boring or unimportant. I hope to persuade you that none of these need be so. In practice, of course, people do research on a daily basis though it may go unregarded, for example: finding out what friends and family would like for presents; comparing prices when shopping; or working out how much alcohol can be drunk without getting a hangover.

I find it hard to imagine a job graduates of leisure, sport and tourism courses are likely to find themselves in that will not require some dealing with research: commissioning or managing; conducting; assessing its significance for policy and practice; even interpreting its (mis)representations in the media. Within their jobs people have to interpret data from some budget or output figures, gather evidence for reports, work out whether a new product/service will sell better than an existing one, or know whether data published in a professional magazine are reliable.

Is researching leisure, sport and tourism any different from doing research in other areas of social study? In terms of the range of the techniques used, the answer has to be, 'Not a lot'. The practical and theoretical context is different, but it involves the same or similar techniques as many others. Importantly for us though, people 'out there' quite like answering the questions or talking about their leisure experiences. Unfortunately for us though, this is partly because they, with some justification, think they are experts. So while they may be more willing to be involved in the research they are also more likely to be critical of it, questioning the premises and the findings.

In doing my research I like to feel that I am contributing to the wider debate. This means that the research needs to relate to the key concepts people are discussing and using in leisure, sport and tourism, rather than existing in some vacuum. It may sometimes be possible to get away with knowing little about the context of the subject under investigation, but more is needed if the goal is to understand social processes rather than just model their outcomes in describing patterns of behaviour. I want to avoid the misapprehension that research is some superior form of data gathering through which the facts will speak for themselves. Facts, if there are such things in the social sciences, do not speak for themselves. These supposed facts are jointly constructed by the acts of researchers and the operations of the social processes being examined, so need to be interpreted in that light. It is important that we should understand how this knowledge is produced.

Discussion of research methods is often embedded in complicated language that puts people off. As a result I have tried to define key terms as I go along, but at the end of the book have also provided a glossary to aid understanding. The glossary is intended to give you enough information to 'get you through' rather than being the definitive explanation. As you read more widely and your understanding of research methods grows, you will arrive at more refined definitions of these terms.

Can We Identify Good Research?

The challenge I throw out to first time researchers is, 'Why should I believe you rather than my mate, Dave, down the pub?' Believe me, Dave has an answer for everything and can be very persuasive in arguing that I should believe him rather than any alternative explanation. Research has to withstand intense scrutiny. So can we identify 'good' research? What lends a piece of research the kind of credibility that will persuade people of its findings?

Following the apparent success of the scientific approach, many see the goal of social research to be to conduct *objective* studies using *valid* and *reliable* measures to produce findings that can be *generalised* beyond the study to a wider population. The feasibility, usefulness and even desirability of each aspect of this have been questioned and represent themes to which I shall return through the course of this book. In making claims of validity we are asserting that the research is indeed measuring or examining what it claims to. This expectation of research seems eminently reasonable, but involves quite some claim if our research is about complex ideas like flow, fairness, crime, health, patriarchy, power, social inclusion or globalisation. Similarly, although we might want measures that can be relied upon to be consistent (reliable) across different studies by different people, it has to be questioned how realistic a prospect this is in the context of approaches used in leisure, sport and tourism research.

In the introduction to their reader on dealing with data, Sapsford and Jupp suggest that:

> The major concern is with *validity*, by which we mean the design of research to provide credible conclusions: whether the evidence which the research offers can bear the weight of the interpretation that is put on it. Every report of research embodies an argument: 'on the basis of this evidence I argue that these conclusions are true ...' What has to be established in order that the report's conclusions can be believed is that the arguments embodied in the report are *valid* ones: that the data *do* measure or characterise what the authors claim, and that the interpretations *do* follow from them. (1996: 1)

Being objective means adopting a value neutral position free of bias and prejudice. This kind of clinical approach may be intuitively appealing, but I doubt that it is possible in the social sciences. Indeed the pretence may be unhelpful and confusing. It is unreasonable and misleading to see the researcher as a neutral, sterilised research instrument. Different people will respond to the researcher in different ways in different environments; and different researchers will see, hear and understand different things because of their personal experience, knowledge and values. A critical approach to research should be prepared to challenge at every level our presumptions about the way the world works, and indeed about the way we think and do research.

Consideration of the merits of various approaches to research commonly start with a distinction between quantitative and qualitative data. Quantitative data are based on items that can be counted and subjected to mathematical analysis (the number of people with access to a home computer, the number of participant occasions, cost of holiday, age, etc.); qualitative data are words or images that represent phenomena that do not lend themselves to precise measurement.

Different people think about the world in different ways and important philosophical principles underlie these debates, but some people just feel more comfortable with the apparent precision of measuring things, while others want to know about feelings, meanings and processes.

If I were to say, 'I feel 77 bad today', you would probably look at me in a strange way. If I said, 'I feel 77 bad today because I've had 9 negative experiences and only 2 positive ones', you might begin to think that there is some strange logic to what I'm saying, but still be quizzical as I add, 'And on top of that my stress level is 120 because my boss is a 4'.

But then I explain that:

Depression is measured by Roberts' $D = (N^2 - P^2)/d$
(number of negative experiences squared minus number of positive experiences squared, all divided by the number of days over which we are measuring)

Aha, a researcher. He must know what he is talking about.

Of course I made it up. You must not believe everything you read in books.

The methods chosen by researchers reflect assumptions held about the nature of research and the world. Failing to examine carefully what passes for objectivity may result in naive research. This is not to give approval to those attempting to pass off personal opinion as sound research – far from it. Critical research should ensure enhanced not reduced rigour. Being critical in your research approach means trying not to take things for granted. Research is about continually asking questions, not just of people, but of previous research, of the data, of the research process (to try to find the best approach) and of oneself; in short, of everything in sight. It involves a sharp focus and an appreciation of the bigger picture. It also requires an appreciation of the part played by researchers themselves in producing a particular set of findings.

A researcher should always be the most thoroughgoing critic of their own research, constantly asking questions and raising doubts. Approaching research in that way will help to enhance its quality and credibility. Imagine being interviewed on radio or television by a tough, persistent interviewer. All the points of challenge should have been addressed already, prior to, or during, the research.

Returning to my challenge about why I should believe your research rather than my mate Dave down the pub, my suggestion is that it requires:

1. a carefully formulated problem with precise terminology/definitions
2. an understanding of the surrounding context
3. credible data collection from a suitable set of sources
4. appropriate and competent analysis
5. an informed interpretation and preparedness to acknowledge contradictory evidence.

Remember – when doing small-scale research

Don't be too ambitious. Devise a 'nice little project' – it can always expand later.

Rather than covering a wide area superficially, it is normally better to explore a subject in detail so that you can say something substantive.

Be precise and carefully formulate your research task rather than just 'looking at' something. Ask yourself what questions you want to address, what information you need to do that, where you will get that information from and what you will do with it. At the same time you have to cultivate that most desirable of characteristics, an open mind.

Careful planning should involve a full literature search to situate your work in the context of research and others' thinking.

Although you have to 'own' the research, make the most of whatever help you can find: librarians, supervisors, local experts, friends who are prepared to tell you that you are wrong.

Don't procrastinate, but don't leap into the field before making proper preparations. Invest effort in negotiating access to the people and sites you need to involve in your research. You cannot expect everyone 'out there' to drop everything for you. Be prepared to make contingency plans for when that key informant refuses to see you. Persevere rather than give up when you encounter the inevitable setbacks.

Even if you are a slow reader like I am, try not to restrict your reading too much. Read widely round your topic well past your formal literature review so that you can become 'expert'.

Good research projects are a whole rather than a series of discrete entities. Make sure, for example, that the literature review is properly integrated with your own investigations and that the method and techniques you select are a logical extension of that review and the way you have formulated the research problem.

Make sure you don't forget your good ideas. Keep a notebook to record and rework your ideas – they are precious.

If you are engaged in empirical work, don't leave consideration of the analysis until after you have collected the data. Work out early on whether the kind of analysis you think might be most revealing requires data in a particular form. And if you are able to get someone else to enter your data into the computer, check your forms/questionnaires with them early on.

Don't assume that when you have collected the data you have broken the back of the exercise. Detailed analysis takes time and you should make sure you get maximum benefit from the data you have worked so hard to get. This applies as much to qualitative data as to quantitative.

For most of us writing is hard work, so make sure you leave enough time to do this properly, and write specifically for your audience.

Discipline yourself and resist the temptation to bung in everything that just might be relevant.

Don't forget: don't plagiarise by passing off other people's work as your own.

What the Book Offers

The book does not cover the detail of quantitative approaches that are addressed well in other publications. Instead, while certainly not ignoring the quantitative, I shall give more emphasis to the qualitative dimensions of research. I also aim to bring a more critical approach to the arena of leisure, sport and tourism by linking to some of the key concepts to do with academic and professional practice (gender, equity, social inclusion, etc.). Hence readers will be encouraged not just to model outcomes of behaviours, but also to try to gain an understanding of the processes that underpin them.

I find people who just know *the* right way to do research quite worrying. So, I have tried to avoid writing one of those 'how to' books that purports to offer the perfect recipe and cover all the multitude of techniques available. Consequently the chapters are not written to a standard format; they address issues that have been important to me in doing research in leisure.

To avoid purely abstract discussion of research methods, the text makes extensive use of real projects from the field. A lot of the time this means drawing on research I have been involved in myself. The intention is certainly not to parade this as perfect practice (I have a rather better appreciation of its limitations than most), but rather to present a series of exemplars suitable for examination so that you can work out what, to your mind, is good and bad practice, and why. Researchers often do things that they recognise as being 'less than ideal', because they are constrained by pragmatic considerations (logistical difficulties, time or money). They may also be trying to balance conflicting considerations, for example, amount of information gained and imposition on the respondent/participant.

The intention is that the text should pose questions and provide material to help the active reader move towards their own answers. Slightly different research problems may benefit from substantially different approaches. Indeed, two different researchers may approach the same problem from very different angles (Chapter 15). It is possible that on the basis of your own experience or what you have read elsewhere you disagree with some of the points that are made in this book. That does not matter in and of itself – there is plenty of disagreement in research circles about the best way to do research. What does matter is that you should be able to mount a reasoned argument about why you have chosen the strategy, technique or even wording that you have.

The book contains some exercises that can be completed either individually or in groups (or ignored if the reader is already adept) as a means of beginning to get to grips with the challenges posed in carrying out research. Doing these should encourage you to rehearse arguments and play with ideas in working out practical solutions that will shape your research. The intention is to promote a DIY approach, but if you have the opportunity to work through some of these issues with someone else, the ensuing debate is likely to help enormously.

Presumably if you are reading this book you either want to do research or have to do it because your boss or course leader says so. The ideal, of course, is that even if you start doing it because you have to, you finish it because you want to and have become enthused by the process. While books like this can help give confidence in developing research skills, it undoubtedly helps if there is someone around to act as a sounding board. I am fortunate in that I conduct almost all my research as part of a team, but you may need to prevail upon work colleagues, friends, family or fellow students. Those sounding boards will also be helpful in getting the most out of the ideas discussed in this book.

You never know, research may become your recreational drug of choice.

Further Lines of Enquiry

The Higher Education Academy Network for hospitality, leisure, sport and tourism has set up a research gateway that provides useful research resources:www.hlst.ltsn.ac.uk/gateway/gateway.html.

Howard Becker (1998) in his book, *Tricks of the Trade: How to Think about Your Research While You're Doing It*, gives a good insight to this process of continual questioning that I have been discussing. Otherwise, start with the article you've found most interesting over the past year and ask yourself, 'What is going on here?' See if you can reconstruct the story of the research.

2

Ways of Knowing, Ways of Seeing

> The relation between what we see and what we know is never settled ... . The way we see things is affected by what we know or what we believe. (Berger, 1972: 7–8)

Different people do research in different ways. This leads to fierce arguments. I want to avoid suggesting that there is a single right way to do research, and instead provide the means by which researchers can decide for themselves how best to proceed in order to resolve the challenge they have set themselves. Continually improving research practice gives confidence in the quality of the findings. This chapter will address:

- formulating a do-able research challenge and refining a manageable set of questions
- the range of techniques available in the researcher's armoury
- rehearsing arguments and posing questions
- the rationales and remits that establish the point of the research
- research design – from case study to controlled experiments
- the process of doing research.

As I pointed out in the opening chapter, some people have very definite views about *the* way to do research. Having followed many different approaches and used many different techniques, I just do not see the world like that. Everything has to flow from what you decide you need to know. The relationship between the research question, the data needs and the techniques is crucial, and one research style should not be expected to suit all occasions.

Getting Your Research Underway

People often find identifying a suitable research challenge extremely difficult. Some people choose to do an extended literature review. This is not the easy option many imagine it to be because a descriptive account is not acceptable. This route requires considerable powers of synthesis and analysis, and being comfortable with sophisticated theory is a prerequisite. Consequently most students choose to incorporate some empirical component to gather their own data – that at least gives a story to tell.

You should not assume that all research has to be grand or abstract; indeed, for your purposes it is better for it not to be. Equally, you should not undervalue your own interests. So if you have been involved in stamp collecting, Civil War re-enactments or your idol's fan club since the age of 8, why not try to work out how that can be related to ideas addressed on the course? But beware; simply having been mad about football since before you could walk is not enough to provide the rationale for the research. There needs to be something that suggests intellectual inquiry, the wanting to know bit. While university supervisors may emphasise the links to theory, employers may emphasise the link to policy. This may affect the shape of the research itself or the nature of the reporting.

What interests you?
What have others done?

Just jot down any ideas that come into your head. What is it that intrigues you about your area of interest? You cannot just stop there. There then has to be some process of refinement and you have to be convinced that what you are proposing is worth knowing.

Some questions to ask yourself:

- How does my chosen topic relate to the subject matter of the course? If you are doing the research as part of your job, you need to be clear how it will relate to the goals of your department/organisation.
- Do I have the resources to do it (time, money, contacts, means of travel, etc.)?
- Do I have the knowledge and skills to do it? If not, how can I acquire them?

Identifying a Dissertation Challenge

Most dissertations can be seen to address one of just a handful of different kinds of challenge (by all means try to identify more).

Filling in gaps
e.g., *We know _____ about the relationships between work and leisure, but not the reactions of the worker's family. So _____*
or, *Belt and Braces gathered a large amount of data about the relationship between different types of leisure and health. However, in their preoccupation with physical fitness they overlooked the data they had on mental wellbeing. I intend to analyse this to_____.*
(Be careful that the gap you identify is a real one and there isn't already a body of work addressing just that.)

Changes over time
e.g., *20 years ago Long found that leisure activities in retirement were essentially the same as before retirement. Since then _____ changes have occurred, so I shall repeat the earlier study to find out if the same pattern persists.*
or, *Does the trail of abandoned cinemas/bowling greens/tennis courts in Birmingham tell us more about shifts in population or shifts in fashion?*

Evaluation of an initiative
e.g., *Midtown Library Service will be running a read-a-book scheme. I shall monitor its progress and evaluate its success in changing reading patterns among people from different educational backgrounds.*

Cross-cultural comparisons
e.g., *Crompton found this in the US, but Britain is different because _____, so can we expect the same to apply here?*

Applying someone's theory to new circumstances
e.g., *Bourdieu's ideas of 'cultural capital' have rarely been applied to aspects of working class culture. I intend to explore whether the same frameworks can be applied in the arena of gambling, and try to work out the implications for the industry.*

Contrasting the explanations different theories offer for the same phenomenon
(and exploring the consequences for practice)
e.g., *I shall examine the evidence for feminist and anthropological explanations of group behaviour in city centres, and explore the likely effectiveness of alternative methods of control within each of these frameworks.*

Applying someone's model
e.g., *Slack has proposed that the best way for a company to address organisational change is _____. I shall examine how closely Bettalezya followed this process, how issues were dealt with and with what success.*

Research Techniques

It seems commonplace for people approaching social research for the first time to take for granted that they will be doing a questionnaire. There are many good reasons for using social surveys, but there should be no presumption that this should be the approach of choice. Later chapters introduce alternatives, but there are many more.

My apparently trivial example in the previous chapter of feeling '77 bad today' is the kind of issue that underlies discussions about how we find out about the world and what passes for knowledge. Accurate measurement allows comparison. Can we measure the kinds of thing we talk about in the social sciences? Some choose their research techniques in the firm belief that it is vital that we should find a way of doing so; others are equally convinced that such precision is an illusion and a distraction from finding out how social processes operate.

Exercise

It is not unusual to hear professionals and policymakers arguing that leisure enhances quality of life (or promotes social inclusion or aids neighbourhood renewal). This is normally a statement of belief rather than something for which they have any evidence. So if you were set the challenge of trying to do some research that would help address whether or not that kind of claim is justified, where would you start?

Some important principles:

1. *Define your terms* – It is important to be clear and precise about what you are investigating.

   - What is meant by 'quality of life'?
   - Is leisure more than just sport?

2. *Narrow the focus* – You would be well advised not even to think about trying to address the question as a whole. Instead, choose a manageable chunk. So you might decide to examine whether those involved in a wider variety of leisure pursuits report a higher level of life satisfaction. Is 'variety' the most important consideration?
3. *Decide what evidence you will need* – How would you measure variety of leisure pursuits and life satisfaction? Do you need a quantitative measure or is this an occasion when qualitative data would tell you more?
4. *Question the (potential) findings* – If we find a relationship does that imply we know what causes improvements in the quality of life? Suppose that those involved in a wider variety of leisure pursuits did in fact report a higher level of life satisfaction, maybe they are able to take part in this variety of leisure because they have a higher income and it is this higher income that is determining their satisfaction with life.

Research Design

I mentioned in the opening chapter that many social researchers have been bewitched by the scientific method, so I shall take as my starting point here the basics of the *experimental* method which tries to establish causal relationships through examining whether a change in one thing leads to a change in another. In its simplest form:

Step 1   Hypothesise some relationship between a causal variable (the independent variable, conventionally labelled X) and some form of performance (the dependent variable, conventionally labelled Y) [e.g. 'increased stamina improves performance' or, in the previous example, 'a wider variety of leisure activities leads to higher levels of life satisfaction'].

Step 2   Randomly allocate people to two groups.

Step 3   For both groups, measure the key variable you are interested in [e.g., stamina or number of leisure activities and indicator of performance or life satisfaction]

Step 4   Give some treatment to one group (the treatment group) but not the other (the control group) and keep all other conditions the same. [The treatment might be in the form of nutritional supplements, a training programme, classes at the leisure centre or anything that is hypothesised to bring about change.]

Step 5   Repeat the measurement of Step 2.

If some change has been recorded in the treatment group and not in the control group, the cause of the change is attributed to the treatment, as long as nothing else has been changed.

Researchers gradually became aware of various limitations in this approach, and devised more sophisticated designs to try to address those shortcomings.[1] Although sport psychologists often try to replicate the conditions of experimental design, elsewhere in our field of leisure, sport and tourism it is not common. The problem is that in social research it is rarely possible to conduct even the basic experimental design. Instead the research designs are usually less structured, and as a consequence it may not be possible to say confidently that one thing causes another.

---

[1] For example, it was realised that some people may have been affected simply because they were being 'treated', independent of the 'treatment' itself, ie they were responding to something being done or someone taking an interest in them. To counteract this a group was included in the research design that received a placebo, something which of itself should have no impact on the outcome.

Consider, for example, an area of considerable contemporary interest – whether sport, the arts, outdoor adventure or other leisure pursuits can be used to divert people from crime. Quite apart from problems of measuring sport/arts/adventure and crime, the chances are it is not possible to allocate people randomly to treatment and control groups. It may not even be desirable, never mind possible, to administer the same dose of sport to each person in the control trial; it is impossible to hold the other aspects of people's lives constant, and other than in exceptional circumstances you can hardly prohibit those in the control group from taking part in sport. Nonetheless people do try to put together experiment-like research designs to meet such research challenges, and you can try to work out what that might look like in these circumstances. Experimental design is not foolproof though. It cannot protect against a wrongly formulated model. A researcher may think they have established that involvement in sport has turned people away from crime, but the key variable may have been the charisma of the person running the project or the social contact provided by the sessions rather than the activity itself.

Elsewhere the research design problems may be less complex. We may, for example, be interested in how to reduce the amount of litter left at picnic sites in national parks. Assuming we can devise a good measure of the amount of littering that can be administered at different points in time, part way through that sequence we might remove all litter bins from picnic sites in one park (in the belief that people will then take their litter home), mount an anti-litter media campaign in the catchment area of another and leave things unaltered in a third. The consequences can then be carefully tracked in each park, though of course the visitors have not been randomly allocated to the three parks. Alternatively, we may be more interested in why littering occurs and in what circumstances.

Working with a single group receiving the 'treatment', conducting repeat measures (or soundings), still represents a **longitudinal** study. Returning to our sport and crime example, researchers might gather data at the start of a project (or even before) and again some time into the project or at its end. This might be with the same individuals on both occasions, a panel (e.g. the young people on the programme), or with different people drawn from the same population (e.g. for community perceptions of violence/crime). Although this lacks the random allocation to treatment and control groups, the interest is still with change over time.

However, the majority of small scale studies in social research are either **cross-sectional studies** or one-off **case studies** conducted in one place at a single point in time (snap shots).

A **cross-sectional study** might involve a community survey to establish people's views on how threats to safety limit their leisure choices; or it might be a survey of those in a young offenders' institution to identify their characteristics, how they got involved in crime and their attitudes towards crime and corrective practices. What happens then is that the researcher searches for how different groups vary in their attitudes or behaviour. This might mean seeing if there is any difference in the way in which fear of crime varies according to age, gender, how long people have been resident in the area, whether or not they have been the victims of crime or whether there is a diversionary project running in their area. In such circumstances attempts to establish causal relationships come not through allocating people randomly to groups as above, but through statistical procedures to 'control' the effect of different variables to try and identify whether, for example, committing crime can be attributed to educational experience, peers, parental influence or (lack of) involvement in sport.

Continuing with our example, a **case study** might involve examining the success of a project that has been set up among young people considered to be 'at risk' with a view to diverting them from crime. While this might not produce 'hard' data to prove a link between participation in the project and deviant behaviour, it might be possible to identify participants' interpretations of what causes them to engage or not engage in such behaviour and whether they think leisure activities play any part in that. Typically a case study would not be concerned only with those receiving the 'treatment', but all the players in the game (e.g., policymakers, project workers, local residents) as well as the structures and operations of the project.

Of course, anything observed in that case study may be peculiar to that place/project. The research design might therefore be strengthened by examining two or more projects to introduce a *comparative* dimension. It is, of course, possible to introduce a comparative dimension *within* a case study to provide a focus for interpretation and analysis. This might involve comparing how males and females react to the demands and opportunities of the programme. Comparative studies may be either cross-sectional or longitudinal.

Your interest may instead be in the use of libraries or allotments as a leisure resource or the phenomenon of Disney Land/World. It should be fairly straightforward to identify the same kinds of research design that might be put into operation in that context (see also Chapter 16 on writing a research proposal). Whatever the design, researchers should always go looking for alternative explanations and never believe their own publicity. Others will certainly be asking questions about whether or not the research really addresses the issues it claims to (the validity of the measures involved), whether the logic of the argument justifies the conclusions (commonly referred to as **internal validity**), and how generalisable the findings are to other circumstances (commonly referred to as **external validity**).

Most researchers share these concerns, but those who prefer a more qualitative approach may talk about them in a different way (Chapter 15).

Mixed Method and Triangulation

In scientific research researchers are expected to test the reliability, validity and generality of findings. In social science we cannot expect to know things precisely, but the more times we examine something in different ways the more we increase our chances of understanding what we are studying. The term most commonly associated with this in the research literature is 'triangulation'.[2] This is all about taking different fixes, different bearings on the phenomenon under investigation, from different perspectives. These alternative 'takes' can come in several forms, through:

* *Data* – Staying with the theme introduced above, imagine a scenario in which some children are playing in a newly provided adventure play area when a group of slightly older children turns up; apart from one, the younger children soon leave; later a fire breaks out at the play area. The researcher may compare accounts given by different youngsters, then draw in the interpretations of the youth worker and local police officer and compare all those accounts with CCTV footage.
* *Methodologies* – It is not hard to imagine different styles of research in similar circumstances that use personality profiling, observation, interviews or video diaries, so more than one of these might be combined within a single study to gather different kinds of information.
* *Theories* – Different insights might be provided by applying different theories to analyse and interpret the data being collected (in this case we might use theories of personality, territory or gender, for example).
* *Researchers* – Presented with the same data different researchers may offer different interpretations because of their personal background, experience of similar events or academic training.
* *Cases* – scientific replication may not be possible in the social sciences (we cannot treat 'the real world' as a laboratory in which everything is controlled), but we might still want to explore what element of replicability can be established in different circumstances – analogous to the comparative research design discussed earlier in this chapter.

---

[2]I'm not sure of the origins of the term. I first came across it in Norman Denzin (1970) *The Research Act*.

If they come up with the same findings we start to have some confidence that maybe the suggested relationship really does exist. If they do not, it should suggest new ideas and theories to us.

The hope is that different lines of inquiry will be confirmatory, reinforcing each other and our confidence in our findings. However, in the face of the desire to arrive at *the* answer, one of the most important benefits of using multiple methods and different perspectives may be to reduce inappropriate certainty, to avoid us having blind faith in our findings and accepting an explanation that may not be warranted (Robson, 1993).

Although they are not quite the same, other writers use multi-method or multiple strategies to address similar ideas. You need to be clear about what you think each approach will contribute to your research, not use multiple methods just because you think it is 'the done thing'.

The Research Process

When I read about other people's research I am curious to know the story of the research, so I can work out how the conclusions have been arrived at. The research process is a complex mix of the methodical and the creative. One of my previous bosses was fond of describing it as 99% perspiration and 1% inspiration (he did not pretend that was original) in order to make sure I did not labour under any romantic notion that I could get away with not doing the hard graft. The research process associated with the scientific method introduced above might be summarised as being:

> observation ⇒ formulate preliminary theory ⇒ devise testable hypothesis ⇒ collect data ⇒ conduct analysis to test hypothesis ⇒ confirm/revise theory.

Although it represents a model he was not particularly comfortable with Bulmer (1977: 6) identified an ideal-typical approach to social research that he likened to a military campaign:

> design the research ⇒ select sampling procedures ⇒ construct a questionnaire ⇒ collect data ⇒ coding and analysis ⇒ interpretation and reporting.

Like many others, my experience of research in leisure, sport and tourism has been that the process is less straightforward than either of those suggests. In one of our research projects some time ago (Long et al., 1988) the process was more like that set out below.

The Research Process

1. Purpose
2. Audience
3. Focus
4. Questions (hypotheses)
5. Information Needs
6. Information Sources (+ negotiating access)
7. Methods
8. Time and Resources
    (how the practical constrains the desirable)
9. Procedures
    (including sampling)
10. Data Gathering
    (after pilot, pre-test or trial)
11. Data Preparation
    (e.g. coding and data entry)
12. Analysis and Interpretation
13. Writing-up
14. Dissemination

N.B.

(a) all stages are interlinked
(b) think through all stages before starting
(c) data gathering is Stage 10 not Stage1
(d) in practice the process is not as neat as this

That piece of research was done to inform the Local Education Authority's policy on community schooling, but to test the transferability of the process to other circumstances I have tried to work through how it might apply to someone doing their research on that ever popular topic of football hooliganism.

1. *Purpose* – This simply establishes a general starting point. For the current exercise we shall take this as being 'to explore the nature and consequences of football crowd behaviour'.
2. *Audience* – That starting point might suggest any number of possible research projects, and different groups/organisations will have different priorities and push the research in a particular direction. The Home Office might choose a different research project from the clubs, which might in turn differ from the interests of academics. Dissertation research may have to satisfy the demands of both tutors and people 'out there' who have agreed to co-operate in your research.

3. *Focus* – The particular focus may be suggested by a review of the literature. So, for example, you may have identified that a major gap in the literature is the impact the behaviour of the fans has on local residents. The focus may also be suggested by related theories – theories of risk, territoriality, masculinity, the civilising process, cultural conflict …

4. *Questions* – Whatever the focus you choose it is likely to suggest a whole set of more precise questions that you might be interested in, for example:

   • How do the views of business owners and residents compare?
   • Is there a difference in the experiences of white and black residents?
   • Are arrests for incidents between fans, offences against other people or against property?
   • What is the reaction in those communities where the stadium has been relocated away so that it no longer affects them?

   In scientific research such questions would be reformulated into hypotheses (and you may wish to follow that route), but in other styles of research in the social sciences such issues are simply used to give shape and direction to the research.

5. *Information Needs* – It is then necessary to identify what information is going to be needed. In this case we might need some record of offences or people's reactions/feelings.

6. *Information Sources* – The source of the relevant data has to be identified: the archives of the local newspaper, police/club records, police officers themselves, local residents, your own observations in the field. Check that these sources will actually produce the information you need. Check too that you can get access to them (negotiating access may be especially difficult for a student project).

7. *Methods/Techniques* –You might start out doing a statistical analysis of arrest data to try to identify trends, supplement that with individual or group interviews with officers so you can understand how the statistics relate to what happened on the day, and administer a questionnaire to local people to find out how people's attitudes vary.

8. *Time and Resources* – There never seems to be enough money or time, so the practical must constrain the desirable. Map out what can be done with the resources available or heartache will follow. Your friend in the statistics department may tell you that you need 1000 respondents, but if you are the only interviewer that is unlikely. Be realistic about what can be achieved so you don't bite off more than you can chew. On the other hand your tutor/boss is not going to be amused if they think you have been skiving and not doing much work.

9. *Procedures* – Think through what you are actually going to do and then run a pilot (trial run) to see if it works in practice. Where, when and how is it best to do the research? How will you get there, how will the sample be selected and the data collected, what will you do if it rains?

10. *Data Gathering* – Only after all that has gone before are you able to collect your data.

11. *Data Preparation* – You have to get the data into shape so you can try and make sense of it. This often involves coding, whether the data are in the form of questionnaires, lengthy interviews, police reports or your field notes from attendance at matches. Quantitative data, and increasingly qualitative too, have to be entered into computer files.

12. *Analysis and Interpretation* – Pure description is rarely enough, even if you have managed to quantify some component of behaviour/outlook. Reporting that 27% of residents said something may be of some interest, but does not advance our understanding very far (especially if you have to add that they are only four people). So you might at least consider if there is a difference between male and female residents or the behaviour of fans of different ages. What can you say about why or how something happened? Importantly, you need to consider what implications your findings might have for theory, policy or practice.

13. *Writing-up* – I enjoy this, but only if there is enough time to do a good job. Don't underestimate how long this stage will take, especially as it is important to leave time for editing and proof-reading. It is important to take into consideration once again the audience (academics or professionals; councillors or officers; customers or Board members) and to choose an appropriate style.

14. *Dissemination* – Having spent a lot of time doing the research it seems only sensible to make sure that the findings get noticed by as many people as possible.

Four important points should be noted from this.

(i)   The research process is normally far messier than a model like this might imply. By the time the report gets written, it has been tidied-up … and you don't want to know about the mistakes.

(ii)   The different stages are interlinked and, typically, one stage overlaps with another.

(iii) Data collection is only stage 10 in this process. Which particular stage it is matters less than an appreciation that data gathering is not the first step in the research process. A lot needs to happen before that. To coin a popular aphorism, 'prior preparation prevents piss poor performance'.

(iv)   Of course things will change, but it is important to think through all the stages before setting out.

It is good practice to get into the habit of keeping a research diary, noting what decisions have been taken, what has happened to you, your reactions to what you have seen or been told. It is also important to engage in conversations with yourself, asking questions about how the research is being conducted and your own role in that,[3] and possible interpretations of what you have seen and heard.

Research Planning

While you are just talking about the research it is easy to bluster – many of us have become quite practised at that – so it is a good idea to find an alternative way of representing the research. Try drawing a diagrammatic representation of what it is about with boxes and arrows to show the imagined relationships. Having refined the nature of the research challenge it is also important to clarify the data requirements. Completing a simple table like that in Figure 2.1 will help here. For each of the research questions you want to address (sub-divide these as much as possible), record the information you will need if you are to say anything sensible about your chosen topic, and then identify where that is going to come from.

Identify area of research interest … review …focus … and then ask yourself:		
What questions am I interested in?	What information do I need to be able to answer those questions?	How will I get it?

Figure 2.1   Research Planning

When working on an extended research project it is important to have a route map that charts the expected journey through the process. This often takes the form of a timeline, setting out key stages, milestones and thresholds. In any project some

[3]Much has been written in recent years about 'the reflexive researcher', which is concerned with the impact researchers have on the world around them and upon the findings of the research, because of their own experience, their understanding of how the world operates and their impact on others.

things cannot be done until other stages have been completed. A good project plan containing a timeline should make sure that the necessary building blocks are in place at the right time – make sure that important stages like negotiating access/approval are not left out. For all my insistence that the preparatory stages are important, it is vital that you press on at this stage and don't procrastinate. Data collection, analysis and writing all need substantial blocks of time and should not be squeezed so that corners have to be cut. The schedule needs to have enough flexibility to allow time to recover from a computer virus or the Managing Director taking a week longer than expected to grant permission for interviews with the firm's employees. This exercise also helps to maintain momentum through the course of the project, offering a way of monitoring progress and providing reminders.

Those involved in sport may be familiar with ideas of 'the inner game' or mental rehearsal. It is useful to apply the same principles here. Project yourself into the future and imagine you are actually doing each step of the research. If you can do this well it will cut out some avoidable mistakes.

Exercise

Many of these ideas seem very abstract and hard to relate to when talked about in these terms. Find an article that you like in one of the academic journals and then try to work out:

- How has the research problem been formulated?
- What are the key issues and variables under consideration?
- How did the researcher(s) understand/measure these? (It is hard enough to measure, examine or assess something like income never mind more complex ideas like social class or power.)
- What was the basic structure of the research design – experimental, longitudinal, cross-sectional, case study, comparative?

Ask these same questions of your proposed research.

Further Lines of Enquiry

For those working in more scientific parts of the leisure, sport and tourism area, a useful introduction to the idea of experimental research design can be found in Thomas and Nelson's (2001) *Research Methods in Physical Activity*. In the context of social research, try de Vaus's (2002) book *Surveys in Social Research*. For anyone wanting to explore these issues in more detail de Vaus (2001) has devoted a complete book to the examination of research design, in which he presents design as the logical structure of enquiry.

3

Finding What is Already There – and Putting it to Use

How do I know whether or not I need to know it if I don't know what there is to know, so I know if I need to know it. (With apologies to *Yes Minister*)

It seems only sensible to make good use of knowledge already available to us. We can do this either by assessing the findings reported in books, reports and journal articles or returning to the original data sets produced by previous research and re-examining them. To do this properly requires not just description, but a critical eye assessing its potential for the current research. This chapter will address:

- the importance and process of literature review
- the need for selectivity and a critical eye
- referencing and avoiding plagiarism
- electronic searches
- the use of secondary data sets.

Background

Just as John Donne wrote that 'No man is an island, entire of itself', so too no research stands alone. It is surrounded by other grains of sand, some of which may be little gems. Knowing what other research has been conducted may save us going down blind alleys, making mistakes or repeating work that has already been conducted by others. It may also give us the means to understand our own research better and provide insights we would never have arrived at on our own. The nature of the review may vary depending upon whether it is conducted for a dissertation or a work project, but the process of identifying what is available and establishing the contribution it can make to the planned research is common to both. If you are doing your research within a university setting it is almost certain that carrying out some review of the literature will be a requirement. However, there are better reasons for doing this exercise than compulsion.

1. To start with, as Thomas and Nelson (1990: 48) note, 'the purpose of the review is to demonstrate that your problem needs investigation and that you have considered the value of relevant past research in developing your hypotheses and methods'.
2. It should provide reassurance that the research challenge you have selected is appropriate, important and do-able.
3. Beyond that, by the time you submit your dissertation you should have a good knowledge of the main ideas people have been writing about in relation to your research topic. In short you should have become expert in your chosen field. A good literature review lends an air of authority – it helps to establish your credentials and demonstrate that you have some expertise, that you know what you are talking about (so even Dave might believe you).
4. Tracing how others have conducted their research should help in devising an appropriate approach and set of research instruments for your own work.
5. The material identified in your literature review should provide a route into your later analysis, using the categories, theories and speculation you have unearthed.

Some people do worry that becoming embedded in existing ways of understanding the world limits thought, preventing researchers from 'thinking outside the box'. However, the counter argument based on the stimulation of ideas is very strong, especially for those whose natural inclination is to 'argue' with what they read or make links between disparate ideas.

Formulating the initial research challenge is intimately bound up with the review process. From the germ of an idea you have to work to and fro, using the literature in an iterative process of refinement. As you know more about the literature you can be more precise in specifying your research problem, and the more precise you are in specifying your research problem the more focused and productive can be your literature search.

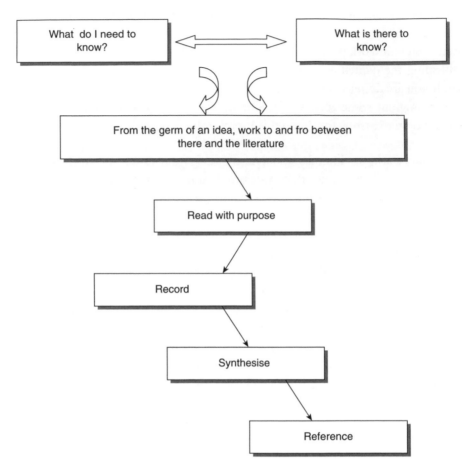

Figure 3.1   Making use of literature

Searching

A common complaint heard by dissertation tutors is that there is nothing written about a student's selected topic. You may not find anything specifically on 'the effectiveness of distributing free shuttlecocks as a way of encouraging single parents to become involved in the activities of the leisure centre'. But there will be plenty of material on differential participation patterns, barriers to participation, policies to encourage the participation of disadvantaged groups, establishing new markets, sports development, management theory, feminist theories of women's involvement in sport and a host of other perspectives. Think laterally. Your challenge is to sift, sort and evaluate.

A library catalogue is a useful start but that is all – even for its own collection it does not cover articles in journals or chapters in edited collections, for example. If you are lucky enough to be in a university the information staff are probably equipped to provide assistance to get you started on your literature search. There are several abstracting services now available electronically that will allow you to search for material on the subjects you are interested in. The resultant listing comes with details of the source of the publication and a short summary of what the paper contains. Two of the most relevant to our areas of interest are *SportDiscus* and *leisuretourism.com*.

Although they may not contain abstracts there are also many general services in the form of either compendiums or catalogues. Popular examples of the former are *EBSCO* and *Cambridge Scientific Abstracts* which contains within it, for example, *Sociological Abstracts*. An example of the latter is *zetoc*, a database that gives access to the British Library's electronic table of contents and as such contains details of the content of a huge number of journals and conference proceedings (other national libraries have their equivalents – perhaps the most well known is the Library of Congress accessed via www.catalog.loc.gov).[1] As a catalogue, *zetoc* does not offer an abstracting service, but does offer the chance to link to the original item if it is available electronically. A more recent arrival is *Google Scholar* which is subscription free and helps to identify academic outputs that fit your specification.

So, there are different levels involved:

1. indexes and catalogues (listings)
2. abstracting services that provide short summaries of the material available
3. full-text journals online.

If you are not part of a university or major organisation, it may be difficult to use some of these. To gain access to most of them you will need an ATHENS[2] password as authentication, *and* (normally) for your institution or professional association to have paid the subscription to the index or abstracting service (and subsequently the journal). Ask your librarian or information officer what you will be able to get access to. Otherwise you will have to fall back on the web.

Even though e-technology makes it unnecessary it is still a good idea to rifle through the pages of the journals in leisure, sport and tourism so that you get a feel for the kind of material they contain and what is considered important at the time.

---

[1]Because of the confusion that can be caused by inappropriate punctuation in web addresses, angled brackets are sometimes used to delimit the address when it is presented in the text. Do not type these as part of the address when you come to use them.

[2]Primarily but not exclusively used by further and higher education and the health sector in the UK as a system to 'authenticate' and authorise users for access to online services from around the world <www.athens.ac.uk>.

Take a Look to Map the Territory

For example:

- *Leisure Studies*
- *Leisure Sciences*
- *Journal of Leisure Research*
- *Loisir et Société (Leisure & Society)*
- *Managing Leisure*
- *Tourism Management*
- *Annals of Tourism Research*
- *Journal of Sustainable Tourism*
- *Sports Sociology Journal*
- *Journal of Sport Management*
- *Journal of Sport & Social Issues*
- *International Review for the Sociology of Sport*
- *Therapeutic Recreation Journal*
- *Journal of Physical Education, Recreation & Dance*
- *Media, Culture & Society* etc...

And don't forget the journals in your mainstream discipline, those in related areas like *Theory, Culture & Society* or the *Journal of the Market Research Society*, and those on research methods (yes there are some).

If your literature search identifies books or articles that are not available at your own library there are alternatives:

- The library you have access to is probably linked with others as part of a network.
- The system of Inter-Library Loans (in the UK) can normally get material that is published in the country (and much from abroad) from the National Lending Library.
- Many public organisations covering sport, tourism, the arts, countryside, waterways, forestry, etc. have their own library and information services that you may be able to sweet talk your way into.
- Increasing amounts of material are available electronically.

Most students and leisure professionals now are familiar with the idea of using the internet for a web-based search, but if this is not your forte, remember there will be plenty of people around who will be only too pleased to help – ask your family, friends and librarians. Of course, the internet brings its own problems. The first is the sheer volume of material, which can become a curse rather than a blessing. The second is the unknown quality of what is placed on the web. You should not believe everything you find there – you may be interested in *The Internet Detective*, which will help you assess quality. This is at www.vts.intute.ac.uk/detective.

Many sites contain useful links to other sites, but some are specifically constructed to act as 'gateways' to several other sites in that particular field of interest. Especially good for the social sciences is the one that hosts the internet detective: www.intute.ac.uk/socialsciences.

The Review Process

In light of what has been said, the bulk of your literature review has to be done early, but it should continue throughout the research. However, there is so much material 'out there' you could go on forever, so make a clear cut-off date that leaves plenty of time for writing.

Reading with purpose

Wonderful though it is, information and communications technology can potentially lead to severe problems of information overload. It is important to be selective and assess what is going to be useful. You have to learn to be a processor, not just a collector, of information.

Recording

Photocopying or downloading and putting it in your file is not enough – osmosis does not work here. You have to identify the major points and assess:

- how they relate to what others have found
- what they contribute to your research.

There is something about physically taking notes that helps to cement this in your brain. But then when you want to check back you have to find the original again… so perhaps there is something to be said for having the full text of *key* articles after all. Whether working with hard or electronic copy you can use different coloured highlighters and annotate the material you have selected. After taking notes, try writing a paragraph that you might later incorporate into your dissertation. This helps to secure the significance of what has just been read.

Every researcher has forgotten to do it at some time (and subsequently cursed themselves), but it really is important to record the full details of the source (see below).

Synthesising

You will have to leave out a lot of the things you have read and made notes on. This can be galling after all that hard work, but you should be aiming for a quality product so think 'relevance'. It is not enough merely to collect and describe. Simply listing material – Smith said this; Kelly said that; in 1987 a study found... – is inadequate for a dissertation. Researchers are often encouraged to 'be critical'. This does not mean finding fault with every piece of research in your review. It may involve identifying shortcomings, but more than that you need to ask yourself, 'What is the significance of this material, how does it fit with what others have said and how will it contribute to my research?'

Some of the key considerations for you to act on:

- Classify the research studies you have found so that you group like with like.
- Order the items to support the logical development of an argument (maybe drawing on a study more than once).
- Explore relationships between the bits of information they present (what is being proposed?).
- Explain and evaluate these 'facts'/interpretations and relationships assessing their credibility (how much faith you can put in them) and their potential contribution to the forthcoming research.
- Compare/contrast the results of different investigators.
- Identify the next step, which should indicate why your research is necessary in that particular form.

Referencing and (Avoiding) Plagiarism

In the academic world there is an expectation that when you make use of work that is not your own you acknowledge where it has come from, whether or not it is a direct quote. Not making proper reference to your sources is known as 'plagiarism' and most institutions impose heavy penalties when this is detected. But referencing is not done just for these ethical/legalistic reasons. It serves other important purposes:

1. It allows the reader to follow-up the ideas being discussed by going back to the original.
2. It helps to demonstrate how you position your work within the theoretical and policy debates around leisure, sport and tourism.
3. If properly handled it should lend added weight to your argument by demonstrating support from elsewhere.

The social sciences have been following the lead taken by the natural and physical sciences in adopting the Harvard System as the normal way of referencing previously published material. Unfortunately, though, this gives a misleading impression because instead of a standard set of rules there is any number of variations on the theme (the version I normally use is not quite the same as the one the publishers of this book prefer). The basic principles are consistent, but styles vary. It is important though to be consistent in presenting standard units of information so people can track down the literature you have been using.

There are many guides to referencing, so I only intend to provide a summary here. Always check if your institution/organisation has its own guidelines. If it does, it makes sense to follow those.

In the text:

- author, date: page number (if substantive quote)
- if more than one reference, place in date order
- if there are more than two authors for the publication, name the first and then use et al. – all authors should be named in the references at the end
- short quotes are incorporated into sentences, longer quotes (more than two lines) should be set out in a separate block, indented, single spaced.

Examples

Patton (1990) has suggested 14 possible strategies for sampling.

Different levels of involvement can be recognised (Gold, 1969):

… like the leisure boredom scale (Iso-Ahola and Weissinger, 1990; Wegner et al., 2002)

Wolcott (1995: 96) identifies the dilemma of the observer who faces 'the problem of what to look at and what to look for and the never-ending tension between taking a closer look at something versus taking a broader look at everything'.

… but there is also the problem of seeing the past 'through rose-tinted spectacles':

> For example I can distinctly remember saying to myself when I left school for the last time 'never forget how terrible these school years were'. But now I find it difficult to recapture that degree of negative feeling towards my schooldays. The content of my memories for school is more positive than I could have predicted twenty-four years ago. (Coleman, 1991: 124)

In the references:

- Book – author (date) *title*. place of publication: publisher.
- Journal article – author (date) 'title', *journal*, vol. (issue): page numbers.
- Chapter in a book – author (date) 'title', in editor (ed.), *book title*. place of publication, publisher, page numbers.

Examples

Blackshaw, T. (2003) *Leisure Life: Myth, Masculinity and Modernity.* London: Routledge.

Long, J. and Wray, S. (2003) 'It Depends Who You Are: On Asking Difficult Questions in Leisure Research', *Loisir et Société*, 26 (1): 169–82.

Whyte, W. F. (1982) 'Interviewing in Field Research', in R.G. Burgess (ed.), *Field Research: A Sourcebook and Field Manual.* London: Allen & Unwin. pp. 111–22.

All works cited in the text should appear in the references at the end. These are listed in alphabetical order by author. Publications by the same author are listed in date order (if more than one publication by an author in the same year, they are distinguished by a, b, etc. after the date – e.g. 2004a). All works included in the references should be cited in the text.

If you are doing a report to committee you might well be asked to use a different style because this referencing system 'can get in the way'. In such circumstances those who want to remain true to the principle that proper acknowledgement should be given commonly use a system of footnotes to provide the information.

If you get confused you can take a look in any of the recognised journals and follow the model used there. Alternatively, many (perhaps most) higher education institutions produce their own guides (you can find ours at www.leedsmet.ac.uk/lskills/open/sfl/content/harvard/intro/01.html). Guides like this are helpful for sorting out how to reference material that does not fit into these basic patterns, e.g. government publications and acts of parliament.

More and more information is found on the web where place of publication and publisher have no real significance, and it may be difficult to find when it was published or even who the author was. Again, the basic principle is to provide readers with the information they need to locate the material for themselves. This should include as much of the standard publication detail as possible plus the Uniform Resource Locator (URL). Control codes make some URLs run to several lines. In such circumstances it is normally considered sufficient to specify the website where the article can be located. Because the web is continually changing, you should also indicate when you last accessed the item. I was able to find quite a lot of detail on how to reference electronic material on the Flinders University website (accessed 08/08/04) at: www.lib.flinders.edu.au/resources/sub/healthsci/referencing/electronic.html.

There are now several software packages (e.g. Endnote, Procite and Papyrus) designed to help store references and make them available to the document you are writing in a range of formats.

Secondary Data Sets

Behind what can be read about in journal articles, books and reports lie the original data sets. These may provide the necessary context for your own research and even offer direct comparisons. They may provide an opportunity to examine something that the original researchers either lacked the time, skills or interest to analyse. They may benefit from further analysis using alternative statistical techniques, or you may want to re-address the same issues from a different theoretical perspective.

People conventionally refer to data collected specifically for the research project as being primary data. However, sometimes use may be made of data originally collected for a different purpose/study, in which case it is referred to as being secondary data. Just as with recycling aluminium cans and plastic bottles, the extent to which researchers recycle data in this way fluctuates with fashion and most people do not bother. Key statistics may commonly be quoted, but revisiting the data sets to conduct further analysis is uncommon – it becomes more common the more people are aware of the cost of gathering primary data, or when concern grows about imposing unnecessarily on the public. If the data already exist and we already know most of what there is to know about what, why and how, it is hardly fair to add to the public's concern that they are being over-researched (Chapter 14).

Stay alert though when considering the application of secondary data to a new research challenge:

1. *Dated?* – The data may just be too old to be useful because things are likely to have changed substantially since they were originally collected.
2. *Categories?* – You may be interested in tennis and the over 50s while the original survey included tennis in a general category of 'racket sports' and used age groups of 40–59 and 60+.
3. *Who?* – The General Household Survey, like may others, only includes people aged 16 and over, which may not help you much if your research interests lie with participation among those at school.
4. *Time period?* – For example some data sets may relate to participation in the past month and others to the past year.
5. *Geographical coverage?* – Check that national/federal, regional/state areas match your interests.

Quite often when we review these sorts of issues we conclude that the data are not ideal for our purposes. The question then is whether or not they 'will do' because the match is close enough.

Some major surveys are conducted for a long time and then just run out of steam as policy interests change. For example, the UK Day Visits Survey used to be conducted in alternate years and provided an important source of leisure/tourism data, but there has not been one since 1998.

The sports world of course is full of statistics on performance that might sustain further analysis. For example, Grusky (1963) assessed the impact that changes in coaches and managers had on team performance. And many have followed since. So, as part of a research project, sports statistics might be used to establish just how big an advantage playing at home is, or what impact promotion/relegation has on attendance.

Social statistics are a form of knowledge, and like all knowledge they are created by a particular set of procedures – they are not just lying about waiting to be published. All forms of knowledge represent power. Some statistics are collected and others are not, different procedures of analysis can be deployed, and presentation can be very selective. Let me issue a reminder from Chapter 1.

FACTS DO NOT SPEAK FOR THEMSELVES

Gathering together columns of numbers can be quite reassuring. But the numbers are meaningless without an understanding of how they have been collected and a theoretically informed interpretation of their significance. As Tomlinson (1989: 98) urged 'Without theory there is nothing; without concepts lists of facts are simply signposts to nowhere'.

Further Lines of Enquiry

I normally refer people struggling to appreciate what a literature review should look like to Judith Bell's book, *Doing Your Research Project* (3rd edition, 1999), because contained within the discussion is an example that gives a good idea of the style and purpose of a literature review in a small-scale research project.

Many of the data sets collected with public money in the UK are available on the internet at: www.data-archive.ac.uk. This need not be restricted to quantitative data – they also run *Qualidata*: www.esds.ac.uk/qualidata. The Public Records Office makes a huge volume of historical data available online at: www.nationalarchives.gov.uk.

ESDS International provides access to, and support for, a range of datasets with a European emphasis, but extends worldwide: www.esds.ac.uk/international. This offers access to other databases in North America and elsewhere, including the UN Common Database.

The Sport England website includes *The Value of Sport* which contains information on studies that assess the contribution made by sport. It also provides details of how judgements are made about which studies to include on the basis of their methodological transparency and robustness: www.sportengland.org/about _vosm.

Books to which people often refer regarding secondary analysis are those by Hakim (1982) and Dale et al. (1988). A more recent offering is the four volume set by Bulmer et al. (2006).

4

Subjects, Respondents, Participants and Collaborators

People aren't just bodies to be counted in research. On the other hand, accounting for them properly is of utmost importance.

This chapter will consider the people researchers need to deal with, how they are selected, and their relationship with them. This requires an understanding of who the research is about. This chapter will address:

- different forms of sampling and procedures for implementation
- issues of representativeness
- a consideration of those left out and those not responding (response rates)
- relationships between the researcher and those they are researching
- responsibilities of the researcher to the participants.

Although it is possible to avoid people in social research, most empirical investigations involve dealing with them. In doing so it is important to remember that they are people, not just items that are researched – they have feelings too. Consequently the more people can be made to feel valued for their knowledge and expertise the more likely they are to agree to be involved in the research and the better the quality of data they provide. In acknowledgement of this, recent research accounts are less likely to refer to them as subjects, and more likely to refer to respondents or participants – which implies a more active part in the research. In some research designs they may be so central to the development of the research that they become collaborators in the research process. To some extent this is the case no matter what the research design, but normally the key decisions are taken by the researcher(s).

Selecting Research Participants

> Sampling is a major problem for any kind of research. We can't study every case of whatever we're interested in. ... Every scientific enterprise tries to find out something that will apply to everything of a certain kind by studying a few examples, the results of the study being, as we say, 'generalizable' to all members of that class of stuff. We need the sample to persuade people that we know something about the whole class. (Becker, 1998: 67)

Because we cannot include in our research all the people in whom we have an interest, there has to be a basis for selecting some rather than others (not just whim). Of course, what is being sampled does not have to be people; your research might involve selecting:

- Which leisure centres, heritage sites, etc.? If you are not going to use a truly random process, how will these be selected? Because they are 'typical'? Because they are 'the best'? Because they will let you?
- Which matches, tournaments, re-enactments? Similar issues apply here.
- Which month (season), day, session? Seasonality in particular is a major issue in understanding leisure, sport and tourism, but differential patterns of participation through the day and week are also crucial to our studies.

Moreover, in selecting the questions to be addressed we are effectively sampling from the infinite number of possible research challenges. I hope you can then see why I become concerned if people conducting qualitative research suggest that sampling has nothing to do with them. Whatever the research there is sampling, and the sampling is inescapably bound to the formulation of the problem, the analysis and the conclusions, not to mention the confidence they command. If you expect people to set any store by your research you therefore have a responsibility to make this selection extremely carefully.

Different styles of research have different approaches to this set of issues. In survey research the emphasis is on representativeness, in experimental research the emphasis may be on random selection and allocation to control and treatment groups, and in qualitative research the emphasis may be on giving voice to different interests. Whatever the approach, Darren's and Jess's mates from their Leisure and Sport Management course probably will not provide an appropriate sample, certainly not one representative of 'the public'.

Even carefully constructed selection procedures may not allow all an equal chance of being included. In tourism surveys, for example, the more independent travellers are less likely to be at the survey points; street surveys exclude or under-represent, those at work, those living in rural areas or those who for whatever reason 'get out and about' less. Even with home interview surveys it is not easy to construct a truly random sample. Those who are most active in their external leisure activities are least likely to be at home; those most likely to be at home may be least likely to answer the door. Well resourced studies have a number of 'call-backs' to try to address this. Some element of pragmatism enters most research design, but try to work out how you can maximise the inclusiveness of the study.

I shall take as my starting point some of the conventions and practices associated with sampling in the context of survey research, draw attention to some of the alternatives and conclude with a more detailed consideration of some approaches used in qualitative research.

Important Concepts

Population	All the people, facilities, etc. that fit the description you establish, e.g. all sports clubs in town, all visitors to the resort. To allow the sample to represent the population properly, it is vital that the population is first defined precisely – be clear about location, characteristics, settings, etc.
Sampling frame	The listing of those examples/members in the population so that the selection of the sample can proceed.
Sample	A selection of elements from that population – the most desirable characteristic of a sample is that it should 'represent' the larger population.
Sampling Error	The difference by chance between the sample and population simply by virtue of measuring a sample rather than the whole population – typically measured in terms of the standard error.

How Big Should My Sample Be?

This is probably the question most commonly asked by those doing their first survey. Frustratingly the answer from the expert is not likely to be what the researcher wants to hear. The first response is likely to be: 'It depends'. When pressed, and the problem is analysed, the final answer may be a number much bigger than the researcher wants to contemplate. 'Real' statisticians will almost always try to persuade you to get a larger sample than you can afford (in terms of time and money). Certainly, other things being equal, the larger your sample, the more reliable your findings. Sadly though, doubling the size does not double the reliability. It may not seem fair, but in order to halve the sampling error the sample size has to be not doubled but quadrupled.

It is the absolute size of the sample, rather than its size relative to the population, that is the key consideration. Commonly heard statements like, 'The sample is only 0. 1% of the population so it cannot be representative', should be challenged immediately. Survey researchers will trot out explanations about only needing to try a bit of the soup or cake to know what the whole pot/cake tastes like. People are a bit more complicated than cake ingredients, but reasonably confident estimates can be made from relatively small numbers. Next time you see an opinion poll reported in the paper, check the sample size. In the UK, surveys of voting intentions are typically based on about 1000 respondents (perhaps 2000 in the run-up to a general election) who are taken to represent an electorate of something like 44 million.

> Sample size is dependent upon the amount of variation in the key variables, the degree of statistical confidence aimed for and the balance between the probabilities of accepting something as true when in fact it is false and rejecting something as false when it is true. Then you apply the formula to calculate the size of the sample that will be needed.[1]

Table 4.1 gives an indication of how much confidence we can attach to our findings given different sample sizes (these apparently precise figures only apply in certain circumstances – see, for example, de Vaus, 2002). The figures produced from the sample are estimates of what the population is likely to be. In crude terms this suggests that in the opinion poll with a sample of 1000 we can be 95% sure that the true figure lies within plus or minus 3 percentage points of our estimate. Hence, if a party's support stands at 42% in the poll, we can be reasonably confident that it lies between 39% and 45%. But that is still quite a big range, which suggests that we should be cautious in how we treat such data. So be careful in the claims you make if you are working with small sample sizes.

How big the sample needs to be will vary according to the nature of the variation in the group, the level of accuracy needed and the nature of the analysis you want to do. There are various 'rules of thumb', one of which (Hoinville et al., 1977) suggests that you should aim for a minimum of 50–100 in each sub-group (e.g. age group, sex). The combination of statistical principles with pragmatism explains why the kinds of variation social theory suggests are important are often not addressed in

---

[1]To be honest, most of us don't. We use tables that have already been calculated (e.g. Cohen, 1977).

Table 4.1 Confidence in Samples

Sample size	Tolerance 95% probability (percentage points)	Tolerance 99% probability (percentage points)
10	30.1	40.1
25	19.6	25.8
50	13.9	18.2
100	9.8	12.9
200	6.9	9.1
400	4.9	6.5
1000	3.1	4.1

Note: This is irrespective of the size of the 'population' unless the sample size gets close to the size of the population. So be very careful in interpreting the findings of surveys based on a small number of respondents.

the presentation of research findings. With relatively few respondents, variables like ethnicity or class are often collapsed into a few sub-groups (e.g. black/white and working class/middle class respectively). This is done to create larger sub-samples that will command greater confidence, but at the expense of overriding the theory that stresses the importance of disaggregating such categories.

De Vaus (1991) recommends that when dealing with nominal/categorical data there should be a minimum of five people/units in each cell of the matrix when some form of table is produced. (I think this is because for proper use of the Chi-Square statistic, often used in these circumstances [Chapter 11], there should not be more than 20% of cells with an expected frequency of less than 5.) *So, if you are interested in how five age groups are distributed between four categories of physical activity, what would be the minimum number of respondents needed?*[2] In practice of course many more than this minimum are needed because it is unlikely that there will be an even distribution of respondents between categories.

Within qualitative research projects the nature of the exercise is rather different and the sample size is typically much smaller, with anywhere from half a dozen to 30 or 40 respondents. Occasionally sample sizes, even in qualitative research, are considerably larger than this, whereas some studies are based on intensive biographical work with a single respondent. I shall return to this after discussing the associated sampling procedures.

---

[2] 5×5 (age) $\times 4$ (physical activity) = 100

How Do I Select My Sample?

A random sample is a very precise statistical concept. It most certainly does not mean the people I happened to meet while I was out doing my shopping on a Saturday morning. Random or probability sampling involves each person/item in the population having an equal chance of being selected. There are four main types:

1. *Simple Random Sample (SRS)* – Random selection from a known, complete **sampling frame** (exhaustive list) such that every person/unit has an equal chance of being included. When you think about it, it is not always easy to establish this list.
2. *Systematic Sampling* – For example, every 10th person on your list.
3. *Stratified Sampling* – For example, by age, sex, department/centre.

   - Group according to strata and then just systematically sample through the population; or
   - SRS within each stratum to get the same percentage sampled from each.

This helps to reduce sample error insofar as each category can be appropriately represented.

4. *Multistage Cluster Sampling* – National random samples are expensive to recruit and this is often used as an alternative.

   - Randomly select a sample of areas – start large, e.g. constituencies, then select smaller units within them, e.g. wards.
   - Having selected a sample of small areas, enumerate the households within those areas, then random sample.
   - Then select individuals within households.

For various reasons research studies may use non random samples (though they are often treated statistically as though they were randomly selected). These can be broadly grouped as:

- *Quota Sampling* – Often used by market research companies because it is cheaper than random sampling. Identify the proportion in the population in particular age, sex, etc. groups (chosen because they are thought likely to influence responses) and get the interviewers to interview respondents selected in those proportions. This process is non random as the interviewer can select anyone as long as they fulfil the quota.
- *Purposive Sampling* – people selected specifically because of what they know (e.g. the former chair of the Leisure Services committee).

- *Convenience Sampling* – uses those at hand. For example, some nameless researchers often seem to derive their samples from students because they are compliant (?) and available.

If you have a complete membership list of those belonging to a particular club, you have a ready made sampling frame (if it is up-to-date) from which you can devise a procedure for selecting a random sample using any of the first three procedures above. But there is a difference between selecting them from a list and locating them for interview. That is when some researchers give up and just interview the first 100 who come through the door – try to resist that urge. If your research is also interested in non-joiners, you might ask each of the selected respondents to refer you to a friend or neighbour who is not a member.

If, more generally, you want a sample of local residents, it may be possible to use a register of electors or of addresses. Some people do not appear on the former because they are too young (what is the minimum age you plan to interview?), because they only moved in recently, because the system is inefficient or because they have deliberately tried to keep out of official records. As an alternative, some researchers use a random walk method to decide which doors to knock on. To do this requires a start point (e.g. the first or randomly selected address in the list or the crossroads nearest the centre of the chosen area), a way of deciding which direction to go in at junctions, and a way of deciding which door to knock on next (e.g. every 7th or a random selector – dice or cards might do). If you just choose a door, you still have to decide who in that household to interview. And if you only choose one person from each address, you will underrepresent those who live in large households. The same problems have to be resolved if you approach groups at the airport or in the park. The Kish grid and some version of a birthday rule (e.g. Kish, 1949; Hoinville et al., 1977) are the most common ways of dealing with this.

For some people the idea of cold calling at a door is too daunting and they look for an easier entrée. This might be provided by working through a residents' association or PTA. These clearly are not going to provide you with a random sample though, so it is important to try to work out just how they differ from the population at large.

Those geared-up to do a lot of telephone interviewing may use random number dialling systems or have an electronic listing of telephone numbers from which they can select. These are not likely to be available to people reading this book, but if the research is being done for your employer you may be able to hire a company that can do this easily.

Table 4.2 Sample proportions and weighting

Stand	Number of spectators	Number of questionnaires	Sampling proportion	Weighting
North	5,000	100	1:50	×50
South	7,000	100	1:70	×70
East	10,000	100	1:100	×100
West	10,000	100	1:100	×100

Sample Proportions and Weighting

You might be very proud of having got 100 questionnaires completed by the spectators going through the turnstiles for each of the four stands for a sell-out match at your local stadium. However, this will have produced different sampling proportions if the stands have different capacities (5, 7, 10 and 10 thousand). While the purpose of the study is to examine the differences between spectators in the different parts of the stadium, this is entirely appropriate (it gives you a reasonable number in each sub-sample for your comparisons). However, assuming there are differences, you have to be cautious in producing aggregate statements about the crowd as a whole. Simply treating all your questionnaires the same would then give an inflated significance to the responses from those in the smaller stands. Had the 400 respondents been divided proportionately between each of the stands there would have been 62, 88, 125 and 125 respectively. Suitable 'weights' have to be given to each of the questionnaires to make sure the overall picture properly represents the crowd as a whole – see Table 4.2. Major statistical packages like SPSS are perfectly capable of dealing with this kind of manipulation of the data.

Exactly the same issue applies in other fields: e.g. a sample containing both members and casual users of a leisure centre or elite and recreational tennis players. Take another example in which you want a sample of tourism businesses from your local resort in order to gauge the response to a particular policy initiative. Perhaps you have made a heroic guess and decided that 100 businesses would be a suitable sample size. You also know that you need different sectors of the tourism industries represented (a form of stratified sampling). The initial plan was to have 25 businesses from each sector. Again, if the main interest is in the differences between the various sectors this is quite sensible, but could misrepresent the overall response of the tourism industries. Working hard through business directories and the like provides an estimate of the size of each of the four sectors (Table 4.3). *If each of the sectors is to be represented proportionately, what should be the size of the sub-samples in the last column in Table 4.3?*

Table 4.3 Sample of tourism-related businesses in Brightsea

Sector	Proposed sample size	Size of sector	Proportionate sample size[3]
Accommodation	25	350	
Retail	25	350	
Catering	25	200	
Amusements	25	100	
All	100	1000	100

How is this Different in Qualitative Research?

> The logic and power of probability sampling depends on selecting a truly random and statistically representative sample that will permit confident generalisation from the sample to a larger population … .The logic and power of purposeful sampling lies in selecting *information rich cases* for study in depth. (Patton, 1990: 169)

Qualitative research is normally associated with a different approach to sampling. Most commonly this will involve some form of *purposive sampling* in which people are chosen quite deliberately for who they are and what they know. You may also encounter the related term, *theoretical sampling*. Like many terms in research, writers often use this in slightly different ways. For some it is derived from the theory that is being used as the basis for the investigation which determines who should be selected – for example, if examining the decision-making around the formulation of policy in leisure/sport/tourism, my sample selection may be determined on the basis of the theory of power that I am working with. For others the sample is carefully selected to check the theory that is gradually emerging through the research. It is quite possible for both aspects to be evident through the course of the same project.

The very word 'purposive' implies that this is anything but a haphazard approach. As Mason comments:

> theoretical sampling means selecting groups or categories to study on the … basis of their relevance to your research questions, your theoretical positions … and most importantly the explanation or account which you are developing … [using] criteria which help to develop and test your theory and explanation. (1996: 93–4)

Patton (1990) has suggested 14 possible strategies for sampling. In fact he actually identified 16, but dismissed convenience sampling (the most common, but least desirable) as being neither purposive nor strategic, and identified a final approach

---

[3] 35, 35, 20, 10

Table 4.4 Procedures for qualitative sampling (after Patton, 1990)

1. *Extreme or deviant case sampling* – chosen because they are troublesome or enlightening.
2. *Intensity sampling* – seek out rich/excellent examples, but not the unusual.
3. *Maximum variation sampling* – capture central themes or principal outcomes that cut across most of the variation in participants/programmes.
4. *Homogeneous sampling* – sub-group investigated in depth. (But [when] can we consider any sub-group to be homogeneous?) Patton suggests this is the norm for focus groups.
5. *Typical case sampling* – use key informants/survey/demographics to identify typical cases. For illustrative not definitive purposes.
6. *Stratified purposeful sampling* – capture major variations by sub-dividing into (say) upper, mid and lower, and then use typical case sampling within each stratum.
7. *Critical case sampling* – the archetype where we would expect the desired outcome, on the basis that if it doesn't work there it won't work anywhere (cf. the key marginals in trying to predict election outcomes).
8. *Snowball (chain) sampling* – continual referral from one respondent to the next.
9. *Criterion sampling* – review and study all cases that meet some pre-determined condition (e.g. those who fail to renew their membership having been members for at least five years).
10. *Theory-based sampling* – Patton sees this as a more formal version of 9 – incidents, times, people sampled on the basis of their representation of theoretical constructs (e.g. different risk strategies).
11. *Confirming and disconfirming cases* – used later in the process to check out the viability of emergent findings: the former to add richness and credibility; the latter to suggest alternative explanations and define boundaries.
12. *Opportunistic sampling* – taking advantage of opportunities arising during data collection to follow new directions.
13. *Purposeful random sampling* – selection randomised to avoid criticisms of bias, designed to maximise credibility rather than representativeness.
14. *Sampling politically important cases* (variation on 7) – select or avoid the politically sensitive (e.g. choosing the ward of the council leader may get more attention paid to the findings).

that is a combination of others. Hunt around and you will be able to find further suggestions, but those summarised in Table 4.4 should provide sufficient ideas.

Qualitative researchers usually work with small samples of people set in the detail of their context and studied in-depth (Miles and Huberman, 1994: 27). Validity and meaningfulness owe everything to the richness of the data derived from the cases selected rather than the size of the sample. As we have seen, in quantitative research there are formulae to allow the appropriate sample size to be calculated, and 'rules of thumb' to fall back on. Are there equivalents in qualitative research? Patton is not very reassuring for those who like certainty:

> *There are no rules for sample size in qualitative inquiry.* Sample size depends on what you want to know, the purpose of the inquiry, what's at stake, what will be useful, what will have credibility, and what can be done with available time and resources. (1990: 184)

Reading accounts of the methods used in qualitative studies, if there is any consideration of the size of the sample the authors may well refer to 'closure', 'theoretical saturation' or 'data saturation'. This occurs when each new respondent gives you the same message as the others. Assuming there is no fundamental flaw in your sample selection, recruiting further respondents would be redundant. In practice this is difficult to judge; just as you think you are getting there something new may pop up. And of course, your boss or dissertation supervisor may be fretful and expect to be told at the outset how many people are going to be included.

In the special case of *focus groups*, the norm seems to be to have groups of six to eight people, but that depends on the expected group dynamics. Don't forget when you are recruiting your group that, whatever they say, some people will probably not turn up – make allowances for that. Then, of course, you have to work out how many focus groups you need (doing just one may not be convincing). Consider too whether the people in the group should have similar experience and views or whether you want them to be really diverse.

The Human Dimension

Discussion of sampling frames and standard errors sounds mechanistic, but it is important to keep in mind the human dimension. Bear in mind how you would feel if you were one of the people asked to take part in your research project. Researchers are dependent upon the people they embroil in the research, so the least that should be done is to make those participants feel valued. For example, if you are interviewing people with disabilities about their holiday patterns, make sure you address them rather than their carer.

Presumably you want people to agree to take part in the research – apart from the depression you may feel from rejection, there is the danger that you will recruit a biased sample if many refuse. So think carefully about how to approach potential participants in the research. You need confidence, a smile, as much charm (not smarm) as you can muster, and an air of competence. The way in which researchers present themselves and the research affects not only the initial agreement to be involved, but also the nature of what is subsequently reported. It is well recognised that most people try to please the researcher. This can operate in all sorts of quite subtle ways to influence the 'findings'. For example, conducting research into people's sporting behaviour while wearing a track suit may lead to inflated levels of participation being reported as people feel they *ought* to say they are active. Similarly, a study of drinking as a part of student lifestyles may get very different responses depending upon whether those being interviewed think the researcher is teetotal or a bit of a lad(ette).

For a similar reason, although you must provide enough information for potential respondents to have a reasonable appreciation of what the research is about, providing too much information may encourage them to respond in a particular way. Presumably you are interested in what they have to say rather than what they think you want them to say.

Non-respondents

In addition to those who may have been left out by the sample design, it is always important to consider who refused to be included in the sample – the issue of non-response. The more who refuse to take part, the more concerned we should be about the representativeness of our sample. While survey researchers would expect to report the response rate or level of non-response as a matter of course, qualitative researchers normally seem to believe (wrongly) that they should be exempt from this good practice.[4] If those who refuse are otherwise much the same as those who are included, no harm is done. But our default position should be to assume that the reverse is the case – certain kinds of people are more likely than others to opt out.

When the opinion polls got the result of the 1992 general election in the UK badly wrong (they greatly over-estimated the Labour vote) there was a post-mortem of polling procedures. Several explanations were offered (and it is likely that 'the answer' lay not in one reason, but some combination).

(i)   There was a late 'swing' as voters changed their mind when it came to marking the ballot paper.
(ii) Conservative voters lied about their intentions.
(iii) Conservative voters refused to be involved in a survey that would make them disclose their intentions.
(iv) Labour voters looked more friendly and approachable and so were disproportionately selected by the survey staff.

It may be that the researchers could do little about some of these, but this experience is a reminder that problems may be compounded by the sampling process that has just missed out or under-represented certain types of people. Our own research, of course, is never subject to such failings.

If you have details of the population from which you are sampling it makes sense to compare the characteristics of the sample with those of the population.

---

[4] We tend to presume that non-response is less of an issue in qualitative research than it is in quantitative research because the goal is not to draw statistical inferences about the population. However, we should be concerned if some voices are systematically excluded.

You can then compare the two and, if you find, for example, that young males 16–24 are under-represented you can apply a correction by weighting the sample. Market research companies using telephone surveys may do this, for example, because low levels of phone ownership among certain groups mean they would otherwise be under-represented.

Those with the strongest opinions (positive and negative) are most likely to opt in, while those with less conviction will tend not to bother. In some cases that does not matter (indeed it may be those strong opinions that you want), but it may give a very peculiar impression of the performance of your health club, for example.

In considering whether those included in our research are representative of some larger population we should also consider whether they are made different by being in our research. In experimental research this has been recognised as the *Hawthorne effect*. If people are likely to be changed by the attention they receive by being part of a research study we need to be alert to this whatever the style of research.

Some Questions to Ask Yourself

Can you establish who or what constitute the population you are interested in and devise a suitable sampling frame?
Have you really got a random selection? Have some been systematically excluded?
Does it matter how many are in your sample?
Can you justifiably claim that your sample is representative of the population?
Will it allow the kind of analysis you want?

Further Lines of Enquiry

There are many detailed accounts of sampling, but I find *Surveys in Social Research* by de Vaus (2002) easy to follow. The UK's National Audit Office also provides a useful guide on its website (listed as NAO Sampling Guide): www.nao.gov.uk/publications/other_publications.htm.

It is informative to see how samples are selected for some of the big surveys. I was looking recently at one investigating attitudes to the quality of life and the environment: www.defra.gov.uk/environment/statistics/pubatt/annex2.htm.

Nigel Gilbert has put together a simulation that allows you to examine the effect of using different sample sizes and different sampling procedures: www.soc.surrey.ac.uk/samp.

5

Social Surveys

> Surveys have a lot to offer. … Since experimentation cannot be used to investigate a wide range of macro-social processes, there is often no alternative to considering variation across cases in a systematic fashion. (Marsh, 1982: 147)

Surveys involve the systematic measurement of a standard set of variables for each of numerous cases. This popular form of data gathering is sometimes trivialised through the media, sometimes given an inflated and unjustified status. Comments in Chapter 2 notwithstanding, many people do conduct social surveys, and they come in many shapes and sizes. This chapter (combined with Chapter 6) rehearses the arguments for the initial selection and also offers practical advice on how to conduct them. This will mean addressing:

* the rationale – selecting from different forms, when and what for
* different types of survey – household, site, telephone, postal, street … doing it – including the pros and cons of self-administered and researcher administered
* 'reading' surveys – how many of whom were asked what, how, etc.

Mills (1959) famously considered that the design and conduct of surveys involved no sociological imagination. This may be true of any number of surveys, but 'it ain't necessarily so'. Any researcher using a social survey should be exhorted to engage their disciplinary imagination. Many people seem to think that surveys are intrinsically neutral activities, simply gathering data, and that ultimately 'the facts will speak for themselves'. This is far from the truth. Different procedures and different definitions may result in very different conclusions. Remember, there is no escaping the link to the concepts integral to the research. For example, what is taken to constitute 'leisure', 'sport', 'tourism', 'race', 'health' or even 'employment'? So in a study of the impact of tourism on employment, would researchers be trying to capture information about day trips or people going to visit friends and relatives, and how are temporary, part-time casual workers to be set alongside those in permanent, full-time jobs? It should not be hard to see that the decisions made about such questions will have a profound effect on the eventual conclusions.

If you are doing your own small-scale research you are likely to conduct a one-off survey that results in a snapshot of behaviours and attitudes at a single point in time (the cross-sectional design referred to in Chapter 2). However, it may be important to use a repeated measures design (sometimes with the same sample, sometimes a different but still hopefully 'representative' one) before and after an intervention or participation in some activity. More generally, the survey may just be repeated at a later point in time to record change (this may be taken a step further to gather continuous data). There is then the opportunity to conduct longitudinal analyses; and repeated often enough it produces 'time series data'. With experience, researchers may decide that they can devise a better way of measuring whatever it is they are interested in. What then to do? Retain the established categories and procedures to allow direct comparison, or seek to improve/keep up-to-date? People get suspicious when the government changes its way of measuring unemployment or inflation, but may think nothing of changes to definitions in leisure, sport and tourism, though the issues remain. If 'better' ways are designed to measure participation or ethnicity, it is then hard to judge how much of any apparent change over time is the result of real change in behaviour and how much is attributable to methodology. In your small-scale research you are more likely to have to address whether to use established procedures, questions or instruments (for the sake of comparison or because they have been previously validated), or to adapt them to make them more appropriate to your context.

Direct Data Gathering

It is tempting to equate surveys with questionnaires (Chapter 6). But many questionnaires exist outside surveys and, more importantly here, not all surveys depend on questionnaires. For example, a survey of the accessibility of leisure centres, sports clubs or museums may involve the researcher directly recording data during visits to the facilities concerned. Quite apart from avoiding problems of non-response, this might produce rather different findings from a questionnaire administered to the managers of the facilities, who may 'see' things in a particular way. Nonetheless this kind of audit still requires a form to record the key details.

Site Surveys represent probably the most common type of survey in leisure research, being conducted at theatres, heritage centres, leisure centres, gyms, etc. By definition they cover users only, so non-users are ignored, but not all non-users are potential users anyway. For example, if 10,000 use the Kirkstall Leisure Centre and there are 740,000 living in the city, there are 730,000 non-users. Are there really? Some users will come from out of town, which suggests there are more non-users; some non-users will be closer to other centres, which suggests there are fewer non-users; and others would not dream of using any leisure centre under any circumstances whatever the inducement. Nonetheless, it is generally useful to make some comparison between users and the population in the catchment area, however defined.

People should be asked on leaving, otherwise they are being asked hypothetical questions about their visit. An interviewer can probably expect to take about five minutes of the respondent's time (sometimes longer) so each interviewer may do about six in an hour, allowing for getting organised or waiting for the next respondent during quieter spells, though there will obviously be variations.

Even though the population of users can readily be identified (by definition they are on site), one of the key challenges is still how to get a representative sample. Simply because of the logistics of survey work, those using the facility/amenity during quiet periods are more likely to be selected as interviewers pounce hungrily on them (during the day at the sports centre, a damp day at the park, the smallest car park at the beach).

Site surveys are typically used to establish:

(a) catchment areas (how many people come from how far away)
(b) user profile (the private sector may want to maximise market share; the public sector may want to attract cross-section or particular target groups)
(c) opinions – though the dissatisfied may have already left/given-up. Moreover, many cannot be bothered thinking about what is right, wrong or needs changing. As a result complaints/recommendations may only come from 10%, so do you act on that or say that 90% did not suggest that change?

Street Surveys are a quick and cheap route to gathering survey data. The 'street' in this sense may represent any convenient location for 'capturing' respondents (e.g. the mall or refectory/canteen). The questionnaire needs to be short because of the circumstances in which potentially uninterested people are approached.

If all you need is a general 'feel' for the way people are thinking, this may be quite adequate, but there are three interrelated problems in particular:

- The environment in which such surveys are conducted often means that response rates are low.
- The amount and quality of data gathered may be similarly low.
- It is difficult to make the sample representative of anything/anyone. Quota sampling (see Chapter 4) is often used, but can you set quotas for the right characteristics? By definition those who are housebound or in employment are likely to be underrepresented. Similarly, the location of the interview point has to be carefully considered. For example, a survey of tourists conducted on the promenade/boardwalk will ignore those in the resort for alternative types of tourism.

Home Interview Surveys can be designed with proper sampling procedures to be more representative of the whole population. However, those who take part in leisure activities may be out doing those activities, so the interviewer has to call back in order to avoid a biased sample. When conducted in major studies these may commonly last an hour or even longer, gathering a large amount of data in the process. The detail that this allows is not easily covered in the alternative forms of survey. These sorts of consideration mean that home interview surveys are usually expensive, but respondents are likely to feel safer on their own territory (as the interviewer you may not though) and be more forthcoming as a result. It is also possible to make arrangements for responses to be entered directly into a laptop computer. The major public bodies may commission their own dedicated survey or may buy some space in a survey covering many different topics. If the number of questions can be contained this is a relatively cheap way of reaching a representative national sample.[1]

Telephone Surveys have been used to reach respondents more cost-effectively. However, multiple providers and unlisted mobile phones[2] make it difficult to establish a sampling frame, and there are still households without a phone at all (particularly important in research concerned with issues of disadvantage or low participation). These variations are not randomly distributed in the population. Some opinion surveys seek to apply a correction factor based on a comparison of the characteristics of the sample and the characteristics of the population to make sure that the poor are not under-represented. An option now being used by market research companies is to use Random Digit Dialling – a computer programme

---

[1] The Mintel leisure reports commonly also use data gathered in this way.

[2] I have been told that this is less of a problem than I imagine because those with mobile phones tend to live in households with a landline as well. I am sceptical.

randomly generates numbers in specified areas (e.g. defined by postcode). This will pick-up unlisted landlines, but not mobile phones or people with no phone at all.

Irritation with direct sales calls increases resistance and it is also harder to establish rapport over the phone. On the other hand the more anonymous procedure may help some people to answer more fully and honestly. Some surveys involve showing people lists or asking for responses to images, and this cannot be done over the phone (technology will eventually resolve this). Again, responses can easily be entered directly into the computer.

A consideration of some of the other standard issues associated with surveys demonstrates the wide range of circumstances that may be involved. In terms of the length of the questionnaire, 10–15 minutes is generally thought to be acceptable for the general public, but much longer questionnaires are possible if dealing with specialist respondents. The cost too can vary enormously depending on the charging policy of the phone company and how dispersed the respondents are. Of course, the cost of phone charges may be more than offset by savings on travel and the efficient use of interviewers' time.

I used to be fiercely resistant to this way of gathering data, and am still unsure of its appropriateness for questionnaire surveys, though it is undoubtedly becoming more popular. However, because of a rail strike some years ago I had to use telephone contact instead of travelling to interview representatives of sports governing bodies against a very open-ended questionnaire. Despite my concerns this worked well because we were gathering data from people selected because of their expertise who already knew about the survey and had been sent a copy of the questions/issues in advance.

Postal Questionnaires can be very useful and appeal to inexperienced researchers who lack the confidence to speak directly to respondents. Their big advantage is that they are able to accommodate a wide geographic spread of respondents at little cost. Unfortunately the levels of response are usually very low if sent to the general public, though they can be higher when dealing with a specialist audience that might consider it has a stake in the research. Response rates are even lower if the questionnaires are distributed in magazines as a readership survey. As discussed in the previous chapter, the big question then is just who is responding?

Response may be improved by:

- including a letter explaining the importance of the survey
- offering a reward (some researchers strongly disapprove on the basis that this changes the relationship between researcher and respondent and the way in which people respond as a consequence, and also alters the public's expectations of other research/ers)

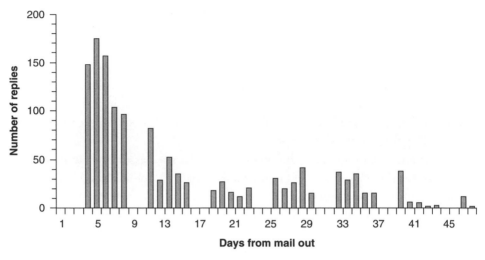

Figure 5.1   Responses received for a postal survey

- keeping it simple and relatively short so it will not be too off-putting (we try to make sure it will fit onto a sheet of A3 paper folded to give four sides of A4[3] without looking too crowded)
- setting a date by which they should reply to create a sense of urgency (but make it realistic)
- sending reminders (this is only possible if the questionnaires are not anonymous and you know who has not responded)
- providing a reply paid envelope.

In a recent study we conducted a postal survey around the country of organisations that had received a grant from a national award scheme. There was no particular reason to expect large numbers to respond, but we managed to achieve a good response rate of 69%, and tracked the arrival of the replies (Figure 5.1). The initial mail out was on days 0 and 1 with a reminder sent to non-respondents three weeks later.

Electronic Surveys are becoming more common because of rapidly evolving technology. These may typically take two forms: one is the electronic equivalent of the postal questionnaire; the other is the electronic equivalent of leaving questionnaires at the reception desk for people to pick up if they are interested. The former makes use of an established email address list and sends the questionnaire to known

---

[3]If you are in North America, that is roughly equivalent to one sheet of paper folded to produce four sides of letter size.

individuals. The latter posts a questionnaire on some part of your website. Extrapolating from either of these to suggest general patterns of behaviour/opinion is likely to be unjustified. However, the very particular group of respondents may provide good quality data that allow the formulation of hypotheses or the development of theory (e.g. if you can identify one group of respondents as different from another and think you can see why, then you have the beginnings of your theory).

Timing

The experience of just going out and doing surveys ought to emphasise the link between practicalities, more general methodological issues and theory. For example, seasonality is so influential in much of leisure, sport and tourism. Like many others I have completed questionnaires by writing inside a plastic bag to keep the paper dry, wondering how I'm going to keep warm. In such circumstances people naturally give shorter answers and spend less time trying to think of all the things they have done on their visit. Maybe that is why we have a rosy picture of the niceness of leisure – data are predominantly gathered in good weather.

A little thought should demonstrate that a dissertation conducted between October and April (in most northern climes) is limited in how it can address issues associated with open air music festivals, just as one on rugby union or ice hockey is constrained if conducted in the summer. Even big organisations get caught out, having to produce answers too quickly or wait for budget approval.

Seasonality affects not just your likelihood of getting cold and wet. Theatre programmes, political activity, television schedules, patterns of eating out all have seasonal variations, and most surveys you are likely to do will be snapshots. Some major surveys, like the UK's General Household Survey, are conducted through the year, which helps to provide a better representation in the aggregate.

At the park or visitor attraction does it matter that you miss the early morning use because you were still having breakfast, or the early evening use because you had to get home? The questions go on. At the outset ask the questions of yourself as a researcher and as a participant, and then just keep asking.

One last point about timing relates to how many questionnaires or other data collection procedures will be completed in a given time span. In addition to the length of time productively collecting data there is also travel time to and between sites, the time spent waiting for the next respondent to appear, and the time necessary for recruiting and wrapping up. All of which means that it will take longer than you first think.

Self-Administered Questionnaires?

You need to consider whether your survey instruments will be administered by an interviewer (face-to-face or over the phone) or self-administered (filled-in by the respondent).

Interviewers can:

- encourage participation by people who would otherwise not bother to respond
- encourage people to take it seriously
- clarify any confusion about the meaning of the questions (though interviewers are normally instructed to read only the words written on the page to make sure everyone is responding to the same question without any prompting)
- include those who cannot read – not a trivial point when a significant proportion of the population, even in supposedly well-educated societies, is 'functionally illiterate'.

But *interviewers can also put people off, record what they say wrongly or encourage a particular response.*

Self-Administered Questionnaires (SAQs) can:

- get to a large number of scattered people quickly and cheaply
- lend anonymity, which may be very important if asking about sensitive issues.

But *SAQs typically have a low response rate, the nature of the non-response is unknown and any misunderstanding of the questions cannot be corrected.*

These considerations need to be weighed carefully depending upon the particular research in question, but on balance it is normally better to have an interviewer administer the questionnaire (even better, a good interviewer). Perhaps this is not what you are wanting to hear if you are reticent about approaching people and asking them questions.

It is considered bad methodological practice to combine data from these two different formats even if the wording of the questions appears the same. For questions about attitudes and beliefs it is considered important that all respondents should be responding to the same stimulus. If some are asked the questions and some read them for themselves this is not so, not least because they may be read out of sequence or people may return to amend their responses later.

Evaluating Survey Data

I started the chapter by encouraging you not to take for granted the findings of surveys. Whether it is your own research or something you are reading about (from however eminent a source), you should ask yourself a series of questions in appraising the work:

- *Focus* – Was there an appropriate focus? Remind yourself of the starting point and consider whether the research challenge was an appropriate one or was based on a misreading of the issue.
- *Sample Design* – How was the sample drawn up? Was it just of participants or were non-participants included as well? Was it really 'the public' or readers of a particular newspaper/magazine or account holders with some bank … ?
- *Sample Size* – How big is the sample and what levels of statistical confidence, margins of error and significance are associated with the findings as a consequence?
- *Response Rate* – What was the refusal rate? Who did not respond? Are the respondents 'typical' of the population or dominated by Mr and Mrs Angry?
- *Questionnaire Design* – What questions were asked? Are these a reasonable representation of the issues? For example, did they just ask about what is provided or what should be provided? As with all research we need to know if there are any 'interested parties' behind the research. Does the research have a particular angle because of the vested interests of the researchers or the people who funded it?
- *Question Wording* – Were neutral or leading words/phrases used in the question and were appropriate categories offered for the possible responses?
- *Interpretation* – Are the conclusions justified on the basis of the data?

Even in survey research objectivity may prove elusive, but transparency of process should be prized. It should be quite clear to others how the findings have been arrived at. In the conduct of surveys themselves, being methodical and rigorous is highly commended.

Conducting the Survey

Think about presenting yourself and the survey to your potential participants and review the likely impacts of your appearance, approach (e.g. body language) and introduction (including why the data are necessary). These will affect whether or not people respond and how.

Make sure all survey workers are trained so that they know why the data are needed, ask confidently questions about age, income, etc., and if using a questionnaire make

(Continued)

(*Continued*)

sure they read the questions exactly as they appear on the page. Interviewers need to know the reason for each question so they can explain to inquisitive respondents. Enough information needs to be provided to explain and inform without unnecessarily colouring their responses.

Devise appropriate sampling procedures and stick to them.

Ensure clarity of instructions to your respondents so they know what is expected of them, e.g. how many answers to each question, and clarity of instruction to your survey workers (even if it is only you) to ensure consistency throughout the survey, e.g. in coding responses.

On a more mundane level, make sure you know where you can find toilets, food and shelter.

Make sure you have all the bits and pieces you need, e.g. pens, questionnaires, survey report forms, show cards, instructions for which respondents to select from a group/household, clip boards, waterproof clothing.

If you have others working with you, make sure they know what to do to find out what to do when they don't know what to do.

Think about your personal safety. I count myself fortunate that neither I nor my colleagues have had serious problems when conducting surveys, but you need to recognise that you are vulnerable when surveying in the park, at the football stadium or in other people's houses. I have been caught between two groups of sparring football supporters, but their aggression was mainly for show and they weren't interested in me. Don't let worries stop you, but be sensible and work out what you can do to reduce the risk. In different circumstances you might leave details of your whereabouts with friends, work in pairs, conduct interviews near police/stewards, etc. See the SRA website for some useful guidelines: www.the-sra.org.uk/staying_safe.htm.

Further Lines of Enquiry

For a robust defence of social surveys, see Marsh's (1982) book, *The Survey Method*.

In Appendix 1 to *Bowling Alone* (one of the most discussed books in leisure policy circles in recent years) Putnam (2000) discusses the methodology he used to assess the extent of social change. His discussion of the use of surveys offers useful insights (pp. 416–24).

An example of a standardised visitor survey developed by Veal for Centennial Parklands in Australia can be found at: www.cp.nsw.gov.au/about_us/super_group/standard_visitor_survey.

The UK's data archive, which contains the outputs from the major publicly funded surveys, has links to those in other countries: www.data-archive.ac.uk.

6

Setting Questions

Any fool can design a questionnaire.

Enquiring researchers set questions in all sorts of different research forms, though the focus of attention in this chapter is on questionnaires. Of course 'any fool can write a questionnaire', but the challenge is to write one that will produce good quality data. This chapter will address ways of posing questions in different environments and explain the importance of considering the meaning of words to try to avoid a casual approach to research. It will address some of the most commonly asked questions:

- How long should my questionnaire be?
- Can I measure what I'm interested in?
- Can I ask people their age/income/etc.?

As you read through the chapter, try to identify what you think constitutes good practice in questionnaire design and then compare it with the box at the end. This chapter should be read in conjunction with Chapter 7 which addresses questions within qualitative interviews. The challenge for the researcher is to identify what can be transferred from one form to another.

What Do You Want to Know?

No, what do you really want to know?

This question should represent the starting point for any questionnaire, but it is all too easy to get carried away and start dashing off questions that 'feel right'. It is important to be quite clear about the research question that you are trying to address.[1] You should be able to identify the link between each question and that central challenge. If you fail to ask the right questions (and enough of them), it is self-evident that you are going to end up frustrated with no real evidence at your disposal. Equally, asking questions that are not necessary to your research challenge is a waste of your respondents' time and an unfair imposition on them. 'I thought it would be nice to know' is not an adequate justification for posing a question; make sure you have a use for it. If you have worked through the procedures discussed in Chapter 2, it ought to be fairly clear how things slot into place. This also implies that some attention has been given to how the data will be analysed.

> ... *the world is a vast sea of potential data in which one would swim aimlessly in perpetuity (or drown) without criteria for selecting and organising data. (Bulmer, 1977: 3)*

This then forms part of the response to the question about how long the questionnaire should be; it depends on the data needs. However, it also depends on the circumstances in which the questionnaire is conducted and the interest of the respondents. I have just thrown in the bin a questionnaire I got sent by the manufacturer asking me about my new car. I started out with good intentions because, as a researcher, I feel an obligation, and in any case I wanted to explain my reservations. But eventually I gave up because I felt they were taking me for a ride and pushing my goodwill too far. I was being asked for huge quantities of extraneous data and not being allowed to convey the messages I wanted.

So consider:

Where are you? On the street, in the heritage centre, in the car park, on the doorstep, in the home? The more comfortable the respondent is, the longer your questionnaire can be; so if you are outside the weather comes into consideration too.

How motivated are your respondents likely to be? The more interested they are in the subject or the more they are likely to be influenced by any outcome, the greater the input they are likely to be prepared to make.

How good is the interviewer? You need to allow people time to consider their answers, but also be efficient in dealing with the questions. An experienced interviewer can cover a lot of questions in five minutes.

---

[1] As will be discussed in later chapters there are approaches to research that are more tentative and speculative, but even then the best studies are characterised by a clarity of purpose.

Strip out any questions you cannot justify – you owe it to your respondents – but make sure you get the detail you need. It is painful to read superficial research reports, so make sure that any important issue is addressed by more than one question. I remember being at a conference once when the presenter (Roger Jowell) insisted that 'good questions travel in convoys', and this strikes me as good advice.

Different Circumstances, Different Questions?

There is a need for different types of question to serve different purposes. Questions can be asked in many different formats, and a bit of variety normally helps to retain the respondent's interest. Any of the standard texts will make the distinction between open and closed questions, but there are several variations on that theme.

Closed questions	Closed questions restrict responses to pre-coded categories. The most simple form of this is the Yes/No distinction, but it may be any set of categories that have been determined in advance. The usual advice is that the categories should be:

(a) mutually exclusive – i.e. if the response is in one category it cannot be in another, so you need carefully defined rules of assignment; and

(b) mutually exhaustive – i.e. together they account for all possible responses, hence the appearance of 'other' at the end of the list. However, if 'other' turns out to be the most frequent response, it is not very informative.

Open questions	Open questions allow a free response so that people answer using their own words. These responses are then typically coded into a set of categories that are drawn-up to fit the answers provided. They can then be analysed quantitatively in the same way as closed questions. However, sometimes the responses are treated purely as qualitative data.
Open questions/preset categories	An alternative is to offer people the freedom of an open question, but to code them straight into pre-determined categories. Like many compromises it is not clear that it resolves the problem it was designed to address. Predetermined categories presume that the researcher knows the most likely responses. Quite often they do, but it does amount to imposing the researcher's view of things onto the research and the respondents. This is less a case of leading questions, more one

of leading answers and is likely to be a particular problem when dealing with opinions. Not only is choice apparently restricted to an 'acceptable' set, but undue prominence may be given to the first option. (To counter this aspect survey staff are often instructed to rotate the order in which potential answers are presented to respondents. This is easily achieved if the questionnaire is computer administered, when the programme can ensure this happens.)

Checklists

These are often used as a means of gathering data on participation. For example, rather than asking people an open question about which sports they participate in, they are presented with a list and asked to say which they have taken part in during the past 12 months/four weeks/one week. Not surprisingly this approach records people as taking part in more activities than if an open question is asked and people have to trawl through their brains. Does it just remind people of things they would otherwise have forgotten or artificially inflate participation rates by 'putting ideas into people's heads'? Especially if presented with a long list (the last time the question was asked in the General Household Survey in Britain there were some 30 activities – vastly reduced from some of the earlier ones) there is subtle pressure on people to say that they have taken part in something, whether or not they really have.

Rankings

These might be in the form of asking respondents to place a given set of items/activities/reasons in rank order, or identifying their own set (e.g. of leisure activities) in some order of preference. At the outset this seems intuitively appealing, but has been found to be very difficult for respondents, and such rankings are not easy to deal with analytically.

Attitude scales

These are an attempt to put numbers on (quantify) people's ideas (see the section on the semantic differential and Likert scales, p. 64). They are standard fare in sports psychology, but are found in many parts of leisure and tourism research as well. Perhaps the best known is the POMS (Profile of Mood States) scale, developed to assess mood states and applied commonly to sports men and women, but there are many others like the leisure boredom scale (Iso-Ahola and Weissinger, 1990; Wegner et al., 2002). However, beyond those standard instruments, a large proportion of questionnaires include questions that ask people to score themselves on a multi-point scale.

Preferred statements These are a bit like multiple choice questions in an exam, but in this case there is no 'right' answer. They are very difficult to construct in such a way that the choices reflect the same evaluative dimension, so are more often used to represent different positions in a 'political' debate. For example, in one of our surveys (Long et al., 2000) we adapted a question used in the FA Premier League National Fan Survey administered by the Sir Norman Chester Centre for Football Research (now the Centre for the Sociology of Sport: www.le.ac.uk/so/css). Our version read: Are you concerned about the number of foreign players in the professional game? (Tick one box only)

- ☐ No they improve the standard
- ☐ We are close to the limit of foreign players
- ☐ Yes, foreign players limit the opportunities for British players
- ☐ Don't know/not sure

Some questions explicitly or implicitly invite multiple responses – e.g. *Why did you come to this visitor attraction today rather than any other?* This may apply to both closed and open questions. In such circumstances some people may offer four or more responses and others only one. This may cause problems in data entry and statistical analysis using your favourite package, and may also have the effect of giving increased significance to the more articulate who are the ones likely to identify more reasons/activities. The alternative would be to ask: *What was the main reason you decided to come to this visitor attraction today rather than any other?* But that may cause frustration for people who made their decision on the basis of a package of criteria.

While some people resent being constrained by boxes, others find it difficult to express themselves if given a blank canvas. Faced with this, questionnaire designers typically seek to offer a mix of different question types. On a good day this variety will serve to maintain the interest of the maximum number of respondents; on a bad day most respondents will get irritated by something in the questionnaire. Fortunately a survey has found that the number of good days exceeds the number of bad days …

An Introduction to Scaling Techniques

The basic idea behind psychometric scaling is to try to formalise what is going on in somebody's head with regard to our chosen area of study and to quantify it. Before getting into the detail of the scaling techniques, it is probably sensible to rehearse the distinctions between the different levels of measurement in the box below. Those who are confident in these can just skip this box.

Levels of measurement

Conventionally four levels are identified: nominal (categorical); ordinal (rank); interval; ratio.

Nominal – simply allocated to one of a number of categories, most simply the Yes/No distinction, but applied to any set of categories, such as why the respondent came to this centre rather than any other. These categories have no significance other than as a means of labelling; we know that they are different, but that is all.

Ordinal – allows the distinction that one category is greater than another, but provides no indication of by how much (e.g. allocating a star rating to the films currently showing).

Interval – allows us to measure by how much one thing differs from another (e.g. the temperature in centigrade of the leisure centre's pool).

Ratio – a measure that allows us to distinguish how many times greater one unit is than another (e.g. ticket price). This is not true of interval data because there is no 'absolute zero' (base point).

In practice there is no real need to worry about this last point as social researchers typically conflate the third and fourth levels (interval/ratio). However, the distinctions between the others are crucial in determining the kind of analysis that can be conducted.

Don't leave it until the analysis stage to work this out – that way lies heartache. In the current context, the 7-point (etc.) attitude scales are ordinal variables, but they are commonly treated as though they represent interval data and are subjected to sophisticated multivariate statistical analysis on that basis. This has attracted considerable criticism from statisticians.

(Note that questions involving measurement at the nominal level can produce ratio scales. For example, whether or not an employee is registered disabled is a nominal variable. However, when the measure is changed to represent the proportion of disabled employees in a leisure services department, a ratio variable is created that allows comparison with other departments.)

In the following box is a set of questions taken from a longer questionnaire that was part of a study undertaken for a policy review (Best Value) in Mansfield by the Centre for Leisure and Sport Research to examine the use of parks and associated attitudes. To check that you know the distinction between the different levels of measurement, identify the level for each question and check against the final box at the end of this chapter (p. 74).

A. Can I just check how long you have lived in Mansfield? **WRITE IN NUMBER OF YEARS AND MONTHS AND CODE BELOW**

_____ YEARS _____ MONTHS

1 LESS THAN ONE YEAR
2 MORE THAN ONE YEAR, BUT LESS THAN FIVE YEARS
3 MORE THAN FIVE YEARS, BUT LESS THAN TEN YEARS
4 TEN YEARS OR MORE

B. Have you noticed any changes in the park you go to most often in the past year?
1 YES
2 NO – **GO TO Q_**

C. Overall do you think these changes have been for the better or worse?
1 BETTER
2 WORSE
3 NO DIFFERENCE

D. Have you used a football/rugby/cricket pitch in Mansfield in the past 12 months?
1 YES
2 NO – **GO TO Q_**
3 CAN'T RECALL – **GO TO Q_**

E. How would you rate the quality of the pitch you used most recently? **SHOW CARD AND CODE ONE ONLY**
5 EXCELLENT
4 GOOD
3 AVERAGE
2 POOR
1 VERY POOR
6 DON'T KNOW

F. What do you think the Council could do to improve safety? **DO NOT PROMPT. CODE ALL THAT APPLY**

1	Better Lighting	5	Softer Surfaces
2	Remove Shrubs	6	Better Maintenance of Equipment
3	More Park Staff	7	Clean Up Glass Etc.
4	Get Police To Stop Gangs Gathering	8	Other (please specify)

G. On the basis of what you know about Mansfield generally, how would you rate the quality of the following? **SHOW CARD WITH RATING SCALE. READ OUT ITEMS AND CODE ONE FOR EACH**

EXCELLENT 5
GOOD 4
AVERAGE 3
POOR 2
VERY POOR 1
DK 6

H. What was your age last birthday?

The most frequently used techniques of scaling are derived from two basic approaches: the Semantic Differential and Likert Scales. Both ask respondents to assign themselves a score on a (series of) numerical scale(s).

Semantic differential

These scales are based on bi-polar adjectives:

good/bad
accessible/inaccessible
clean/tidy
friendly/unwelcoming
efficient/inefficient etc …

We might then ask the staff of a Leisure Services Department (or Company Head Office) to score each of the local leisure centres on each of our scales. These scales can have as many points on them as you believe appropriate. The classic semantic differential scale has seven points, but researchers have chosen other sizes. The two main points to consider are:

(1)   How many gradations can your respondents cope with/distinguish between? 3? 5? 7? 10? 100? Too few and they feel frustrated because there is insufficient sensitivity to represent the distinctions they want to make. Too many and the distinctions become arbitrary.

(2)   Do you wish them to have a non-committal mid-point? You can force respondents to come down on one side or the other by having an even number of points on the scale, but that may make them feel uncomfortable and resentful.

(N.B. There may also be questions on which people have insufficient knowledge to make a decision. It may be important to distinguish these people from those who have considered the issue and find themselves right in the middle.)

These scores can be combined to get overall estimates made by all respondents on a scale, compare the ratings of different leisure centres, see if different staff (e.g. 'front line' *v* 'backroom') view the centres differently, etc. That operation, though, invites the question, 'Do I mean the same by '6' as you do?'.

Likert scales

These present respondents with statements and ask them the extent to which they agree/disagree. They might take the form:

Please indicate the extent to which you agree with the following statements by ringing the appropriate answer.

'The level of racism has fallen in football over the past 10 years.'

| Strongly agree | Agree | Neither agree nor disagree | Disagree | Strongly disagree |

'On holiday I prefer to go to places I've never been to before.'

| Strongly agree | Agree | Neither agree nor disagree | Disagree | Strongly disagree |

It is very difficult to get statements that really say what you want and are completely unambiguous. If you don't believe me just try it with a group of about four questionnaire designers.

A true Likert scale is essentially a composite scale. In other words, responses to statements are not treated separately, but summed (added-up) to produce an overall score for each respondent's reaction to a particular issue. The idea is that most of the important issues we are interested in are multifaceted and cannot be addressed by a single question. Each statement therefore addresses a slightly different aspect of the central issue, but it is the overall response that we are interested in (e.g. whether people are competitive or collaborative in their approach to sport). This means that the individual statements (items) should 'hang together' as an entity. The relationship between individual items and the overall scale should then be checked (typically done by using a statistic known as Cronbach's alpha).

It is important that people should consider each item separately rather than check their agreement all down the left hand side of the page. So to avoid unthinking responses some of the statements should have a positive orientation to the issue being considered, and some negative. You then have to be careful how you 'add' the various statements together (so that the positive end of the scale is always scored higher).

There are many other psychometric scales that you may come across, and many different kinds of scaling task. For example, not so long ago the overriding concern of socio-economic policy was with unemployment, so in one of our studies we were interested in tourism's ability to reduce unemployment and provide an economic generator (Vaughan and Long, 1982; Duffield et al., 1987). The concern was that if tourism jobs were regarded as undesirable then they would have limited success in stemming the flow of out migration by those in search of employment. We therefore reviewed the employment literature and identified what were considered to be the key aspects/characteristics of a job (e.g. good pay, security, providing a challenge, variety, promotion prospects, etc.). We then asked people employed in tourism to assess the extent to which their job satisfied those various characteristics (using a set of 7-point scales), and also asked a sample of unemployed people in the same areas how important those characteristics of a job were to them (and whether they expected those most important to them to be supplied by a job in tourism).

The Significance of Language

One of the objectives in using a questionnaire is that it should be designed in such a way that all those sampled are responding to exactly the same stimulus. This idea is borrowed from scientific research where, for example, each participant in the experimental group might be given exactly the same amount of the same dietary supplement in the same circumstances in order to measure the effect on performance. Of course, for the equivalent to be true in relation to questionnaires people do not just have to be presented with the same wording, but they have to understand the question in the same way. That is why survey staff are often instructed to read out exactly what is on the questionnaire, and only what is on the questionnaire. For the questions to be understood in the same way, they need to be straightforward (using simple language) and not open to misinterpretation.

To ensure clarity, imprecise terms should be avoided. For example, 'often' can be interpreted very differently by different people and for the same person may vary between activities – going to the theatre often may equate with five times a year, while playing squash often may be five times a week. Words like 'normally' may appear in institutional documents precisely because they are not too precise and so allow 'room for manoeuvre' in their interpretation. For just that reason they are not good for questionnaires (but of course they often appear in questionnaires). Because of this it is better to ask people for an actual number of occasions or particulars of given events (the most recent/the most fulfilling) rather than some general pattern.

If there is a particular target population, whether football fans, youngsters on the street, Trekkies or trekkers, use the language your respondents will be familiar with. However, beware an artificiality that may easily be interpreted as patronising.

In dealing with more general populations, though, it is important to avoid jargon. Moreover, there should be no presumption that respondents will have heard of things that are central to the research – e.g. the government department responsible for funding, public agency instituting policy, the latest curriculum initiative or training regime

These problems, of course, are exacerbated if respondents have a different language as their first language. This is a particular problem in cross-national studies, surveys of tourist visitors to a destination, studies of minority ethnic groups, or indeed a study of 'the public' which must include minority ethnic groups. Comprehending the questionnaire you have written may be difficult for them, and even if the questionnaire is translated it is difficult to ensure that exactly the same meaning is retained (languages tend not to work like that).

Question Framing and Sequencing

We are advised to avoid long and convoluted questions, leading questions, ambiguous questions and hypothetical questions. A little thought will normally resolve the first, but the others may not be quite so straightforward.

Respondents should feel that they can give any answer they want rather than 'the right one'. *Leading questions* are sometimes easy to spot, but others may simply steer people away from the response they want to give:

Why do you think that women are not interested in rugby?
What could you do to make your club more open to other groups?

Inviting the respondent to agree is also leading, as is the association of emotive words with certain positions (e.g. Do you think the evil/unfairness of drug taking has to be … ?). Moreover, unless the researcher is extremely careful, the very fact that a question is being asked at all may imply a particular response.

Questions may be *ambiguous* because there is in fact more than one question implicit in the wording, or if people may give the same answer for different reasons. I now cringe at one question we used (Long et al., 2000) that seemed like a good idea at the time (yes, it was piloted). Club secretaries were asked the extent to which they agreed/disagreed with the statement:

Too much is made of this black/white thing – in football they're all the same.

This was chosen because it was a phrase commonly fed back to us in our investigation of participation in sport by minority ethnic groups and was intended to provide an indication of racialised thinking. Quite apart from the objectification and 'othering' implied by the use of 'they' rather than 'we', it is essentially ambiguous. Consider how people with the following views would respond to the question:

- Different racial groups do have different sporting abilities.
- Sport as an institution tries to make out that everybody is treated the same, and fails to recognise the racism experienced by many people from minority ethnic groups.
- Too much is made of this black/white thing with people always whingeing about how badly treated minority ethnic groups are (and sport is only interested in talent).
- Too much is made of this by people with racial stereotypes and everyone should be treated according to their sporting aptitude (but in fact in sport they are not).

Memo to self: 'Try harder next time'.

Faced with a *hypothetical* question about 'what if', people find it difficult to divine what their attitude/behaviour would actually be. I remember hearing on the radio about a study that had tried to establish how much the environment was worth to people. In order to put a price on this people were asked how much they would be prepared to contribute to clean up a recent oil spill in order to restore the environment of the Alaskan coast. The average figure was $85; but when this was contextualised in terms of the competing demands on their purse it came down to 29 cents. In a recreational context a similar approach might be used, for example, to try to estimate the value people place on retaining a pristine environment rather than allowing a proposed development, like a ski slope on a mountainside.

In practice of course, in the kind of area we work in, hypothetical questions are often of great interest.

> The City of Benton is investigating setting-up a museum to tell the story of local people. If this happens, how likely would you be to visit it: 'very likely'; 'possibly'; 'unlikely'; 'definitely not'; 'don't know'?

> If the price of a swim increased by $1 would you: 'still come as often'; 'still come, but less frequently'; 'stop coming'; 'don't know'?

They are the bread and butter of people wanting to plan future provision. We like to have this kind of information, but it is not easy for respondents to foresee what would actually happen in these circumstances. It is therefore not sensible to rely on this source, but to think of how different questions might be asked of different sources in different ways. It might be possible to examine what had happened elsewhere in similar circumstances or to conduct a small piece of action research to see what happens in response to small changes prior to making decisions with more long-term implications.

One of the most common challenges in our areas of research is to establish levels of participation and the frequency of that participation. This is not as straightforward as might first be imagined. Once again the key is to clarify just what you want to know: the number of people who participate; the number of participant occasions (tickets sold); the percentage of the population who (do not) participate. Think about how the data are going to be described in the final report for some of the common formulations:

Have you taken part in _____ in the past week/month/year?
How many times have you taken part in the past week/month/year?
Do you take part in ____   Daily
                                          At least once a week
                                          At least once a month
                                          At least once a year
                                          Less than once a year
                                          Never

As discussed above, terms like 'rarely', 'occasionally', 'frequently' are not very helpful because they lack precision.

Many of our activities in leisure, sport and tourism are seasonal. The contrasting seasonal patterns of rugby union and cricket are obvious, but there are also variations in listening to live music, going to visitor attractions, even visiting the local park. A moment's thought will demonstrate the difficulties this causes in establishing levels of participation and the consequent implications for the formulation of the questions asked. Think too of the implications for the leisure centre manager of figures on participation in swimming that include swimming while away on holiday, not just in local pools.

Measures of participation over the past year as a whole help to address problems of seasonality, but may be more vulnerable to inaccurate recall than those based on the past week or month. Just how far back can we expect people to remember, with what accuracy and level of detail? Imagine being asked how much you spent on your last holiday on travel, accommodation, food and drink, excursions/activities, souvenirs/gifts. Then consider what difference it makes whether this is immediately on your return, a month later when your credit card bill comes in, or several months later when the tan has faded and you just have some photographs.

Questions sometimes ask: 'When you participate … ?'. This presumes a normal standard of behaviour. In some cases this may be justified; more often it is not. One of the supposedly validated measures of physical activity (the EPIC Physical Activity Questionnaire)[2] includes as one of its questions:

> In a typical week during the past 12 months, how many hours did you spend on each of the following activities? Can you tell me this for the summer and the winter?
> Walking, including walking to work, shopping and leisure
> Cycling, including cycling to work and during leisure time
> Gardening
> Housework such as cleaning, washing, cooking, childcare
> Do-it-yourself
> Other physical exercise such as keep fit, aerobics, swimming and jogging

This is presumably an attempt to avoid the problems posed by seasonality discussed earlier. However, although my life is not particularly complicated, I cannot conceive how I could answer that question accurately, because I have no idea what a 'typical week' might be over the course of a year. Nonetheless, heroic stabs in the dark by thousands like me have been used to produce precise numbers that are presented as fact.

It is better to ask about a specific occasion – usually the most recent, or perhaps the favourite. Some researchers worry that will miss the typical behaviour, but how representative is a research world made up entirely of 'usual' experiences? In survey work that typicality comes from the aggregate of all responses – a little bit more than usual by one person is assumed to be cancelled out by a little bit less by another. In other styles of research you may want to include supplementary questions to identify variations from the norm.

A question within a questionnaire is not a discrete entity. The order in which questions appear not only affects respondents' enthusiasm for the task, but also influences the way they respond to each question in light of what has gone before. Questions need to be grouped in a natural, logical order that flows from one section to the next. Filters are used to make sure respondents are only asked those questions that are relevant to them. For example, if respondents have no awareness of an anti-racism campaign in sport, there is not much point in asking them how effective they

---

[2]EPIC stands for 'European Prospective Investigation into Cancer and Nutrition'.

think it has been. A question to establish whether or not they have heard of it should therefore be followed by routing instructions to the next appropriate question.

The general advice is to start with questions the respondent will enjoy. They should be easy to answer, obviously relevant and 'concrete'. This means that early questions are normally closed, with open and more abstract questions addressed later once respondents have become engaged with the exercise. Contrary to some people's natural inclination to start by asking for personal details, these should be left to the end. If they are getting weary by then they do not have to exercise much brain power to provide such routine information, but the more important issues in this context relate to concerns over intrusion.

Asking Sensitive Questions

Many people object to being asked questions that they think are no concern of anybody else. Dealing with this is not easy because people certainly do not respond uniformly. What represents gross impertinence to one person is a matter of no consequence to another. Ask yourself first whether there is a real need for such data. There is no point in running the risk of alienating some respondents if you do not need it to address your research challenge.

This sensitivity is one reason why personal details are normally left until the end of the questionnaire. By that time the respondent should be clearer about the purpose of the research and have more confidence in the researchers. Questions on age and income, for example, should then be asked in a matter-of-fact way, presuming that there is no problem associated with answering them. Respondents should be reassured of confidentiality at this stage if necessary, but avoid making a big fuss over it or you may put the idea into their head that there is something to worry about.

There is a common belief that people are more likely to be prepared to answer if they are asked to choose between a limited number of categories/bands rather than provide their exact age or income. This is probably true, but there are two powerful arguments for not doing that because of the implications for analysis:

(1) Some statistical techniques require interval rather than ordinal data.
(2) Even if grouped data are to be used in the analysis, pre-determined categories deny flexibility, whereas interval/ratio data can be grouped using natural breaks in the distribution, or used to provide similar numbers in each category.

Leisure questionnaires may also be centrally concerned with sensitive matters, like gambling, the consumption of alcohol or sexual behaviour. These are circumstances in which respondents may be inclined to conceal the whole truth. Blunt, direct questions may not get truthful answers and a more indirect approach may be required. So in our work on racism in sport (e.g. Long et al., 2000) we asked questions about related issues (e.g. reactions to campaigns against abusive chanting), asked about the racism of other people, and addressed personal attitudes obliquely. An example of the latter was a question we used in various circumstances:

> Most players at one time or another will receive abusive remarks from both players and spectators, but sometimes players get abuse because of the colour of their skin.

> Do you think this is:

> Acceptable/part of the game ☐

> Sometime acceptable when they play badly ☐

> Never acceptable ☐

The nature of the response and the quality of the data depend in large part on how good the interviewer is and whether the respondent can recognise the context and purpose of the question.

Increase Your Chance of Getting 'Personal' Data

- Consider the wording carefully.
- Give thought to using categories of response.
- Be friendly and create an air of competence.
- Treat in a 'matter-of-fact' way.
- Offer reassurance of confidentiality.

Pilots

Everyone I have ever met who is involved in questionnaire design stresses the importance of piloting the questionnaire – i.e. having a trial run. I am persuaded this is not just a coincidence; it really is important. Properly conducted, the pilot provides:

- an insight into whether the respondent understands the question as it was intended – what may seem obvious to the writer may be confusing for the reader
- a check that people feel comfortable with the scaling, ranking, etc. tasks that have been set
- an indication of whether any predefined categories are appropriate for the kind of answers people are likely to give

- reassurance that the questions flow in a proper sequence
- a check that the mechanics and logistics of the whole process of administering the questionnaire in the field work effectively.

To fulfil this purpose the pilot does not have to be a huge undertaking. However, it does need to be conducted using people as much like the intended sample as possible.

Sometimes the pilot is also used to provide training for the interviewers. However, it is better to separate these processes as it is hardly a fair test of the emergent questionnaire to have it conducted by inexperienced staff. Some people use pilots to provide early day findings. This strikes me as very strange. For those findings to have any value there would need to have been a piloting of the pilot. Although no guarantee of a perfect questionnaire, a pilot can make a big difference by picking up and correcting mistakes.

Good practice in questionnaire design

Thinking about the points made already in this chapter will have suggested some principles for guiding the design of questionnaires. Here are some of the key points that most experienced researchers would subscribe to.

Clarity – Make sure you work out what you want to know and why. Don't waste your respondents' time. On the other hand, if the issue is important to you make sure you ask enough questions to do it justice – one question is rarely enough. With a carefully designed questionnaire you can ask a lot of questions quickly.

Communication – Make clear to respondents why they are being asked the questions, which questions they should answer and how many responses they are expected to provide.

Questions – Try to avoid hypothetical questions, ambiguous questions, leading questions. Consider carefully the advantages of using open or closed questions.

Define – Specify exactly what you are referring to. For example, if you are asking about participation, specify the time period and avoid terms that mean different things to different people, like usually/occasionally.

Categories – Do not use overlapping categories. So for age you might use 20–29, 30–39, etc., or 20–24, 25–29, etc.

Flow – You need a logical sequence, starting with questions that are easy to answer before moving on to more complex/abstract ones. Except in special circumstances leave personal details until last.

Administering – Make the layout appealing and easy to follow for you and for your respondent. Read questions exactly as they are on the questionnaire. Probe for detail, but do not prompt by suggesting answers (it is not meant to be your thoughts that get recorded).

Coding and Data Entry – If you are going to allow your respondent more than one response to a question, make sure you know how the statistical package on your computer will cope with this. At the design stage, think about how you will code and enter data into the computer.

(Continued)

(Continued)

Piloting – Find some people as like your respondents as possible and see how they react to your questions. Review and revise the questionnaire. Practise interviewing too – a good interviewer will get a higher proportion of people to respond, get honest answers to sensitive questions and prevent the respondent fretting about how long it is taking (think also about dress, body language, etc.)

Advice – Seek the help of experts. Examine what others have done in writing their questionnaires and critique it.

Further Lines of Enquiry

For an easy to understand introduction to constructing scales and designing questionnaires, I find *Surveys in Social Research* by de Vaus useful (2002, 5th edn). More detailed advice on questionnaire design can be found in Oppenheim's (1992, 2nd edn) *Questionnaire Design, Interviewing and Attitude Measurement* or Fink's (1995) *How to Ask Survey Questions*.

The Centre for Applied Social Surveys has a useful website: www.s3ri.soton.ac.uk/cass. It used to host the ESRC question bank that gives access to the standard formulation of questions in public surveys in the UK. This is now at: http://qb.soc.surrey.ac.uk.

Some of the validated scales, like POMS, are copyrighted and their use has to be licensed (check the appropriate websites), but many articles on their use can be found through electronic abstracting services discussed in Chapter 3.

Checking levels of measurement questions (Box p.62)

Variable	Level of measurement
A	The original variable provides ratio data, but is subsequently reduced to ordinal data on a scale 1–4
B	Nominal data
C	Nominal data, but if reorganised to better/no difference/worse it could be treated as ordinal
D	Nominal data
E	Ordinal data, but be very careful about how you treat the last category or the computer might conclude that those who 'don't know' think the pitch is super excellent because it is coded with the highest value.
F	Nominal data
G	Ordinal data
H	Ratio data

7

Interviewing – Openness with a Sense of Purpose

Like the therapist, the research interviewer listens more than he [sic] talks, and listens with a lively and sympathetic interest. (Whyte, 1984: 98)

Some people construct interviews just like a questionnaire, but allow more qualitative responses. Other interviews are very different, being much more interactive. At its core, the art of interviewing develops questioning and listening over an extended exchange, typically with several people. It has become customary to label almost any form of interviewing that does not involve a questionnaire as being 'in-depth'. Particularly for those more familiar with questionnaires it is important to identify what 'in-depth interviewing' really means. This chapter will address:

- different styles of interviewing
- the characteristics of good interviews/interviewers
- the relationship between the researcher and the respondents
- the special case of interviewing 'experts'
- an introduction to group interviews and focus groups
- practical aspects of organising and running interviews.

Do you pose questions differently when conducting an interview rather than using a questionnaire? For some people (whether researchers or respondents) the questionnaire, with its standardised structure and restricted responses, is too constrained in its ability to gather important information from people. The very features which give it its strength can be disadvantages in other circumstances. Undoubtedly it does make for easier comparisons and simpler data handling, but at the expense of allowing respondents the opportunity to express what *they* see as being most significant. Interviewing techniques offer an alternative to the rigid format of the questionnaire with its predominantly 'closed' questions.

Different Styles of Interviewing

Nowadays we have plenty of experience of interviewing courtesy of the mass media. Unfortunately, neither the political interviewer nor the chat show host provide good models for the researcher. *Before getting involved in the following discussion, try to identify what you think might be the top half dozen or so characteristics of a good interviewer.* I shall provide my list later in the chapter for you to compare.

Whether the research is designed to find out how people decide where to go on holiday, what their experiences are of racism in sport or how they escape from their family responsibilities to enjoy their own leisure without feeling guilty, the first inclination of most social researchers would be to conduct interviews. When interviewing the intention is to discover how people think about the world and what is important to them rather than what is important to the researcher. In-depth interviews are typically used to gather detailed, 'rich', qualitative data from a small number of respondents instead of the quantitative data usually gathered from a larger number in a questionnaire survey.[1] While the emphasis of questionnaires is on producing quantitative data, interviews seek mainly (but not exclusively) qualitative data.

Interviewing is not, however, the easy alternative that some people imagine – thoughtfulness, skill and sympathy are paramount. Clearly it helps if you feel comfortable talking with people you have probably not met before, but being good at talking is not what it is about. It is the respondent who is supposed to be encouraged to 'open-up' and do the talking, the skill of the researcher is to listen. But this is a special kind of listening – active listening. Merely being a sponge is inadequate. What is required is someone capable of recognising the meaning of what is being said so that they can use that to guide the discussion and ask sensible follow-up questions.

---

[1]Psychological research may, of course, use questionnaires within an experimental design requiring relatively few respondents

Some people like a fairly structured approach, while others want it to be as free-flowing as possible. At one end of the continuum are interviews that are essentially questionnaires with a series of open-ended questions; formal questions are posed in a set order, though the interviewer may have the opportunity to probe with follow-up questions. At the other end of the continuum are interviews with no set questions and where the goal is to get as close as possible to reconstructing a chat between friends. Although some will disagree with me, I believe you must have some idea what your research is trying to achieve, otherwise your respondent will wonder what on earth is going on. 'Whatever its merits for therapy, a genuinely nondirective interviewing approach simply is not appropriate for research. Far from putting informants at their ease, it actually produces anxieties' (Whyte, 1984: 97).

Framing Questions

So, most researchers using this approach will have an interview schedule or checklist to provide a framework. Some have more detail than others, but typically identify key topics and some suggested issues to explore within those. Below are two checklists that we used on past projects that demonstrate this variation in detail. The first one is taken from a study of the changing significance of leisure in the period around retirement (Long and Wimbush, 1985), and was used prior to retirement. You can see that this identified rather more topics for discussion than the second, which left the interviewers with more room for manoeuvre. This latter study was part of an examination of the nature and extent of racism in grassroots football (Long et al., 2000), done to inform the campaign, *Let's Kick Racism Out of Football*.

Checklist for Pre-Retirement Interview

1. Current Lifestyle

(i) Job

[ ] what is job?
[ ] how long worked there?
[ ] happy with job?
[ ] anything wrong with job?
[ ] overtime?
[ ] unusual hours?
[ ] skills required/developed?
[ ] meet many people at work?
[ ] many of their friends come from work?
[ ] non-work activities linked to work?
[ ] leisure opportunities around work?

(ii) Important Aspects of Life

[ ] important aspects of life?
[ ] anything particularly interested in?
[ ] anything make them depressed?
[ ] life have a routine?
[ ] activities they go out of their way to make time for?

(iii) Non-work Activities

[ ] what is done outside formal work hours?
[ ] why do these things?
[ ] satisfaction derived?
[ ] activities with wife?
[ ] holidays?

(iv) Social Contacts

[ ] visitors?
[ ] visits?
[ ] geographical extent?
[ ] who else?
[ ] and for what purpose?

(v) Locale

[ ] how long in the area?
[ ] social facilities/amenities/ resources available locally?
[ ] extent of use?
[ ] what is lacking (for them)?

(vi) Past Spare Time Activities

[ ] any given up?
[ ] why?
[ ] anything else replace them?

2. Expectations of Retirement

(i) Planning and Preparation for Retirement

[ ] plans to move to other area?
[ ] financial plans?
[ ] pre-retirement courses attended?

(ii) Attitudes to Retirement

[ ] what do friends who have retired do?
[ ] what do neighbours who have retired do?
[ ] enjoying their retirement?
[ ] ever think of retiring earlier?
[ ] if did, what prevented them?
[ ] even if hadn't thought of it, would have liked to?
[ ] wife's attitude to respondent's retirement?

(iii) Use of Time

[ ] what will they do in time available to them?
[ ] anticipate having a lot of spare time?
[ ] who will time be spent with?
[ ] most time at home or elsewhere?

(iv) Constraints

[ ] what will facilitate or impede them doing what's mentioned above?
[ ] factors within/outwith their control?
[ ] advantages and disadvantages of retirement?

3. Anything to Add

[ ]

Checklist (2) for Interview on Racism in Football

Black Players	**White Players**
1. Careers How introduced to football? Father involved in football? Directed to particular positions?	Same
2. Any difference between footballing characteristics of black, Asian and white players? Why relatively few Asians?	Same
3. Any different if play for/against all black rather than mixed team (or vice versa)? Any different if play against all white team?	Any different if play for mixed or white team (or vice versa)? Any different if play against all black/Asian team?
4. *Kick Racism Out of Football* had any impact in the grass roots game? Would similar campaign in the grass roots game be a good idea?	Same
5. Experience of racism in football? Form it took? Frequency? What is most damaging? If not verbal, how do they know it was racism and not down to something else?	If suggest there is none, probe – None at all? If insist, move to 7 and ask why they think it's different from professional game. Check – Directed at them or at black player?
6. Check – Apart from other players anything from refs, club officials, leagues, county?	Same
7. Comparison Variation by clubs. Worst offenders? Variation by leagues or district. 5-a-side *v* 11 cf. professional football cf. other sports	Same
8. Improvements in the future?	Same
9. Would they referee?	Same

In both studies these interviews were only one of several ways of gathering data. As you can imagine it is quite challenging to get people to talk freely about a subject as sensitive as racism. So in an earlier study of cricket (Long et al., 1997), in order to encourage them to talk, we put to them three related controversial topics of the day, which they would probably have discussed several times before:

* Why there were no Asian or Black players in the county side.
* Whether Asian and Black players could be expected to perform to their full potential when playing for the county or national team.
* Whether black and ethnic minorities living in England should support the England cricket team.

The basis for the questions posed in the interview may come from 'brainstorming', a literature review or preliminary discussions with 'experts' (the experts on these occasions may be people very like your eventual respondents). Just because you are expecting the respondents to play a large part in shaping the interview is no reason to underplay the importance of proper preparation. Standard wording is replaced by questions that slot naturally into the flow of the conversation, and the interviewer will typically try to use the language of her/his respondent. Some of the principles that apply in questionnaire design are equally appropriate here – group questions together in blocks and work out logical sequences, learn your 'script', but be prepared to be flexible. It is the follow-up questions that are crucial if this approach is to produce the rich information that is supposed to be its hallmark.

It is still best to avoid long, convoluted questions and ambiguous or hypothetical questions, but this approach is more forgiving in that there is room to clarify and expand if the respondent misinterprets or struggles with a question. Don't be afraid to ask 'Why?' Some young children have a very annoying habit of repeatedly asking why, no matter what the response to their question. If your interview is genuinely to be 'in depth' you need to be similarly persistent and inquisitive, but find ways of doing it that stimulate rather than irritate.

Writers on the topic identify different kinds of question that are used in interviews. I draw your attention to two of these below and hope the originators will forgive me because this is not exactly what they said, but basically they suggest the following distinctions.

1. *Non-verbal response*   e.g. 'Uh-huh' – indicates the interviewer is listening and interested.

2. *Verbal encouragement*   e.g. 'That's interesting' – encourages respondent to keep talking/expand on current topic.

3. *Reflection*	repeats last statement as a question, e.g. 'So you don't like sport?'
4. *Probe*	invites explanation of the last statement, e.g. 'Why don't you like sport?'
5. *Back tracking*	returns to something the respondent said earlier and seeks further information, e.g. 'Let's go back to what you were saying about your school days'.
6. *New topic*	e.g. 'Can we talk about other leisure activities – what about entertainment?'

After Whyte (1982; 1984)

1. *Experience/behaviour*	past and current activities, e.g. playing careers
2. *Knowledge*	of structures, initiatives, procedures, e.g. 'What is the governing body's policy on women's participation?'
3. *Opinion/value*	e.g. 'Do you believe that has been successful?'
4. *Feeling*	e.g. 'What do you feel about that policy yourself?'
5. *Sensory*	e.g. 'What's it like to line-up on the pitch at the national stadium?'
6. *Socio-demographics*	Age, education, income, etc.

After Patton (2002)

There are many such classifications. Which particular set you identify with most closely is less important than recognising that not all questions are of the same form and an interviewer needs to be alert to the variations on offer.

Good Practice

Trial runs are as important to pilot this kind of interview as they are with question-naires and other research approaches. In so far as no two interviews are likely to be run the same way, the pilot cannot fulfil quite the same purpose as it would with a questionnaire, but you need to know how to introduce the various topics in such a way that you will get a full, honest and informative response from the person you are interviewing. The 'trick' is to get people to talk freely about what they think are the most important aspects of the subject you are examining, without going off at a tangent. The interviewer then acts as a guide.

Characteristics of Good Interviews and Interviewing

1. Know your schedule/checklist (be prepared – and know your recording equipment too).
2. Establish rapport, be sympathetic, encourage respondents to talk, don't patronise.
3. Tune in to their language, use appropriate language yourself and phrase questions clearly.
4. Accept the value of respondents' views – don't be judgmental.
5. Listen to respondents and pick up on important issues they raise.
6. Read between the lines, pick up on non-verbals, but don't make assumptions – check.
7. Probe and explore – follow-up. Don't content yourself with the initial response.
8. Recall and relate questions to what has been said.
9. Allow space to answer – don't fear silence – try not to restrict.
10. Avoid irrelevant rambling – guide (but don't lead).

As you may be asking complex questions you need to give your respondents time to think about what they want to say, so don't rush them – let them compose a thoughtful answer. Wherever possible you should use that answer to shape your next question. Sometimes you will need to shift the line of questioning, but even then it may be possible to relate it to what your respondent said some time earlier. This allows the respondent to feel that what they have to say is important and you are taking it on board.

It helps if you try to put yourself in their shoes and imagine what would make you most forthcoming in your responses. You would probably want to feel comfortable, able to relate to the person you are talking to, who in turn needs to appear non-judgmental. Good interviewers give the impression of being 'good listeners', but also carefully guide and draw out by probing beyond the initial responses to get at underlying reasons.

It has been suggested that we should try to escape the authoritarian approach of questionnaire surveys where all the power rests with the researchers, and establish a more equal relationship so that the experience is less like an inquisition. It takes time for a trusting, relaxed relationship to be established, and it is important to give some effort to building rapport. If at all possible it is sensible to get the respondent talking before the interview starts.

Some researchers believe that the relationship between researcher and respondent is so crucial to the success of the research that they should be carefully matched, according to sex, ethnicity, age, etc. (Long and Wray, 2003). The argument here is twofold. First, the proposition is, for example, that a woman is less likely to be open with a man than with another woman. Second, even if the same information were to be forthcoming, it would not mean the same to a man, who would not be alerted to the same kind of follow-up questions and would be less capable of appreciating the significance and meaning of the material provided. As a consequence, it is suggested, the analysis would be less insightful than that conducted by a woman.

Inevitably there are a number of complicating factors.

(a) *Wrongly identifying the distinguishing characteristics* – In some circumstances innocently assigning an Asian interviewer to an Asian respondent may cause as many problems as having a white interviewer if, for example, the interviewer were a Hindu from Delhi and the respondent a Muslim from Sylhet.

(b) *Identifying the wrong variable* – We may succeed in matching male and female interviewers and respondents, but in circumstances in which the most telling distinction is class.

(c) *Resources* – In practice, unless there is a large budget for the project the decision is likely to be made on pragmatic grounds. The interviewer can only be chosen from those available – often just you.

These interviews will normally, but not necessarily, take longer than questionnaires – an hour is not unusual, and sometimes longer. Select your venue carefully so that your respondent feels comfortable and can give you their full attention.

Recording

A while ago it was assumed that people were phobic about tape-recorders. In my experience this is no longer the case (if it ever was). In all bar a few circumstances people are prepared to let you use a recorder (now more likely to be digital than tape). You can always offer them the option of asking for it to be turned off at any time in the interview if there is something they would rather keep 'off the record'. Recording the interview offers you the major advantage of being able to concentrate on what they are saying and guide the interview rather than having to scribble notes all the time. Maintaining eye contact and interacting with your respondent are important if a conversational feel is to be achieved.

There are still occasions when it is more appropriate to write notes:

(a) when the use of a tape recorder would make it a more formal event than you want to suggest
(b) when the interview is conducted in surroundings that would make it difficult to pick out what the respondent has said (e.g. in a bar)
(c) when your technology lets you down.

Make sure that you have a blank cassette and life in the batteries (or that the power supply is connected and switched on), and that the machine and the microphone are both working efficiently. Any problems like these undermine the respondent's faith in the interviewer (it doesn't do much for the interviewer's self-confidence either). Please do not imagine that I am being patronising in pointing these things out. I have made all these mistakes and more.

You may end up with hours of tape recordings. What are you then going to do with all that material? Transcription and coding as part of a rigorous process of analysis can take a lot of time (Chapter 12).

There may be occasions when you feel it would be inappropriate to record the interview in any way at the time, and then you have to write soon afterwards as full an account as possible. This is surprisingly difficult, so be suspicious of those reports where the researcher describes this process and then manages to provide word-for-word quotations.

Don't forget, some of the most interesting things are likely to be said before the tape recorder is switched on or after it is switched off. Doctors are familiar with this experience as many patients only manage to steel themselves to raise the matter that is troubling them as they are about to leave the surgery. Particularly if you have conducted the interview at their home, you may also have observed various things that help you to understand the respondent. You will therefore need to remember to make a note of these extra pieces of information. Or is that unfair to your respondent – catching them with their guard down, outside the 'contract' of your agreement? Is it admissible evidence?

Interviewing Key Informants and Experts: a special case

Everybody is an expert on their own life and millions think they are sports experts, but beyond that some people are chosen for interview because of their specialist knowledge/experience (e.g. interviews with board members, policymakers or club secretaries). This is very far from a random sample. People have been purposively selected and cannot easily be replaced in the research, so special attention has to be given to their recruitment and the way the interview is conducted. Don't forget that the research that seems so vital to you is not likely to have the same importance to these key people. I don't mean to be offensive, but why should the Chief Executive of the record company or the manager of the top football team be bothered with your research (especially when they probably get a sackful of such requests)? The same issue has to be addressed whoever is recruited to whatever kind of research, it is just that it is even more relevant here.

Gaining access is often one of the hardest parts and you may have to use the techniques of the sales executive – get your foot in the door and don't let them say 'no'. Did I hear you say 'that doesn't sound very ethical'? It is often easier to get the collaboration of an ex-minister or ex-chairperson who will have fewer inhibitions about disclosing what was or is still happening. Historical data are likely to be less sensitive, and supporting official statistics may well be available.

The approach needs to be to an individual rather than an organisation. Get the name of the person in the organisation who is likely to be of most use to you. This person may be the one best qualified to deal with the issues you are researching; or get someone to identify the best person to speak to – many organisations have 'gatekeepers' who you may have to go through in order to get to your target. They may provide a formal introduction or just a set of recommendations. Just being able to say that 'so-and-so said I ought to speak to you' is a big advantage in persuading people to be interviewed, but you may be being directed to people likely to present the organisation in a favourable light. It is difficult to know which medium is best for the approach to invite participation, but I think that if you have a referred lead it is best to phone and follow with a letter; otherwise send a short letter and promise to contact by phone.

Somehow you have to secure the interest of the key informant. This applies whether you want them to be a respondent themselves or you need their permission to do the research with the staff/members of their organisation. When trying to get agreement for setting up the project, try to get your targets to talk about their interests and then explain your own. They will need something to let them understand what you want. It may be better to take an example of the type of research you want to do rather than *the* research you want to do. This allows them to understand what might be involved, but prevents them picking holes in your work. Objections have to be removed. Assure anonymity and confidentiality, and be reassuring but honest about the amount of their time that will be needed. Explain the benefits to them – e.g. information, stimulation, cheaper than consultants, knowledge of what (anonymous) others are doing. They hold most of the cards so a bit of flattery will not go amiss and you can try to persuade them that it is an honour to be selected, reflecting their (organisation's) pre-eminence. If you've got to the Chief Executive or Managing Director it might be sensible to invite them to pass you down the hierarchy to sort out the details.

I remember being at a seminar once when a researcher gave a tip about offering alternative 'closes'. This might be in the form : 'Would ____ be OK, or would ____ be better?' Ensure that both are positive. This may seem cheeky, but he insisted it worked. Finally make sure that both parties are clear about what has been agreed.

It is important to clarify the role of the interview in your own mind, and subsequently for the interviewee. Are you trying to establish 'facts' or to get their views of how the organisation operates or are they the objects of the study (e.g. revealing the 'assumptive worlds'[2] that underpin their decisions)? The nature of the bargain struck at the start will influence the information given – who it is for, what use it will be put to, what the readership will be.

These respondents have been targeted because of their specialist knowledge so when interviewing them you need to accept the concepts/ideas they use and allow their knowledge to shape the interview – people want to feel the interview is unique to them/their organisation. While this means one interview may be very different from another, my preference is still to use some kind of pro forma to underpin it. These are usually busy people who are likely to get frustrated if they feel that you are just there for an aimless chat. The more you know in advance, the more you are likely to get out of the interview, so find out as much as possible about your respondent and their organisation. Present yourself as an informed outsider (when dealing with people 'at the top' it is often the case that interviewers are more acceptable the further away they come from). This will establish your credibility and helps to get past the first round of standard responses to the more revealing material that will set your research apart. And, importantly, it allows you to do a responsive interview properly.

Although they are 'key' informants they may not know the proper response to a question. Allow them to say 'don't know' or 'will have to check that one out and come back to you'. If they flannel, go down the hierarchy to get the answer. Those at the top may tend to generalise; those further 'down' the organisational hierarchy are more likely to use concrete examples.

Because of their eminence, it may be easy for such respondents to be identified however you try to conceal them in your writing. Processes that give participants the chance to check you have got it right (member checking) then become especially important. Some researchers send transcripts of interviews back to informants for their approval; others send the resultant analysis from the final report (quote plus surrounding context).

---

[2]The unwritten beliefs and values.

Group Interviews, Group Discussions and Focus Groups

These all operate with the presumption that different ideas will be expressed as a result of people sparking off each other rather than just holding a series of one-to-one meetings with the researcher. As these techniques were developed important distinctions were made between group interviews, group discussions and focus groups in terms of their structure, purpose and operation. In some, standard information may be sought from each member of the group (group interviews); others have a looser structure, promoting debate (group discussions); and others use group interactions to address some challenge (focus group). Perhaps unhelpfully in terms of the variation involved, these seem increasingly to be given the generic label of 'focus groups' as they have become popular with 'the creatives', market researchers and politicians. All the more reason, if you use them, to be careful to provide sufficient detail in your project report/dissertation about what was entailed.

What could be better than getting data from several people at once? However, unless you have experience of running/facilitating groups and have developed the specialist skills needed, any of these are difficult to manage as a productive research tool. The whole intention of these approaches is to exploit the interaction between the various members, and if you are unable to handle the group dynamic it is better to stick to individual interviews. There are circumstances in which I would change that advice. For example, when interviewing school children there are advantages in running small group interviews. First it helps avoid the threat of being accused of any wrongdoing (don't forget in the UK you should get your Criminal Records Bureau check). Second, it begins to redress the power imbalance between the child and the researcher, giving them more confidence through the presence of their friends.

Now you not only have to persuade people to contribute to the research, but you have to persuade them all to come to a common venue at the same time. Because of this some researchers use naturally occurring groups (e.g. members of a supporters' association, a club, a residents' association or a friendship group). In relation to your research you may identify different 'communities of interest' (e.g. policymakers, managers, front-line staff and users/customers). Do you want representatives of each grouping mixed together in each of your focus groups, or would you rather assign each grouping to its own focus group?

I remember that for one of the early groups I was involved with we had invited 10 people, expecting a couple not to turn up. But they did turn up, and some brought reinforcements with them – 14 people and not a shrinking violet among them; they were all determined to have their say. It was not the most comfortable night of my life. If people have been selected because they have special knowledge of the subject being investigated, it is probably better to have slightly fewer than if they are just a general group. The most common size of group seems to be six to eight people. The running time can vary too, but in our projects they have normally lasted about an hour and a half with 'bits' on either side while people gather and then run down.

This group has to meet somewhere. Clearly convenience is important, as is the size of the venue and the kind of atmosphere it creates (you can help that by providing refreshments even if it is only tea and coffee). More subtle though is the significance of territory. In a study designed to explore people's attitudes towards sports provision, their awareness and channels of information, we arranged to use a room in the council offices (because it was central and available). I don't know why I said the influence of territory was subtle. Putting together the location with the agenda led to the conclusion that we were council employees looking to close local facilities. We were left in no doubt about one message (no closure of facilities), but it was hard to address more subtle points about what might represent good practice in leisure provision.

The role of the researcher in these circumstances is often referred to as that of a moderator. It helps if there is a second person who can take the lead from time to time, and it also means that a note can be taken of who is speaking, which helps with transcription and interpreting what has been said. To encourage people to open up it may be useful to borrow projective techniques from market research and advertising: e.g. filling in speech/thought bubbles in a cartoon or creating a collage/story board from images cut from a colour magazine. These allow people to put forward ideas without feeling they are being interrogated and help to support a collective creativity within the group.

Elsewhere you may have come across debates about the way in which groups operate. One well known approach suggests that any group goes through a series of stages:

- *Forming* – making sure everyone is included
- *Storming* – establishing roles and balance of power
- *Norming* – moving from difference and disagreement to agreement
- *Performing* – working together as a group
- *Mourning* – winding down the group.

Assuming there is some truth in this, you need to match your research agenda to these different functions. The most useful phases in terms of gathering research data are likely to be 'norming' and 'performing'. Of course, if all these phases are to be concentrated within one meeting, it leaves relatively little time for the productive payload.

In those groups where the emphasis is on solving a problem (appropriate policy initiatives or advertisements, for example) there is pressure to reach consensus, thereby running the risk of not giving proper attention to dissenting views. It is possible to extend the analysis by treating not just the words as data, but also examining the way the group operated in order to explore: how the opinions of different members influenced the group; where opinions were most strongly held; how group opinions were formed; what empathy there is for other points of view; what causes shifts in opinion.

Further Lines of Enquiry

There is no shortage of advice on conducting interviews. Judith Bell's (1999) book *Doing Your Research Project* offers an alternative easy introduction. For further issues associated with different forms of interviewing, Tim May's (2001) *Social Research* is clear and relatively easy to follow.

For an interviewing case study, go to the associated research methods resources at: www.leedsmet.ac.uk/carnegie/1030.htm.

8

Observation Techniques – Using your Eyes and Ears

A central paradox of the participant observation method is to seek information by not asking questions. (Frankenburg, 1982: 50)

All good social researchers of course benefit from being good observers, so they see what happens around them, not just what they are told happens. The spectacle and public behaviour associated with leisure, sport and tourism make ready material for different styles of observation. This chapter will try to convey the challenge involved in something that initially sounds so ridiculously easy. Addressed carefully, observing behaviour rather than relying on reported behaviour can provide not just a realistic alternative, but one capable of unexpected insights. The chapter covers:

- When different styles of observation are used
- Moving in, creating a role and establishing rapport
- What to look for and how to record
- Difficulties of inference and proof
- The arguments for and against such approaches.

Observation

The main concern of this chapter is with participant observation and the orientation to research that this implies. However, observation is used as part of very different styles of research. For example, formal observation may be used to record the number of people using the trim trail in a public park or a long distance footpath. The electronic records that leisure centres might hold of numbers engaged in certain activities are not available in these circumstances and an alternative is needed even to gain simple measures of usage. Elsewhere, it might be possible to record quite accurately how much erosion occurs on various paths across a hillside, but to make sense of that we would need to know how many walkers, mountain-bikers, horse riders and motor cyclists use each path. Observation may also be used as a way of calibrating research instruments. Having conducted a questionnaire survey of people using a stretch of coast, the survey responses should be calibrated (weighted) to reflect the number of people recorded as gaining access to the beach by each of the car parks at which the survey was conducted. Or it might be important to establish response rates (and associated levels of use) by knowing what proportion of visitors/trail walkers/shoppers picked up a questionnaire and returned it to the collection box.

Thus, observation can be used as a technique to gather quantitative data, and quantitative data may be incorporated into a participant observation study. But participant observation is most commonly associated with qualitative research derived from an ethnographic tradition of studying different people's way of life. In practice those doing participant observation may use a suite of techniques, for example:

- using and observing at local facilities
- attending meetings, gatherings, etc.
- informal visiting to friends and neighbours
- formal and informal interviewing
- special informants
- day-by-day observation (Gans, 1962).

Becker suggests that:

> The participant observer gathers data by participating in the daily life of the group or organisation he [sic] studies. He watches the people he is studying to see what situations they ordinarily meet and how they behave in them. He enters into conversation with some or all of the participants in these situations and discovers their interpretations of the events he has observed. (1958: 652)

The emphasis then is on trying to find out *their* understandings on the basis of *their* behaviour in response to circumstances you observe. The normality of the everyday is crucial to this. Just to give you an insight into the circumstances in which participant observation is used in the field of leisure, sport and tourism, some studies that may repay reading are indicated in the following box – the date refers to the date of publication (so you can check the reference at the end) rather than the fieldwork. This is certainly not intended as an exhaustive list.

William Foote Whyte (1943)	A study of an immigrant Italian community in an American city, focusing on the young men hanging out on the street corners of a slum (Cornerville). This covers leisure forms like gambling, bowling and the community club.
August Hollingshead (1949)	Elmtown – a North American study of the link between class and behaviour among adolescents and how that behaviour is determined by how they are regarded within their culture.
Mass Observation (1987)	A study of people's behaviour in the pubs of Worktown in the north of England during the war years (for a discussion of this study see below pp. 93–4).
Loic Wacquant (1992, 1995, 2003)	An ethnographic study of boxers in Chicago, making use of Bourdieu's theoretical frameworks.
Maureen Glancy (1986)	A study of the group surrounding a softball team (players, friends and hangers-on).
Chris Ryan and Amber Martin (2001)	A study of the rituals in a strip club, which the authors present as a forgotten aspect of sex tourism. They draw parallels with other forms of tourism in which the normal is made strange and vice versa.
Belinda Wheaton (2000)	An examination of the gendered nature of the sub-culture associated with wind surfing (see also Wheaton, 2003).
Nick Holt and Andy Sparkes (2001)	A study of 'cohesiveness' within a college soccer team through the course of a season.
Tony Blackshaw (2003)	The leisure lives of working class 'lads' of 30-something. This examines the pubs, clubs, fashion, fights and sex that dominate the lives of those often overlooked by the preoccupation with leisure consumption.

The largest single exercise in the use of observation techniques in the UK was the work of Mass Observation, which was developed as 'an anthropology of ourselves'. In addition to full-time observers, there were literally thousands of volunteer observers through the course of the project. The full-time observers tended to focus on working-class life, but the bulk of the volunteer observers were middle-class people reporting on what they saw and heard around them. Work started in the 1930s and, amazingly, continued through the war into the 1950s. Being interested in social formations and 'the ordinary', much of the material relates to people's leisure lives. This was gathered through various forms of observation, formal and informal interviews, overheard remarks, life histories and documentation.

One of their focuses in the study of Worktown was the pub (Mass Observation, 1987 (originally 1943)). There they gathered quantitative data which, for example, recorded the speed of drinking and the frequency of occurrence of various topics of conversation, but these were accompanied by more qualitative detail. So, in addition to knowing that people drink faster on a Saturday than a Sunday, they also observed that there is a certain pressure that results in what they called 'level drinking':

> But all our observations show that the majority of pub-goers tend, when drinking in a group, to drink level; and very often there is not a quarter of an inch difference between the depth of beer in the glasses of a group of drinkers. (1987: 169)

This was even found to occur when the drinker was blind. They also recognised the ritual of standing rounds and its social as well as economic significance:

> In gossip or anger one man may accuse another of not paying his turn, but it is an accusation that is seldom substantiated. The consequences of proving such a thing are too drastic, and would bring about an intolerable situation ... Standing rounds is a form of social compulsion of great advantage to the brewers. It makes people drink more, and even spend what they can't afford. (1987: 178–9)

Other observations related to 'swiggling' (swirling the drink round the glass), drunkenness, smoking, spitting and the use of spittoons:

> One, the most drunk, who calls for drink for the others spits nea[t]ly into the spittoon under the table and pleasedly cried 'Reet in'. Another young man tries, amidst laughter. The first one says 'Take it quietly lad don't rush it'. He misses and the first chap does it again, this time hitting the table. He is called a 'filthy bugger' and belches in reply. The observer notes: spitting not previously seen among the young. And adds that when it takes place it is the subject of notice and laughter and backchat. (1987: 207)

This process led not just to 'rich description', but also reflection on the links to social processes (as can be seen in the observation about buying rounds).

Participant observation is much harder than it initially sounds, but it can be very rewarding. It typically involves spending a lot of time with the people the researcher is trying to understand; 'living it'. McCall and Simmons (1969: 3) describe this as 'repeated genuine social interaction on the scene with the subjects themselves as part of the data gathering process', which is intended to produce an analytic description of a complex social organisation. McCall and Simmons have a more formal approach than some advocates of participant observation. They insist that participant observation employs the concepts, propositions and empirical generalisations of a body of scientific theory as the basic guides in analysis and reporting, employs thorough and systematic collection, classification and reporting of facts, and generates new empirical generalisations based on these data. Others insist on the 'tabula rasa' approach – going into 'the field' with a completely open mind so that the researcher's preconceptions do not colour what they observe. The idea is to learn to see things through the eyes of other people. Henderson notes that: 'One has to overcome years of selective inattention and learn all over again how to watch, listen, concentrate, and above all, how to interpret data apart from gathering it' (1991: 60). Perhaps more than any other research approach participant observation elevates empathy (putting yourself in their shoes) to pre-eminence through immersion in the world being researched and a process some call 'indwelling'.

Like social anthropologists studying 'primitive' tribes, sociologists have used participant observation to try to understand 'the other', as with middle-class Americans in the slum (Whyte, 1943; Gans, 1962). Further, it has commonly been used to study 'deviant' groups – acts that are more easily observed than talked about – hence studies of criminals, hooligans, drug addicts, etc. (Patrick, 1973). It is also used when people might be motivated to distort what they do when questioned on subjects such as drinking behaviour. By examining behaviour *in situ* it allows the examination of structures not recognised by those taking part – the researchers are less dependent on others being able/prepared to tell them how things work.

Outsiders and Insiders

In traditional routes to participant observation the researcher embarks on a journey from being an outsider looking in to being (more like) an insider. However, some researchers use participant observation as a means of understanding better their normal milieu. In these circumstances the researcher starts as an insider ...

but not quite. Although Blackshaw (2003) wrote about the mates he had grown up with, the fact that he had become an academic set him apart. Even though his mates treated him fondly, and despite those years of identification, his education meant that his eyes were not their eyes; his mindset no longer fully theirs.

If conducting the research as an outsider, the initial challenge has to be to 'find a way in', establish a rapport, win trust and be accepted. An illuminating account of this process is provided in Whyte's classic (1943) study, *Street Corner Society*, in which he explains the crucial role played by Doc, initially giving Whyte an entrée to the life of the Italian immigrant slum-dweller in America (he subsequently became a key informant and another member of the local community became a collaborator). Ironically some researchers' success in becoming a part of this new world has been challenged by critics on the grounds that it is important for social researchers to remain objective and avoid 'going native' (a reference to the anthropological traditions) and over-identifying with the people involved in the study. The concern is that those involved then suspend the critical faculties of the researcher, who (they argue) should be capable of standing apart from the observed behaviour to produce a detached analysis. This either misses the point of participant observation or rejects its methodological rationale (more of this in Chapter 15). For Patton the challenge is 'to combine participation and observation so as to become capable of understanding the program [setting, participants] as an insider while describing the program for outsiders' (1990: 128).

Different levels of involvement can be recognised (Gold, 1969):

(a) *complete observer* – detached. It has been argued that it is not possible to be a non-participant observer as any observation will have some impact on the observed. One of the classic examples of researchers seeking to be complete observers is with the use of one-way mirrors in research on child development – the researcher can see without being seen. In the study of crowd behaviour at sporting events this can now be achieved via the CCTV cameras installed in stadiums.

(b) *observer as participant* – observing *in situ*, but as a formal task for a short time. This happens when the researcher attends matches, perhaps to record behaviour in different parts of the ground.

(c) *participant as observer* – getting involved, but with the role as researcher recognised. In the crowd behaviour example this might involve 'hanging out' with those who like a fight or with the police/stewards responsible for crowd control so that the researcher can be close to the action, but slightly apart.

(d) *complete participant* – living the life. This would involve joining/infiltrating the gang/team/firm and taking part in all their activities.

That there may be variations on this is not the important issue here. What is important to consider is the extent of involvement of the researchers and the implications that this has for the kind of knowledge they then have access to. Closely associated with this is whether the researcher operates on an overt or covert basis. If you explain to people what you are doing, you are more likely to influence their behaviour (a research version of performing for the cameras). On the other hand, being covert is arguably deceitful and unfair to those being observed. It is sometimes suggested that if the behaviour occurs in a public arena it is there for all to see anyway. But even then matters are not quite that simple. There is a difference between the casual glance of the passer-by and the sustained observation of the researcher, or at least there ought to be.

If you are going to conduct covert research you need to identify a role for yourself. It is not easy to hang out in the club, observing closely while looking as though you ought to be there as part of the fittings. This is not just a matter of convenience, the nature of the knowledge you acquire will be different depending upon whether you attend the aerobics class or run it. Whyte (1943) was lucky, such was the power of Doc's presence, all Whyte had to do was 'be with' Doc to be accepted and pass without comment. He rehearsed explanations about writing a book about the area, but it didn't matter, he was with Doc.

Exercise

Consider what you might do to look natural while you are observing, perhaps for hours at a time, in the amusement arcade, the swing park or gallery. Not many universities or employers want their researchers arrested as voyeurs or paedophiles. Most of the obvious suggestions make you look suspicious, don't allow enough time, or mean adopting a role completely different from that of your 'participants'. If you use friends as camouflage in these social settings, it is hard not to be rude by ignoring them while concentrating on what is happening around you.

Assuming you want people to behave naturally around you, a lot of time has to be given to gaining acceptance, winning trust and establishing rapport (unless the position adopted is that of the complete observer). To this end some writers counsel against asking questions and challenging what is happening. On the other hand complete compliance on the part of a new arrival might equally be viewed as suspicious. Certainly it seems sensible to adopt a low profile and there seems to be agreement on the importance of not passing moral judgements while in the field. Researchers similarly have to consider the extent to which they can intervene in the action when the intention is to study participants' customary behaviour rather than the consequences of the researcher's actions.

Observing, Noting and Recording

Much as with qualitative interviewing (Chapter 7), there are different levels of structure used by participant observers in recording what they have observed. Equally, the same researcher may adopt a different approach at different stages of the research. Observation at a children's playground might be based on a methodical recording of when children arrive and leave, what equipment they play on, for how long, with whom, how many accidents occur at each piece of equipment, etc. Alternatively, the challenge may be to observe and describe the interaction between children playing in same sex and different sex groups in the playground.

Wolcott identifies the dilemma of the observer who faces 'the problem of what to look at and what to look for and the never-ending tension between taking a closer look at something versus taking a broader look at everything' (1995: 96). Typically, the 'observational lens' becomes more focused in the later stages of enquiry as attention is directed to more salient features. In the list below I have loosely interpreted six of Spradley's (1980) nine suggestions about the kind of data that might be collected, and then added six from Denzin (1978). I have done this in the context of observations at a sporting event.

Key features	Example
Spradley	
Actors and their relationships	The different kinds of people involved, e.g. among the crowd. Try also to note how they relate to each other – e.g. (un)friendly rivalry between fans and the relationship between players and referee.
Doing what with what consequences	e.g. chanting directed at the opposing fans or players, its purpose and the response.
Use of space	e.g. for meeting, showing-off, play, conflict.
Time – what happens when for how long	e.g. what happens as the crowd gathers, during the game, at half time and as people leave.
Impact of key events	e.g. a penalty miss or a sending-off.
Feelings – theirs and yours	The feelings of others might be evidenced through smiles, cheering, abuse, etc., but

don't forget to record your own emotional response.

Denzin

Dress	e.g. replica shirts.
Speech or behaviour patterns	e.g. conversations or chants (outside the stadium too); take a look at the body language of the various people involved at the press conference where the manager is given the ominous 'vote of confidence' by the Board.
Non-verbal gestures	e.g. when the team concedes more points/goals.
Salient social objects acted upon	as above for Spradley, key events.
Relationships of one actor to another	as above for Spradley, actors.
Rules of conduct displayed	e.g. in relation to the ethos of the game or conversely in relation to gamesmanship (sorry – I don't know the non-sexist equivalent).

It should be relatively straightforward to transpose these into your own research setting whether it be the gym, the club or the airport terminal, and to think of other categories. The field notes will then contain a log of all those things seen and heard in the setting (events, relationships, etc.). But more than that, they also record your thoughts as a consequence (making the link with other observations and beginning the process of interpretation), and your own experiences and how you feel about them. Produced over an extended period of observation these can become extensive.

This is all very well, but how can the researcher make a record of what is happening without revealing their purpose? Even when the purpose is already known, the recording may distract participants from their 'normal' behaviour. Knowing that a pen and note pad would compromise his ability to 'fit in' at the (night)club, Saipe had to adapt.

> Initially mental notes were taken of numbers, atmosphere, sounds and behavioural patterns, and transferred to jotted notes made with small pad and pen in the privacy of the toilet and on leaving in car or taxi. Fuller notes were written upon returning home, but as this was usually in the early hours of the next morning handwritten notes triggered from mental and jotted notes were scribbled down. These were then completed the following day with a clearer mind and when the ringing in my ears had departed. (1995: 53)

Proof, Inference and Generalisation

Few advocates of participant observation suggest that it is free of problems as a means of contributing to knowledge of people and their lives. For example, it is not possible to prove that just because some outcome was observed following an action it was caused by that action. Even if it seems likely that it did, the same causal link may not hold in other circumstances. However, advocates of participant observation point out that the method is dependent upon repeated observation on multiple occasions (see Becker's quote on p. 91) so there is plenty of opportunity to 'check out' such links.

One of the important goals of research is to conduct it in a manner that will allow generalisation from the specific case(s) of the research to the general population. Gans (1962: 348) voices his concerns that of the 3,000 or so people living in the area he was studying he only spoke with 100 to 150 and had intensive contact with 20. Moreover, his contacts were with men rather than women, and with workers rather than those in the worst economic position. He agonises over his ability to generalise on this basis and is acutely aware that the validity of his findings ultimately rested on his judgments about the data. Does that mean that all we are left with in such circumstances is an interesting case study with no broader application to knowledge? That is the only role that some would allow, but others argue that instead of seeking to extrapolate in order to say something about patterns of behaviour in some larger population, the goal here is to contribute to theory by illustrating concepts and demonstrating processes. Inevitably some voices will go unheard. For all its celebrated status, Whyte's (1943) study has been criticised for ignoring women (particularly the role of the mother in the family) and the church, two central pillars in Italian-American communities of the time (Boelen, 1992).

Over the years people have queued up to criticise participant observation studies. Most commonly this takes the form of questioning the reliability and validity of the data, both on the basis that it is vulnerable to hearsay, but more importantly that it is dependent on personal observation and interpretation, thereby lacking objectivity. Moreover, typically lacking quantitative data, it is difficult to offer 'evidence' and proof.

For advocates of participant observation, on the other hand, it is this very subjectivity that sets it above other approaches. The researcher and research instrument become one and the same, and knowing comes from being there and gaining direct experience. Moreover, from a purely practical point of view, the researcher is around long enough to have plenty of opportunity to check both the information provided to them and their emerging theories. These internal checks allow unsatisfactory explanations to be discarded. Far from being a disadvantage, the flexibility of being able to go to different places, observe different people and pursue different lines of enquiry makes it far superior to other approaches where all procedures are set in advance in the name of rigour. As explanations/theories begin to emerge the research can be redirected accordingly. The intensity of the activity allows exploration in greater depth than the alternatives. Of all the research approaches available it gets closest to the realities of social life. It is not divorced from the mess of everyday activities as experiments, questionnaires or even interviews are, but is part and parcel of what is going on.

Arguably dilemmas about 'going native' relate more to the process of analysis and interpretation than to behaviour. Should analysis and interpretation be conducted using the values and knowledge of an informed researcher or those of the group being studied? This is part of a broader debate about whether social understanding comes from the raw perspective of the insider's experience or the outsider's conceptual tools and theories. In practice, as long as the researcher is aware of this distinction it can provide a powerful tool for analysis.

Ethical Issues

Critics point also to the ethical problems associated with this style of research:

- Do you disclose your position as a researcher? The critics expect to win either way here: conceal your purpose and you are little better than a spy; reveal your purpose and the behaviour you observe has been corrupted by your presence. This is independent of the next point.
- To what extent can you intervene when you are meant to be studying them, not the consequences of your own actions? This relates to the role that is adopted, and can be most clearly recognised as an issue by considering the actions of some who work undercover for the media and 'make things happen for the sake of the story'. More generally, it is not always easy to distinguish between fitting-in and urging-on.
- How to report without betraying confidences? The whole purpose of this approach is to find out things that other styles of research would not, but having done so it may not be fair to parade that for all to see. Anonymity may only provide a thin veneer that in some cases is easily penetrated.
- Should the research and analysis be conducted using the values of the researcher or those of the group being studied? After engaging in the common, but illegal, practice of repeat voting Whyte (1943) decided that he had to

remain true to his own values, but if the researcher does not operate with the values of the other participants it has to be questioned whether it is fair to assess/judge people by standards that are just not part of their world.

These are certainly matters that need to be addressed, but then it is hard to conceive of any social research that does not involve ethical issues.

Benefits and Disadvantages

Pros – *Proponents argue:*

- less likely to be biased, unreliable or invalid – provides more opportunities for internal checks
- more responsive to the data than imposed systems – allows flexibility
- gets closest to the realities of social life – not divorced from the everyday
- intensity of the activity allows exploration in greater depth than the alternatives

Cons – *Opponents argue:*

- produces neither reliable nor valid data
- unable to generalise
- observer bias – depends on personal observation and interpretation
- problems of going native and suspending critical faculties
- subject to hearsay
- because it is non-quantitative it is difficult to present 'evidence' and proof

Despite his agonising about the reliability and validity of his participant observation, Gans (1962: 348) finally concluded:

Participant observation is the only method I know that enables the researchers to get close to the realities of social life. Its deficiencies in producing quantitative data are more than made up for by its ability to minimise the distance between researchers and their subjects of study.

Further Lines of Enquiry

In terms of doing participant observation, I still find two of the older contributions very useful. Whyte's (1943) *Street Corner Society* has a methodological appendix of some 100 words in which he discusses how he went about conducting his research. The collection of papers on *Field Research* edited by Burgess (1982) manages to combine practicalities with theory. In his own book *In The Field*, Burgess (1984) has a useful chapter on recording and analysing field data.

9

Interpreting Texts

Words mean what I want them to mean.
(Humpty Dumpty in Lewis Carroll's *Alice Through the Looking Glass*)

It is all too easy to take published material at face value and to accept uncritically the torrent of broadcast messages. For researchers it is important to consider the agendas that are being advanced through different 'texts' – from official documents (e.g. cultural strategies) to newspaper reports (e.g. of sporting events) to advertisements (e.g. holiday brochures). These 'texts' then represent a research resource in their own right. This chapter will address:

- the mechanics of simple quantitative measures of content analysis
- some of the basic principles of semiotics
- the triad of the transmitter, the message and the receiver, and decoding messages
- how values might be embedded in a range of messages.

With the emergence of postmodernism into leisure studies came a renewed interest in language and meaning. But the language considered extends beyond the spoken and written word to any system of symbols, whether that be dress or logos or photographic images. These can all be treated as 'texts' to be interpreted. This is typically done through some form of content analysis, though different versions may draw on ideas taken from semiotics and discourse analysis (you may also encounter conversational analysis).

On several occasions I have heard people insist that words can mean what they want them to mean, but if we are interested in 'communication' the speaker/writer cannot construct 'meaning' independently of how the words will be understood by others. There are coding systems and structures that allow us to work out what is meant. Even when the text diverges from the normal set of rules, we can eventually learn what the replacement structure is. So for example, a noisy hotel may be described in the holiday brochure as 'lively'. Maybe now I've argued that words *can* mean what you want them to mean, but no. One set of conventions has just replaced or supplemented another. In a parallel example, we 'learn to read' new 'fashion statements', from leaving the bottom button of a waistcoat undone, to which ear an ear-ring is worn in or leaving the laces of trainers untied, never mind the shifting credibility of brands.

Most people visiting Edinburgh at Festival time look for a copy of the programme for what is known as 'The Fringe'. This contains information on some 2000 shows, so the fringe-goer has to do a lot of weeding out to arrive at a shortlist of possibles. This involves working out the conventions of the programme:

Companies calling themselves 'Aaaaaaaaaha!' in order to be first in the alphabetical list – beware.

Shows describing themselves as 'hilarious' – beware, they rarely are (don't worry, plenty of other shows are).

Dramatic productions describing themselves as 'intense' – don't go unless other people describe you as intense.

The basic proposition then is that in social life signs are interpreted using systems of code. Manning (1987) uses a sporting example to show how this operates at different levels. 'Adidas' is not just a label, but it carries a meaning as a running shoe. Because these may be used in different forms of 'sport' – for marathons, jogging, or '10K' runs – that meaning will be read differently, depending upon a series of other cues, to communicate leisurewear for some and serious competitive sport for another. Equally, any tourist who escapes the bubble of the all-inclusive package ought to appreciate that the system of codes and meanings can vary from one culture to another (indeed this has been the theme of one bank's advertising campaign). How these systems of shared meanings form a culture and structure in what we do has become of increasing interest to postmodernists.

You can fairly easily see how this can get quite complicated. If you read around this subject you may find that those researchers concerned with language seem to use some of the most difficult language to understand. So let me go back to a more basic, fundamental approach to content analysis. When I first came across this style of research I was introduced to the triad of transmitter, message and receiver (Figure 9.1). Examining the message, the means of its communication and its content, ought to lead us to consider the effect it has on the audience: for example,

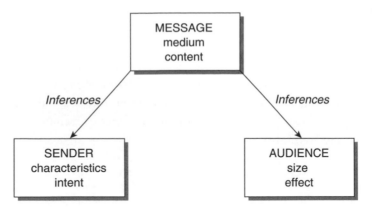

Figure 9.1   The communication triad (adapted from Chadwick et al., 1984: 240)

whether the sports equipment or holiday really is seen as desirable as a consequence of the message or whether violence in films or video games makes people
violent. Importantly too though it should invite us to examine the people who put
it together (whether an arm of government, company, voluntary organisation or
individual) and what lay behind it.

The triad in Figure 9.1 implies a number of focuses for the analysis in addition
to the message itself – who sends it, for what purpose, using what medium, to
whom, with what consequence. When this kind of research is put to work to
examine different problems, the emphasis shifts to different parts of this triad.
For example, in an analysis of graffiti or policy documents the emphasis is likely
to be on the producers of the messages, what they were intending to convey and
what that says about their communities/sub-cultures. On the other hand an
analysis of images used to promote holidays might see the emphasis shift towards
the receivers and how they interpret the messages in deciding which holiday
to buy.

Doing Content Analysis

Let me start with what might appear to be the more formal style of content analysis, and then move to more discursive styles later. The box below indicates some
of the key components involved, and I shall try to explain how one researcher
tackled the problem.

Content Analysis — Typical Tasks

Statement of the problem – important to be systematic – conventionally an appropriate theory is used to devise a hypothesis to test.

Selection of communications for study – these might be: adverts; newspapers; TV programmes; policy documents; graffiti, etc.

Identify basis for sampling these – e.g. which editions of which papers? – selection should be guided by the hypothesis under examination.

Specify the 'bits' to be evaluated – these might be individual words or the overarching theme of the communication.

Devise categories for coding – important to specify what is taken to make a message racist, sexist, homophobic, etc.

Specify form of measurement – e.g. presence/absence, number of column inches, percentage of time.

As with any style of research, how useful content analysis is depends very much on how the research challenge is devised. I have now seen several student projects that tell me that women's sport gets less coverage in the papers than men's sport. I think I knew that already. Of course straightforward counting/measurement can provide some telling data, but there are many ways in which this can be extended and related to leisure, sport and tourism theory.

A tourism example

Pritchard (2001) took as her starting point Cohen's proposition that:

> The representations in tourism brochures and the promotional videos are largely self-conscious constructions ... they are presumably created to be representative enough of what is being marketed to ensure consumer satisfaction upon purchase, while sufficiently idealised to attract and perhaps even to construct a particular tourist gaze. (Cohen, 1985: 411)

Pritchard then set out to examine how images used to represent tourism are created, filtered and mediated through gender-related views of the world that she takes to be pervasive. Her earlier work had demonstrated that these representations were invariably designed to be male-orientated and exclusively heterosexual. In this piece of research Pritchard selected 14 brochures using a stratified sample to cover short- and long-haul holidays and different market segments (seniors, singles and couples). This meant evaluating 12,832 'images', recognising that each photograph could contain more than one image. The way in which each of these images was coded was against a scale that Pritchard had adapted from Butler-Paisley and Paisley-Butler (1974) to assess sexist portrayals of women/men.

Level I	as a one dimensional sexual object or decoration
Level II	in traditional roles – women in passive or beauty activities and childcare; men in sport, authority, etc.
Level III	in non-traditional roles – women in sport, authority, etc.; men in childcare, submissive, etc.
Level IV	as individuals

Pritchard maintains that this escapes the simple sexist/non-sexist dichotomy of a nominal scale, and that by providing a continuum from sexist to non-sexist it represents an ordinal scale (Chapter 6). The images were then weighted according to size in an attempt to reflect their influence/impact. In all categories of brochure images of women represented a clear majority, but more significantly for Pritchard:

> In all the sample brochures the representations of men and women were extremely stereotypical. Men are seen to be active – they swim, water-ski, play golf, hold menus and drive cars; women are portrayed as passive – they watch men, enjoy sedentary leisure or perform 'domestic' tasks, at kitchen sinks in self-catering apartments or looking after children. (2001: 88)

Women tended to be portrayed as being decorative. The same applied to men, though to a lesser extent. The exception to this was in the seniors brochures where women and men are desexualised by tourism marketers. In the singles and couples brochures in particular Pritchard found that even the non-traditional images of men and women did 'not extend to a reversal of submissive and authoritarian roles' (2001: 86). Because of the role representation, Pritchard contends that:

> when female images are *overwhelmingly* restricted to these prescribed and subordinate roles, they serve not only to distort reality, but also, by maintaining sexist stereotypes, to constrain female identities. Such images play a vital role in creating and maintaining everyday perceptions of accepted roles for women and men … (2001: 91)

Intention and Impact

On the basis of the message alone it is somewhat problematic making inferences about the senders and receivers. It seems to me that in the bulk of work in this area the meaning is divined by the researcher without apparent need to ask either the instigator of the message or the people receiving it, about how it was intended and how it was interpreted. One of my former colleagues, who is currently doing his PhD on the meanings carried by replica football shirts, is trying to 'square the circle' by using interviews to identify what the football club and the shirt designers want to convey, alongside what the different shirts mean to the fans (class, community, tradition, loyalty, protest, style, etc.).

A sport example

While he was doing his PhD, Karl Spracklen also wrote for *The Rugby Leaguer*. He reflected on the way in which he constructed one of his reports (in the box below). His analysis was unpublished but is included after the article with some of my commentary added in.

Bram-busters!

Rugby Leaguer, No. 1909, 30.01.95, p. 16

This was a match spoilt by the heavy conditions and the rather lazy interpretation of the new play the ball directive.

Yet the catalogue of errors and the mud bath in the middle of the pitch should not deflect from a sterling second half performance by Bramley, who had effectively won the match around the hour mark when man of the match Wayne Freeman crossed the line twice in three minutes.

Swinton were a shadow of the side that beat Leigh in mid week. Although the younger Tony Barrow put in a hard stint at prop, there was a lack of cohesion between the forwards and the backs. When Brett Clark had to limp from the field at half time their creativity was stifled, and they had nothing to hold up against the home side's tactical genius Ray Ashton and exciting scrum half Gordon Long.

It was the Lions who scored first in the opening minutes when lively hooker Paul Gartland finished a move involving loose forward Paul Barrow and centre David Marsh, which caught the home defence napping. For the next fifteen minutes it was all blue and white as ex-saints Ian Connor and Tony Barrow Junior pounded the Villagers' line.

But that line held firm and the mistakes crept in. When Bramley finally got round to attacking after a Swinton knock on, Gordon Long managed to sneak a try from dummy half.

With both sides deadlocked, Ray Ashton and Dean Hall came on to turn the game in Bramley's favour.

(Continued)

(Continued)

>   *Hall, back from suspension, caused havoc in mid-field and Ashton changed the pattern of the home side's play. Before the interval loose forward Paul Garrett had found a gap and Barry Greenwood capitalised to go in for Bramley's second.*
>
>   *In the second half, the game threatened to degenerate when tempers started to boil resulting in the sin-binning of Swinton prop Ian Connor.*
>
>   *Bramley kept their cool throughout this and Wayne Freeman copied team mate Long in scoring from dummy half, before running sixty yards three minutes later to score his second and kill the Lions' hopes. Dean Creasser then went over after Gordon Long chipped through, before Connor finally returned.*
>
>   *Ian Wrigglesworth could have grabbed another for the home side but for a double movement, and Paul Lord's try on full time for the Lions only contributed to a flattering haul for the visitors.*

Style and Structure

There is a style and structure to a report that has to be followed, a particular language that will be accepted by the editor. When Karl attempted to introduce more thoughtful and humorous writing, it was edited out.

   The style of the *Leaguer* is populist, aiming to give the fan something they will understand, using the language of 'the game'. The paper is still somewhat traditionalist, though the editorial is attempting to subscribe to the newer, Australianised concepts around the game. Hence the expressions of masculinity are removed from the older ideals of drinking and violence to the Lombardian work ethic, the sheer physicality described through war metaphors, and the importance of being 'simply the best'.

   Karl's editor identified two basic structures for match reports: the pyramid and the bulletin. The bulletin is usually short and concise, with snippets of information and no hierarchy of importance between what is more or less relevant. A match report in this style may not say who won until halfway through, or it may even wait until the end. The pyramid is the more usual form with the item of most importance first, so that the essential information of the report can be absorbed at a casual glance. It is no surprise then to see that both Karl and another writer in the *League Express* follow that style for their match report.

   The two papers have differing styles informed by their past history. The *Leaguer* is eager to project a positive image of the game, to tell it as a fan would see it. The *Express* allows for a more reflective approach which can be critical while being 'true to the action', but the structure and language used remain the same, supporting the masculine myth inherent within 'the game'.

Interpreting the meaning

First, a one sentence summary of the match and then scene setting and the key point that 'Bramley ... won the match ... when ...' Next comes a colour remark, which adds cohesion and depth to the text, when I refer back to a match Swinton had previously played. This gives the reporter an air of knowledge and authority. When I say Swinton's creativity was stifled by Clark leaving the pitch, I am saying Swinton could possibly have won the match. After this I mention the players who played well for Bramley (with the exception of Freeman, already mentioned in the second sentence).

One-third of the way through the match report I start to describe the action in the match, exaggerating Swinton's attack and describing their first try and who was involved. This emphasis on Swinton is a defence against any implicit bias, though I return to Bramley to praise their defence and describe their first try.

The match report stresses the war element of the game, praising the confrontational aspect and rewarding players for their toughness and ability to score. The report congratulates victory above all and is designed to stress that victory over the losing team's failings. By recalling masculine highlights (tries, hard work, overcoming adversity, fights, winning), key points and important moments in the game a myth is created over what 'the game' is about. Hence substitutions are ignored as showing weakness, unless it is through those substitutions that better men arrive on the scene to win the game through their strength and skill. The 80 minutes of the match are reduced to a stereotyped view that extols the war and conflict aspect inherent in the game as the most important one.

The match report is littered with masculine symbols, and uses a confrontational, aggressive language. I describe Bramley's performance as 'sterling', an archaic description that resonates with old-fashioned masculinity and courage. I congratulate Tony Barrow Jr for 'hard work' i.e. he tackled roughly, doing his best to inflict injury, and showed no signs of relenting when charging at top speed into other players. He is held up as an example of how to keep going and play strong, an exemplar of a 'rugby man'. Brett Clark has to 'limp off', suggesting it is something he would rather not do, and also that the game can be so tough you get injured but take it like a man. Ray Ashton is a 'tactical genius', equating him with a general at war deciding a plan of action. I call Swinton 'the Lions', an aggressive nickname, and describe the Swinton hooker as 'lively', a coded word that tacitly means tough and feisty, able to play dirty. The home defence is caught napping – a message to kids learning to be rugby players and men to maintain a high work rate all the time if they are to win (and become men).

Next comes another explicit war metaphor. Swinton are described as pounding the Bramley line, but that line held firm! It is the Battle of Britain/Rorke's Drift all over again, strength and faith in one's masculinity overcoming adversity. This is affirmed by the next line, which shows that patience can be rewarded with Long's try. But there is still a stalemate, it is like the Western Front, until the intervention of Ashton (the Napoleon figure of shrewd masculinity) and Hall, who is 'back from suspension', a code for being a strong and short-tempered player. Hall proceeds to cause havoc (he knocks people over and tackles people so that it really hurts, uncaring of his own safety), and it is the intervention of these two that turns the game in Bramley's favour (strength and stamina and know-how = victory).

I brush lightly over the fight, since fighting is not part of the newer expressions of masculinity supported by the Australianised 'game'. But the wording is ambiguous. It can be telling the reader the fight is wrong ('the game threatened to degenerate'), but it uses euphemistic language favoured by coaches, players and the older 'traditionalist' fan ('tempers started to boil'). But having kept their cool (another message to kids about how to behave like a man) Bramley proceed to win. And in winning, they 'kill the Lions' hopes' (aggressive and violent metaphor for victory).

The difference between the match notes and 'the copy'

The style and structure of a match report are important, as these send a message to the readership about 'the game', and what is important in the game. In a sense this is obvious. As a writer, one writes in a specific style for a specific audience. I would not discuss the construction of masculine identity and the imaginary communities of Cohen (1985) in the middle of a Bramley v. Swinton match report; at the same time, I would not write an academic paper in the same way as I speak.

The ethnographic text used for the PhD is truer to my original experience of the match. It was cold, I was not too keen to see a lower second division match, and this is reflected in my perception of what the match was like. In fact, away from the match notes, I only have the vague impression of not being too impressed. This immediate perception of the match is not only stylistically different from the match report, but it also tells a different story: of pessimism, club loyalty, decay, harsh weather and the pub as a social focus before the match.

In direct opposition to the disclaimer about the 'catalogue of errors' not detracting from the match, the reporter was extremely frustrated by the poor quality of the play.

Coda

Karl also compared his account with others. In the process of comparing notes with other reporters a view of the game was debated and agreed upon: the consensus becomes the reality. This makes for more discussion on what happened in the game: 'it doesn't have to be right, only that we are all in agreement'.

Alternative Applications

Exercise

Of course Karl Spracklen's work above is a very particular example, but the same sort of principles apply to any 'text', whether written, oral or visual. See if you can apply the same principles to a newspaper article, an advertisement and a section of a report from a public body.

Although media analysis has attracted much of the attention, content analysis may be used in a range of different challenges. For example, psychologists may use it in interpreting projective personality tests like the thematic apperception test (respondents are asked to make up a story about a picture they are presented with – maybe a picture of some people at a bar in a club or a woman walking the streets at night). Content analysis can also be used as a means of studying social change, e.g.

- the emergence of the concern for sustainability in tourism policy in the face of profit-oriented principles of business management
- the shifting balance between promoting excellence or participation in sport and the arts
- changing priorities afforded to leisure's ability to address unemployment, crime, heath, etc.
- an index of discrimination against minority groups on the basis of negative ethnic stereotypes in books, toys, cartoons, etc.

Just as the examples from the work of Pritchard and Spracklen used in this chapter demonstrate how values are embedded in texts, so this kind of approach can be used to reveal processes of agenda setting. The analysis of policy statements, annual reports and committee minutes can help to reveal how issues are 'framed' and some are just not presented for consideration.

In performing such tasks we have to be clear about the status of the message itself. Scott (1990) suggests that when analysing communications we need to consider authenticity (is it genuine?), credibility (is it undistorted, free from error?), representativeness (is it typical?) and meaning (in a social context).

Questions, Questions – Always Questions

Does the 'text' correspond to the events it describes?
Is there a difference between the intended and received meanings?
Can meaning be divorced from social context?
Do such 'texts' reflect/report social reality or shape it?

Further Lines of Enquiry

Research in this mould has become more common. See, for example: Sirakaya and Sonmez (2000) on the way in which women and men are presented in (US) state tourism brochures, finding that women were more likely to be depicted as subordinate, submissive, dependent; or on the media portrayal of women in sport, for example, Messner et al. (2003) or Higgs et al. (2003); or on the media portrayal of minority ethnic groups in sport, for example, Sabo et al. (1996).

10

Evaluation Techniques

The greatest challenge in assessing the state of sport and physical activity has been the lack of reliable data ... although this does not invalidate the case for action, it weakens our ability to develop evidence-based policy interventions. (Strategy Unit & Department for Culture Media and Sport, 2002: 21)

In the face of stiff competition for resources, advocates of leisure, sport and tourism are expected to demonstrate the effectiveness of investment in new initiatives. Evaluation studies are used to try to examine whether or not some intervention has successfully delivered its goals. These studies may use any number of different techniques. Even where the research is designed to be sympathetic to the needs and feelings of the people involved there is a need for rigour in the approach if doubters are to have confidence in the findings. This chapter will address

- the structure of the evaluation exercise
- different styles of evaluation
- milestones, outputs and outcomes
- selecting criteria, performance indicators and targets
- establishing baselines and benchmarks
- recognising/recording outcomes beyond the programme
- the consequences of who does the research.

Evaluation studies received a big boost in the UK with the election of the New Labour government with its expressed commitment to 'evidence based policy'. Many academic researchers are wary of evaluation because of its close involvement with vested interests keen to shape policy. However, if researchers want their work to have an impact it seems to me these troubled waters have to be negotiated.

Following a line similar to the quote from *Game Plan* at the head of this chapter, the earlier report from Policy Action Team 10 on the contribution of sport and the arts to social inclusion observed that 'there is at present relatively little hard evidence about the costs and benefits of arts and sports in community development or about what sorts of project provide best value for money' (Policy Action Team 10, 1999: 37) and hence we have to rely on 'anecdotal' evidence. This was accompanied by a recommendation that evaluation should be integral to all arts/sport regeneration projects and programmes:

> The team understands well the difficulty of conducting proper evaluation and the need for those conducting evaluation to have appropriate skills and training. It is, however, convinced of the importance of proper evaluation. (Policy Action Team 10, 1999: 37)

You may only want to know whether your arts or sport project is delivering what those attending want. In which case a simple questionnaire (Chapter 6) or round of interviews (Chapter 7) will suffice. However, if you want to know if the project has managed to bring about change by, for example, increasing self-esteem or community cohesion, more attention will have to be given to research design (Chapter 2). There are no special techniques (these may include questionnaires, structured or unstructured interviews, focus groups, observation, and surveys); it is the context and process that differ.

In addition to helping to decide future investment strategies, evaluation may be expected to apply learning to improve future practice. There are any number of questions that an evaluation may be asked to address, but probably the most common are of the following kinds:

- Has a change occurred?
- Can it be attributed to the intervention or would it have happened anyway as a result of surrounding forces?
- Has the intervention/initiative satisfied the proposed goals?
- What made it (not) work?
- Has it been cost effective?

Ideally then we might want to know what the state of affairs was before the project started, formulate some clear measures of performance and see how things had changed by the end of the project. Once again the gold standard (the yardstick by which others are judged) is often taken to be the randomised control trial (RCT) of the scientific experiment (Chapter 2). This is particularly significant if sport and arts projects are competing for funding as part of, or instead of, health spending, an arena where RCTs are taken to be the norm. Leaving aside for the moment whether or not this really is the best approach, it is not likely that this kind of research can be arranged in many of our fields of interest.

1. Random allocation to control and experimental groups is rarely either possible or desirable.
2. There may be multiple interventions each designed to achieve something slightly different.
3. It is hard to ensure that all receive the same 'treatment'.
4. Surrounding circumstances cannot be held constant.

Added to this, some people working in projects 'on the ground' dismiss as naive the faith that is sometimes placed in the validity and reliability of quantitative measures of participation as indicators of social benefit. Confidence, esteem, community cohesion, etc. may not be amenable to quantitative measurement, but the challenge then has to be to identify what does constitute 'evidence'. It is common for project workers to report specific examples of people from the project who have achieved something valuable (e.g. from youngster 'at risk' to Olympic medallist). However, this can easily be dismissed as merely anecdotal evidence. Few people doubt that sport and the arts *can* produce social benefits, which is what such instances demonstrate. The question is to what extent they occur and whether there is something going on that is more than happy coincidence. It would be helpful if such examples could be treated more formally and aggregated to make a compelling case, but this can only be done convincingly if accompanied by a consideration of the counter examples. This has to be followed by a critical examination of why there should be the different outcomes.

Ideally the evaluation should not just be conducted on completion of the project, but designed to produce repeated measures through its course. Not only does that allow some understanding of the project's evolution, but also offers the possibility of feedback before it is too late to do anything about it. This idea of providing feedback seems to upset some researchers wedded to the scientific model because it means that the administered 'dose' may change. The issue drives at the heart of the relationship between research and practice. On the one hand are people who want to be clinical in gathering evidence akin to medical trials as they strive for equivalence of status; on the other are people who want to service more directly the needs of the project they are working with. The latter tend to be keen to devise a form of evaluation that can include the unexpected, which might not be 'counted' if the evaluation is determined purely by the original aims.

Evaluation Processes

Coalter (2002) describes evaluation in the context of what he calls the programme planning process (Figure 10.1). The advantage of seeing it in this way is that evaluation is recognised as being rooted very much in the *aims* of the project and the *interests* of the stakeholders. There may, of course, be a tension between the aims of those responsible for the overall policy and those of the people involved in delivering the project or service. A concern with the impact of a scheme implies a focus on change, which in turn suggests a need for *baseline* data against which future measures can be compared. This might require measures of assessment at the beginning and end to try to calculate total net effects. However, whether or not a project involving youngsters in various leisure activities, for example, is having beneficial outcomes can be assessed over any suitable time period within the programme. Repeated measures or longitudinal data of this kind have to be gathered in exactly the same way on each occasion if using standardised measures. Evaluations using qualitative techniques can be more flexible.

In other circumstances, asking the people involved what change had happened may do away with the need for two (or more) sets of data. For example they may be asked whether they are physically more active as a result of their involvement, or what activity they now do that they did not do previously (or vice versa); or local residents may be asked whether they think the incidence of crime has risen or fallen (fear of crime may be as important as levels of crime).

The challenge of the evaluation may not be just to assess change within a particular project, but to compare one with another. In those circumstances it would seem important that the data be gathered in exactly the same way for each project. This can lead to some very obvious problems. For example, projects are rarely the same and it may not be 'fair' to measure their outcomes in the same way.

In one of our evaluation exercises (Long et al., 2002) three levels of recording project development and delivery could readily be identified.

- Some projects were evaluated only/largely in terms of meeting *milestones* on time: e.g. first consultation meeting, co-ordinator in post. This is done largely to satisfy funding agents regarding due process and is commonly accepted as perfectly adequate to demonstrate proper project management.
- The next level considered measures of *outputs*: e.g. the number of events staged, the number of people attending on at least one occasion or for the duration.
- But a consideration of the power of projects to bring about social benefits required an evaluation of the success in securing *outcomes* which in that case advanced the

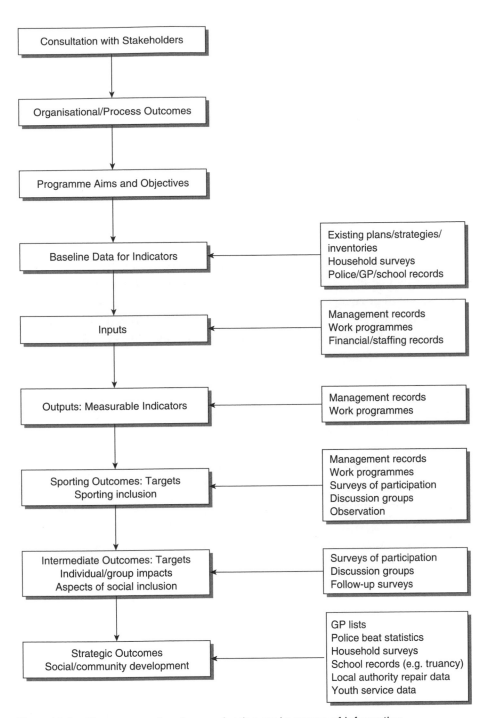

Figure 10.1   Programme planning, evaluation and sources of information
(from Coalter, 2002)

position of socially excluded people. So, did people get jobs, did their health improve, did they move into gainful employment, was crime reduced? In other words, in what ways had the project changed the lives of the participants?

However, Coalter (2002) in Figure 10.1 makes a further distinction in the types of outcomes that might be examined:

(a) *Sporting outcomes* – direct benefits which might include increased participation by women or people from minority ethnic groups, or the development of sporting skills
(b) *Intermediate outcomes* – the impact on the participating individuals such as improved fitness or increased self-esteem
(c) *Strategic outcomes* – broader impacts, like reduced crime or increased social capital, that bring about community development.

Practitioners and policymakers alike may also be interested in *process outcomes*, the processes by which the goals were achieved. For example they may wish to know whether the various agencies have successfully worked in partnership in order to deliver the project, and what the mechanisms were that allowed that to happen. These are normally assessed via qualitative assessments addressed during interview, though other techniques like the analysis of project documentation may also be used.

Policymakers are also concerned with what these outcomes are going to cost, and so want *efficiency* and *effectiveness* to be assessed. Evaluators need to appreciate which of these the emphasis is on as they imply different needs for data. Although these twin concepts are sometimes treated as synonymous, there are important distinctions. This can be illustrated through an everyday analogy (well it is in my life). When cycling up a hill, standing on the pedals may prove very effective, but it is not very efficient in terms of energy consumption. A sport or arts project may be very efficient in terms of accommodating a lot of people, but not prove very effective because they have failed to receive the level of attention necessary. With enough money to throw at the problem many projects might be able to produce very positive outcomes, but not many projects operate in such favourable circumstances. Nichols and Taylor (1996) demonstrated that participation in a sports counselling project was associated with a significant reduction in re-offending rates, but was only really effective for those doing the full 12-week programme. In the next funding round the programme was cut to four weeks. Policymakers do not always hear the message from the evaluation.

Perhaps less often, projects may be assessed on the basis of their ability to promote *equity*. Who benefits is then a key consideration. To what extent is the policy or project successful in delivering benefits to people who are otherwise disadvantaged?

Efficiency, effectiveness and equity may also come to mean something slightly different in shifting policy contexts. In a recent conference presentation we were informed that for the Department for Culture, Media and Sport (presumably like other government departments) an organisation's efficiency is interpreted in terms of the proportion of staff it has 'on the front line' delivering the service rather than doing the administration and organisation. Although this may be a real political imperative, it does not necessarily equate to either efficiency or effectiveness.

Assuming there is a need to know what it takes to secure the benefits hoped for, there has to be a measure of the *inputs* to the process. You might think that is the easy bit, but you may have to work out how to 'cost in' the time of volunteers or a facility/equipment given free (it might also depend on whether other activities have been displaced).

If the evaluation is concerned only with outputs it is fairly straightforward to gather the necessary data, perhaps recording the number of youngsters turning up to each session. However, it is often hard to get agreement on what is a suitable indicator for measuring any of the intermediate or strategic outcomes above. For example, if we want to know whether health has improved as a result of an active lifestyles project, would it be best to measure the number of visits to local doctors, the number of prescriptions dispensed, individual blood pressure or cholesterol levels, or self-reported health? This can often be clarified by adopting an approach that considers what are labelled 'theories of change'. Essentially this involves examining the underlying assumptions that often go unrecognised. So, for example, the evaluators would try to work out what it is about sport/the arts/tourism that might be expected to produce the benefits; what aspects operating in what way?

For the national evaluation of the Local Exercise Action Pilots one of my colleagues used an example from the US Department of Health and Human Services to explain the nature of a logic model (Figure 10.2). This one identifies the various conceptual links associated with a walk to school initiative. Recognising these different elements and their links helps to identify what needs to be examined in the evaluation. It also helps to address the next problem (below) by identifying which links are known on the basis of existing research findings and which are based on theoretical logic.

Attributing Cause and Other Problems

Even when good measures (whether quantitative or qualitative) have produced 'evidence', it is difficult to attribute cause because there may have been many

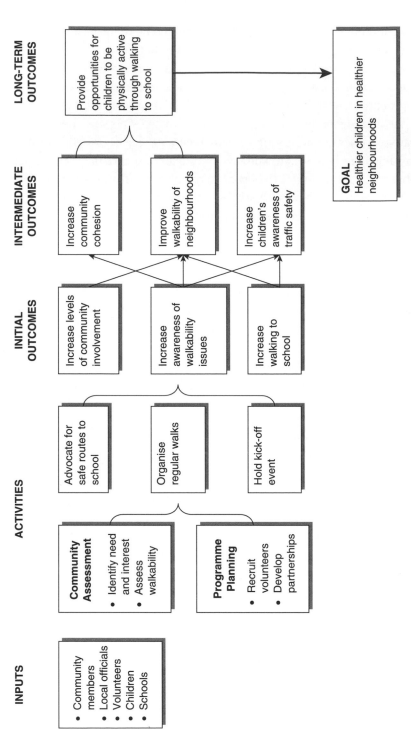

Figure 10.2   A walk to school logic model (adapted from US Department of Health and Human Service, 2002)

other factors involved that have nothing to do with the project or policy being evaluated. For example:

- Youngsters may forsake 'delinquent' or 'deviant' ways because their interests and disposition shift as they 'mature' or they get a job or boyfriend/girlfriend, etc …
- People's health may improve because they change job and experience less stress or they get a job as the economic climate improves so they have the income to allow a better diet or they give up smoking because their best mate dies of cancer, etc …

In the aggregate (i.e. across all participants), perhaps these parallel experiences should not affect the assessment of the project outcomes, but many of the projects you are likely to be interested in will be small-scale and individual circumstances matter. Many schemes that the government is keen to evaluate are directed to areas of disadvantage, and in any one such area there are likely to be many schemes running at the same time. Consequently it may be hard to separate their respective impacts.

Evaluation is further complicated by the bounds of the project. Key outcomes may be evidenced beyond the project (e.g. in schools), and these may easily be overlooked. Many such projects have limited lifespans and the key outcomes may only show up after the project and its evaluation have been completed – alternatively they may be lost/fade over that extended period of time. Problems arise within the boundaries of the project too. Just because a project is delivered in a disadvantaged area does not necessarily mean that the target groups bene-fit. Even delivering leisure opportunities to those target groups may not secure the wider strategic outcomes discussed above.

Earlier in this chapter I suggested that the evaluation exercise has to be grounded in the aims of the project, but in our own evaluations we have some-times found projects lack clarity in what they expect their outcomes to be. This can be further complicated by the organic nature of many projects which leads to evolving objectives, especially when staff change.

Example: Assessing the Contribution of Cultural Projects to Social Inclusion (Long et al., 2002)

This study was set up to use evidence from cultural projects to assess the contribution that could be made to social inclusion (the involvement of people in the processes that deliver the benefits society has to offer). We worked with 14 projects from different parts of England, engaged in activities such as outdoor adventure, performances and exhibitions, football, training in video and recording music, libraries, museums and local history. These activities were being used to promote social inclusion by, for example, helping to prepare people for work, reducing criminal behaviour, improving health. So we:

(Continued)

(Continued)

- examined the different understandings of social exclusion/inclusion
- reviewed evidence of social benefits to provide a context for the practice and achievements of these projects
- examined a range of potential indicators of social inclusion within the projects
- identified evidence of good practice in securing social inclusion goals and evaluation.

The aspects of social inclusion that the funders – the Department for Culture, Media and Sport (DCMS) – were interested in were: improved educational performance; increased employment rates; reduced levels of crime; and better (and more equal) standards of health. On the basis of the most frequently claimed benefits for cultural initiatives we added three more:

- personal development – exercising own ability to act (empowerment)
- social cohesion – interpersonal and inter-group ties
- active citizenship – contributing, accessing privileges, benefits and entitlements, and making structures more open.

We knew these were notoriously difficult to assess, and few projects have the resources to attempt such complex evaluation. Moreover DCMS was keen that the projects should be assessed against their own aims and objectives, which meant that no consistency of practice could be expected. This made it very difficult to generalise about the capabilities of cultural projects. Our challenge was to establish order from disparity. We tried to do this by identifying the set of seven evaluation domains above and then accepted whatever evidence each project could offer within those domains to a consideration of the use of cultural activities to promote social inclusion.

We used a four stage approach with the projects.

1. *Orientation and profiling* – Profiles were constructed of all projects using material deposited on file with DCMS, information gathered from field visits and supplementary information collected by telephone, electronic and written correspondence. Apart from the key contact details each profile contained:

   - project aims
   - funding sources/scale
   - staffing: employees and volunteers
   - project organisation and management
   - activities of project – where and when
   - geographical area covered
   - target population and how engaged/recruited
   - stage of development of the project
   - monitoring and evaluation: process and criteria matched to aims (indicators of success)
   - progress to date
   - future timetable/programme/duration
   - other distinguishing characteristics.

(Continued)

2. *Assisting evaluation and guiding procedures* – We organised a workshop day in London with representatives of the projects and DCMS to consider how appropriate indicators might be constructed and implemented. We distributed information about each project to all those involved, disseminated the outcomes of the day and set up a restricted access web site. Our intention was to try to stimulate interest and activity in evaluation among the projects by fostering a feeling of collective endeavour. These discussions were then followed up in detail in each of the individual projects (see Stage 3 below).

3. *Identifying indicators* – A programme of field visits was supplemented with telephone, fax and email correspondence and was designed to take account of the possible need to observe activities or interview participants as well as interviewing key personnel and collecting relevant documentation. On the basis of the respective Stage 1 profiles we reviewed with each project team the objectives of their project and considered carefully not just milestones and outputs, but what outcomes they hoped to achieve in the context of our seven domains (from educational improvement to active citizenship). We then worked with them to try to identify appropriate indicators of performance linked to these outcomes.

4. *Collating evidence* – The projects involved very different styles of evaluation:

   - external consultants employed either to support the development of the project or to conduct one-off evaluations
   - Consumer Panels run for the service as a whole
   - ad hoc surveys
   - feedback forms from group leaders
   - interviewing intermediaries – e.g. head teachers
   - demonstration through photographic and other evidence.

These evaluations in turn produced different levels of evidence:

   - the (informed) claims of those working on the project
   - feedback from those they work with
   - internal evaluation
   - externally audited evidence.

This is not to infer a truth hierarchy, but it probably does represent a gradient of credibility, even if those who should have the greatest knowledge of the processes and outcomes are those working on the project.

While milestones were registered, some outputs recorded and levels of satisfaction sometimes assessed, outcomes less often played a part in the evaluation exercise, despite these projects being handpicked by DCMS. What was considered to 'work' was primarily the instinctual response of the professionals responsible for the projects. Only rarely were they able to draw on supportive research evidence. In their own projects the project teams took it as an indicator of success that people turned up and stayed. The presumption (perhaps quite correct) is that they will then have benefited from what the project has to offer. The Policy Action Team 10 (1999) report, and the concern with social exclusion generally, imply a recognition of the importance of considering not just what benefits, but also who benefits. However, even at this relatively simple level, few of the projects were able to identify the socio-demographic characteristics of the participants.

Communicating the Findings

The evaluation project cannot be considered successful until the findings have been communicated to other people. In addition to those who have commissioned the research you should consider how to present findings to those who have contributed to your research. Different audiences may want to see the findings presented in different ways. The people you interviewed may be very interested in what you have learnt, but may not particularly want to read your dissertation. A summary of the main points may be more appropriate. Similarly, if a report has been commissioned by an agency or government department, those closest to that policy area may want all the details, while others may only want to know the key findings. Apart from the project report, evaluators produce 'executive summaries' (anything between one and a dozen pages of the main points), papers for academic journals, articles for professional magazines and interviews for the broadcast media.

It may be hard if you are following the prescriptive procedures for the completion of a dissertation, but in other research environments it may be possible to consider the use of innovative and creative ways to disseminate evaluation findings: drama, role play, story telling, videos and other visual feedback through exhibitions, etc. It may be difficult to let people who completed your questionnaires know what the evaluation has concluded, but preparing a story for the local press could go some way to doing this. For many people seeing is believing, so the most effective form of dissemination may have nothing to do with your elaborate evaluation exercise, but be simply inviting people along to an open day so they can witness for themselves the work of the project.

Independent Evaluation?

The Policy Action Team 10 report (1999: 37) on arts and sport recommended that 'wherever possible external evaluation, and the means to carry it out, should be integral to the project/programme'. The use of independent evaluators has several advantages.

- It can relieve the burden on project staff of unwanted responsibilities.
- It can provide the skills necessary to conduct the evaluation.
- It can contribute to the professional development of project staff by encouraging them to be more critical of the project so they can make the adjustments necessary to take it forward.
- It may also increase the credibility of the findings if they are seen to be evaluated by a disinterested party.

Of course, that 'distance' may cause problems if it leaves the evaluators unable to appreciate the day-to-day difficulties encountered in the project or it causes the project workers to feel they are being constantly judged.

In terms of the structure of most of the arts and sports projects Policy Action Team 10 was concerned with, it would probably not be realistic to expect them to take on the complex challenges of researching the relationship with regeneration and social inclusion on their own – and probably not even to take the lead. However, some of the 'evidence' that is likely to be produced is dependent on the 'knowing' (the knowledge that comes from direct experience) of the individuals directly involved, so it is important that both project workers and participants be integrally involved in a collaborative enterprise.

A Political Process

As identified at the beginning of this chapter, evaluation is a political process. The direction of policy, the continuation/extension of funding and individual reputations may all depend on it. Evaluations may put people's jobs on the line so step carefully and be particularly sensitive to how you might be perceived. The different stakeholders identified above in relation to Figure 10.1 are all likely to want different things from the research. As a result a few brickbats are often thrown. This means that evaluators need acute political antennae capable of sensing the voice of vested interest and the implications of the reported findings, and they need to be confident in the methods they have used so that they can defend the legitimacy of their findings. Evaluation has to be thorough to be credible, but should not be so onerous as to be rejected by those in the projects.

For a productive experience, those involved in the programme being evaluated need to feel that they need the research. There are many evaluation reports that do not provide an evaluation so much as offer a justification and applause for the programme. Outcomes, as opposed to milestones and outputs, are not really an integral part of the mindsets of project managers. Evaluation is rarely high among their priorities. They are often preoccupied with organising and managing current activities and planning for the future, particularly securing funding. As one of our contacts observed:

> My sincere apologies for not being able to respond to your email before now. Not only did we spend the summer applying for funding, but the autumn has been taken up with resubmitting new profiles and redesigning all the projects! As I think I may have mentioned to you, we have also had problems with our funding streams for the Programme. The New Deal intermediary in _____ has consistently been owing us

back payments ever since we started, and those have risen to over £40k now. We are trying to contract direct with Employment Services, although this may not help a great deal. The Objective 2 support finished last December, and the new O2 programme will only start at the end of this year. This meant applying for 10 months' gap funding, which still hasn't come through. And the final funding stream is SRB, and this has been delayed and caught up in all sorts of local politics. Our 2000/01 funds only arrived in the summer of 2001, and the 2001/02 funds have still to be formally approved and paid. So you can imagine that it has been a cashflow nightmare to keep the project performing and meeting its outputs and objectives. (Long et al., 2002: 82, quoted with permission from the respondent)

Further Lines of Enquiry

There are many sources of advice on general methods for evaluation. See for example: Weiss (1998) *Evaluation: Methods for Studying Programs and Policies* and Robson (2000) *Small Scale Evaluations*.

Despite its somewhat misleading title, *Sport and Community Development: A Manual*, produced by Coalter (2002) for sportscotland, is in fact a guide to conducting evaluation within one of our areas of interest. The market research organisation, MORI, has produced a report for Sport England (2001) on measuring performance based on customer satisfaction.

Pawson and Tilley (1997) in *Realistic Evaluation* set out a rather different style of evaluation that they label 'scientific realism'. They want to provide a way of conducting evaluation objectively, without getting trapped in the experimental tradition of science, and examine not just whether a programme works, but why it works. Nichols (2005) offers an example of how this might be applied when examining the contribution of sports-based projects to reducing crime.

Other useful web-based material on the conduct of programme evaluation can be found on the site of the US Environmental Protection Agency: www.epa.gov/evaluate; or try www.evaluation.org.uk.

11

Analysing Quantitative Data

> Data analysis is fun. Most students, however, start a data analysis course with two firm convictions: it is going to be dreary, and they are not going to be very good at it. (Marsh, 1988: xvii)

This chapter and the next will emphasise that getting your data isn't everything. Many dissertations and other projects fail to fulfil their potential because insufficient attention is paid to the analysis of hard won data. There is no shortage of books on analysing quantitative data, so the emphasis here is on a way of thinking about and approaching data. This will involve:

- reviewing with caution the levels of measurement
- moving beyond one-dimensional analysis through interrogating the data
- looking for relationships and differences
- some pragmatic guidelines on assessing significance
- interpreting data to give meaning and working out why such patterns should be.

Doing analysis successfully is a continuation of the process of asking questions – asking questions of oneself and of the data. Alongside a recognition that facts do not 'speak for themselves', this is what lies at the heart of any critical research. As Marsh (1988: xviii) explains: 'Instead of testing the data, to see if it can be peppered with one or more asterisks and grandly called 'significant', the researcher interrogates it, often interactively, and has to listen to the response before proceeding'.

Once again there should be interplay between data and theory, so that means constantly considering what the data might contribute to your own ideas and those of others. This is not a text on statistical techniques, so I shall not be discussing probability theories, inviting you to calculate correlation coefficients or dealing with the intricacies of computer packages for statistical analysis.[1] Instead it is more about a mental orientation, encouraging the link to be made between analysis and the spirit of enquiry, and I have to presume that you at least have some vague recollection of many of the sorts of procedure mentioned here and that you will be able to fill in the gaps later.

First, remind yourself of the original research questions and review what kind of data you have. Then get some visual representation of the data so that you can see, for example:

- how the data are distributed on any given variable (e.g. 'normally distributed' in the classic bell curve)
- whether summary measures (e.g. mean and standard deviation) or regression lines are disproportionately affected by a few extreme values
- if there are any clear relationships between variables
- whether it is justifiable to think about a straight line relationship between variables or it is more like a curve.

Such visual representation may be significant for selecting more complex forms of analysis and interpreting the subsequent output, and they are also useful for communicating with your readership. However, I have left consideration of displaying data until Chapter 13.

The choice of analysis is dependent on the nature of the research challenge and what needs to be 'delivered', but it is also dependent on the nature of the data that have been collected. The key characteristics are the level of measurement (nominal, ordinal, interval or ratio – see Chapter 6) and whether or not the data are normally distributed. The majority of the standard statistical tests used to explore relationships and differences in data require at least interval data that are normally distributed. These are the presumptions behind parametric statistics. Although they are often not warranted in the kind of social research conducted around leisure, sport and tourism, many analysts just press ahead as though they were. It has become commonplace, for example, in psychological studies in these areas to apply parametric statistics to ranked data derived from attitude scales. Following statistical principles it might be wise to seek a non-parametric alternative.

The distinction is commonly made between univariate, bivariate and multivariate forms of analysis – i.e. treating one, two and several variables at a time (see,

---

[1] The most commonly used statistical package in the social sciences is SPSS, but there are many others and the statistical function of Excel or whatever spreadsheet you use will cover many of the most common procedures.

e.g., de Vaus, 2002). The other important distinction is between descriptive and inferential statistics. Descriptive statistics summarise the patterns in the responses provided by the sample, whereas inferential statistics allow estimates to be made about the population from which the sample has been derived. Two of the most common challenges are to establish how closely two variables are related (and in what way), and whether the difference we have recorded between two (or more) groups could easily have occurred by chance or if it is big enough to persuade us that the groups are quite distinct. Many reports of surveys get no further than uni-variate analysis, examining each variable in turn to produce descriptive statistics. This can be a revealing start, but more is possible.

Data Preparation and Data Entry

Coding

However data have been gathered they have to be put into a form that can be recognised by the computer for analysis. In quantitative approaches to research this is achieved by giving every item a numerical code. This results in a data matrix (spreadsheet) in which, conventionally, the rows represent the items we are interested in (people, facilities, holidays, etc.) and the columns represent the variables. Most commonly this is done straight from the questionnaire to the computer, but sometimes there is an intermediate stage in which data are recorded onto a separate coding sheet to make it easier then to enter the data into the computer. For some variables the coding process simply involves transferring the number given as the response (e.g. age) into the appropriate cell of the data matrix.

If you have variables that represent scales, for example those that go from 'strongly disagree' to 'strongly agree', it is also fairly straightforward to assign numbers according to where someone lies on that scale (e.g. from 1–7); indeed those numbers may appear on the questionnaire itself. But be careful. Sometimes these scales have to be 'reversed'. Imagine we are interested in how conservative or adventurous people are on holiday and the questionnaire has included the following items and respondents have been asked to indicate the extent to which they agree or disagree with them.

I like to try different foods when I'm on holiday.
I like to be with others from our own country when I'm on holiday.

Agreement with the first might be taken as an indication of being adventurous and open to new experiences, whereas agreement with the second might indicate a more conservative desire for the familiar. It is then important to reverse the scores for the second scale so that the more adventurous end of the scale always receives the high scores (or vice versa). If the items are being treated separately this is just a convenience, but if they are going to be added together to produce a composite score to measure adventurousness, it is essential.

If you simply asked people to choose which category they fitted into (e.g. in response to a question about which ethnic group they belong to), all you have to do is make sure that each category has a number that no other category has, and all people falling into the same category are assigned the same code. Even then though, both interpretation and the coding process itself are easier if 'similar' categories are grouped together (e.g. the various groups representing Asian backgrounds may be coded 7–12).

If you asked an open question (e.g. 'What was your main reason for coming here today?'), you then have to devise a set of categories to group together similar types of response, and then assign them codes as above. Remember the advice from Chapter 6 that the categories should be mutually exclusive (each response is assigned to one category and one category only) and mutually exhaustive (all possible responses are accommodated).

More complex designs

Whether using open or closed questions you may have allowed/encouraged people to give more than one response: e.g.

> Why did you decide to come to this centre today rather than any other?
> [*Code all that apply*] [*Probe: And was there anything else?*]

Not only have you got (potentially) more than one answer to the same question, but different respondents will have given different numbers of response. Check very carefully how your computer program deals with questions like this. For some programs this is too complicated and you will have to treat each of your categories as though it was a question in its own right, e.g.:

> Was it because it is nearby?   Yes/No
> Was it because of price?   Yes/No
> etc.

Some questionnaires ask people to identify which sports/leisure activities they have been involved in, or the holidays they have taken, over the past year, and then ask a set of questions about each of those: frequency, duration, cost, distance travelled, etc. One person may have two activities to report on, the next seven. That makes for a complex data set, so make sure you plan it carefully.

Missing data

There are several reasons why there may be missing data and it may be important to distinguish between them (though not always possible):

- The data are not missing at all. Some respondents may not have had a holiday last year (for example), so there are no details to be provided.
- The respondent just missed the question, perhaps because they got the routing wrong and skipped to the wrong question, or just never saw the back page.
- The respondent just did not understand the question and so in their confusion left it blank.
- The respondent did not know the answer.
- The respondent refused to give an answer.

Check your computer program to see how it deals with missing data.

Data entry

Unless responses to the questionnaire are sent electronically to a linked data matrix, the data entry process can be lengthy. Most readers will be working laboriously through the process themselves. Take care – this is a vital link in the chain.

Statistical packages have their own procedures for creating a data set, but it is common for them to have procedures to allow data to be transferred from an existing spreadsheet. So if you normally work with Excel, for example, it might be easier to enter data using that and then import it into SPSS (or another package) to do the statistical analysis.

Despite your best efforts some of the values in your data matrix may be wrong. This can happen because the original questionnaire was completed incorrectly, the coding was done wrongly or the data entry was inaccurate, whether through striking the same key twice, getting the data in the wrong column or simply hitting the wrong key. There is little that can be done if what was recorded on the questionnaire was not the right answer, but careful checking can resolve the other problems. Doing this properly involves going through each questionnaire (or corresponding record) and checking it against the values on the respective row of the data matrix. Some errors can be identified by doing a frequency count and if, for example, this shows that some people are recorded as answering 7 for a variable that should only be coded 1–5, it is possible to go back to the original questionnaire to find out what the correct value should be. To be able to do this without too much difficulty requires you to have a unique identifier (ID) in the first column of your matrix that matches the number carefully stamped on the front of the questionnaire.

Descriptions of Single Variables

The most important descriptive statistics relate to:

1. *Frequency* – How common are different states or responses/readings?
2. *Average* – Where is the 'centre of gravity' of the responses/readings?
3. *Spread* – Are responses/readings concentrated or dispersed?
4. *Shape* – Are responses/readings distributed evenly and symmetrically?

Some people, who have no intention of doing any more analysis than producing frequency counts, still use tally counts (the old five-bar gate system of counting frequency) produced direct from the questionnaires. If you have no access to a computer this is reasonable, but most people do have access to a computer and it is much more sensible to enter the data into some form of spreadsheet for computer analysis. This makes it easier to:

- calculate summary statistics
- group responses in different ways
- produce graphical displays of the data
- move on to more detailed analysis once the basic patterns have been revealed.

Frequencies

If you want to convey scale or have only a small sample then it is best to use absolute numbers (a simple count). Otherwise it may be easier for readers to understand the significance of findings by using relative frequencies represented as percentages. The crucial thing then is to be clear what the figures are percentages of. Let me demonstrate with a hypothetical example. Say we are interested in the balance between holidays taken in the home country and those taken abroad and conveniently we have a small sample of 100 respondents.

Respondents were asked first if they had taken a holiday of one night or more away from home in the past 12 months and 70 indicated that they had done. Those respondents were then asked whether their *most recent* holiday had been in this country or abroad. Thirty reported that holiday had been abroad – a 40/30/30 split (this country/abroad/none). So **30%** of our respondents had taken their most recent holiday abroad, but **43%** of those taking a holiday had been abroad on their most recent holiday.

People were then asked if in the past 12 months they had taken *any* holidays (a) in this country, or (b) abroad. This identified that 35 had taken a holiday abroad and 50 had taken a holiday in this country. So by this measure **35%** of respondents had holidayed abroad, representing **50%** (35/70) of those taking holidays.

Finally respondents were asked to identify <u>each</u> of their holidays away from home in the past 12 months and indicate which had been in this country and which abroad. This revealed 70 and 40 respectively (110 in total), indicating that **36%** of all holidays taken had been abroad.

Averages

These are referred to in the statistical literature as 'measures of central tendency'. When most of us think of averages we think of what is known as the arithmetic mean, but there are two others less commonly used: the mode and median. The mode is used with nominal (categorical) data. In the example above if people had been asked which country they had visited abroad, the mode would be the most frequently occurring country (or continent if the data were aggregated further). If respondents had also been asked how exotic they thought various countries were as holiday destinations, using gradings ranging from extremely exotic to mundane, with the ordinal (ranked) data produced it would still be possible to identify the mode, but an alternative is offered by the median which identifies which category the middle person falls in when all responses are ordered from high to low. Ordinal data may also have been collected for respondents' age by asking the age group they fall into. Because this represents an underlying continuous variable it is then possible to calculate an estimate of where the median (middle) value lies, rather than just the median category. To calculate the mean age of respondents instead, all respondents' ages are added together and divided by the number of respondents. This requires interval or ratio data – i.e. their actual age. A friendly computer program will calculate any of these 'at the touch of a button'.

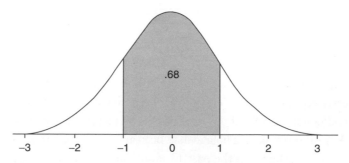

Figure 11.1   Normal distribution showing standard deviations either side of the mean

Spread

Another important characteristic of data is the degree to which they cluster around the average or are spread out. The simplest measure of this is the 'range' which is simply the difference between the highest and lowest values. More complex statistically, but also more revealing, are the variance and standard deviation. You are more likely to encounter the standard deviation which is the square root of the variance. Although statisticians would probably tear their hair out, I find it easiest to think of the standard deviation as the average distance from the mean. Importantly, it can be linked to probability theory to tell us that 68% of any *normal* distribution (Figure 11.1) lies within one standard deviation either side of the mean (95% for two standard deviations and over 99% for three).

Shape

A graphical representation of how the values of a variable are distributed (Chapter 13) may show very different patterns. The key things to look for are:

* Is it a flat (even) distribution or very peaked with some values being much more common than others?
* Is it regular or skewed (lop-sided or squint)? In most (predominantly 'western'?) societies the distribution of income, for example, has a long 'tail' produced by some people extending well above the average.

These considerations become even more important when comparing the 'distributions' for two or more groups. They are also, importantly, interrelated. For example, although income is an interval/ratio variable for which it is easy to calculate the mean, the median is often considered to be a better measure of 'central tendency' because the mean is overly affected by relatively few very high values, giving a misleading impression. But be careful. I recently saw a report of a survey in which respondents had been asked how many hours in a typical week they had spent doing various activities. The statisticians had used the median in preference to the mean because the data set had a few extremely high values that they thought 'infeasible'. They were right that the median is less susceptible to being corrupted by extreme values, but the consequence was that many of the activities had an average of zero because more than half the respondents had not participated at all, not because no one had participated – not very helpful in terms of analysis.

Considering Two Variables

By examining single variables it is possible to provide simple descriptions of how people behave or respond to a particular question (it may equally be about the characteristics of a company, scheme or park). However, it makes for a more interesting analysis if it is possible to say how, for example, different types of people behave or think about something – to examine the views of different age groups, or kinds of littering behaviour in different parks, etc. The next order of question is whether, for example, the responses of one group are essentially the same as those of another group or significantly different.

Consider the following table which presents data on attitudes to expenditure on leisure services, and write a description of what it tells you.

While Table 11.1a represents the basic data, in practice it is easier to see what is going on by representing the absolute numbers as percentages within each political grouping (Table 11.1b). By convention it is done for columns rather than rows (which would show for example that 64% (30/47) of those thinking that more should be spent on leisure services are in the party forming the current administration), but sometimes as a percentage of the total (i.e. in this case that those in the current administration who favour increased expenditure on leisure represent 40% (30/75) of all councillors). Statistical packages like SPSS will provide you with all four sets of data.

It then becomes clear that a majority in both groupings is in favour of increased spending, but those in the governing party are more likely to be in favour. This is where the mind of the detective should be taking over. If a majority of both groupings, but particularly the administration, is in favour of increased spending, why is it that more is not spent on leisure services? The answer has to lie in the (bottom left)

Table 11.1a *Responses from councillors to the question: 'Do you think that more should be spent on leisure services by this local authority?'*

Response	Administration	Opposition
	number of councillors	
Yes	30	17
No	13	15

n = 75
Source: Councillors Survey (2001)

Table 11.1b *Responses (%) from councillors to the question: 'Do you think that more should be spent on leisure services by this local authority?'*

Response	Administration	Opposition
	percentage of councillors	
Yes	70	53
No	30	47

n = 75
Source: Councillors Survey (2001)

cell of Table 11.1a, with 13 councillors from the governing party who are opposed to the idea. It turns out that they tend to have more power generally within their party, and are also in positions where they see the bigger picture within the council, having to review competing priorities. You may work this out anyway, but you can only be in a position to say this with certainty if you do not have strict anonymity and are able to return to the original questionnaires – either they can be identified by name, or else other data in the questionnaire record what position they hold.[2]

You may recall from Chapter 4 the issues around small sample sizes and the need to be careful because of the way in which few responses might be taken to represent the larger population. In this case it is not an issue because the sample is virtually the same as the population. More significant in this case is that small differences are magnified by representing them as percentages. It would only take one of the opposition councillors who replied yes to reply no for the majority (a six point gap) to be eradicated. So statisticians insist we should use absolute values rather than percentages (I prefer to use and present both in a composite table with percentages in brackets alongside the absolute values).

---

[2]Before you start quoting this in your assignment on leisure policy I should point out that although the conclusion did come from empirical investigation, the data are not 'real', but have been constructed for current purposes. The source appears at the foot of the table to indicate good practice in presenting tables of data.

In other circumstances you may be interested to know if two variables are associated: e.g. is there a relationship between people's age and their participation in leisure? The way in which this is calculated depends again on the level of measurement. If you have interval data, the normal procedure is to use what is known as Pearson's Product Moment Correlation Co-efficient (a bit of a mouthful, and usually referred to as 'r'). When you get your computer output or read someone else's account you will see reference to both r and r^2. The first is a measure of how closely the two variables are related, and the second is an alternative that represents the amount of variation in our measure of people's participation in leisure that can be explained by the variations in their ages. The values of r can range from −1 to +1. If the value is around zero there is no relationship between the two variables, the nearer it gets to either −1 or +1 the more closely they are related. The sign is important because it represents the direction of the relationship. If it is positive it means that as one variable increases the other tends to increase with it – typically we might expect income and participation to be related in this way (of course it depends on what exactly we have been measuring). On the other hand a negative correlation (inverse relationship) means that as one variable increases the other decreases – for many measures of participation in leisure this is the kind of relationship typically observed with age.

There are equivalent procedures for ordinal data, of which the most commonly used is called Spearman's Rank Order Correlation Co-efficient or 'rho' (the Greek equivalent of r), which also varies between −1 and +1. Don't forget that much attitudinal data should, strictly speaking, be treated as ordinal data. Equally, in our current example we might have allocated people to age bands (ordinal) and used the data on the questionnaire to assign them to a category representing how 'active' they are – e.g. vigorous activity, moderate activity, light activity, sedentary (also an ordinal scale).

r (correlation coefficient)	
+1	Perfect positive correlation – as one variable increases so does the other
0	No relationship between the two variables at all
−1	Perfect negative correlation – as one variable increases the other decreases

If you have interval data you can calculate a *regression* line that allows you to estimate the level of participation someone might have in leisure for any given age. This is the line you would draw to *best fit* the data if you had a graph of age on the x (horizontal) axis and participation in leisure on the y (vertical) axis (see Figure 13.9b for an example). This provides a simple form of statistical modelling as it allows a prediction of participation to be made for any given value of age. How effective it is in this regard depends on the 'goodness of fit' of the regression line, which in turn is a reflection of the strength of the relationship between the two variables. I have been reliably informed that there are ordinal equivalents of this procedure too.

Multi-Variate Analysis

If you've been keeping up with your other reading about leisure, sport and tourism you will be aware of the argument that people have multiple identities and that it is misleading to see them in terms of a single variable, whether it be class, race, gender or whatever; thus, our respondent Mary is not just black, she is a black, working-class woman, aged __, with … Multi-variate analysis allows several variables to be considered at the same time. These might be demographic characteristics, personal attitudes or attributes of a hotel, for example.

The mathematical models that lie behind these are complex and I have no intention of trying to address them in detail here, but I want to provide a pen portrait to indicate the potential, and then if you see something that fits your research goals you can follow it up. There are various forms of *analysis of variance* that deal with more than two variables, and *multiple regression* similarly is a more sophisticated version of the procedures for simple linear regression mentioned earlier in this chapter.

Major Multi-Variate Techniques

Factor analysis (FA)[3] – is used to examine the underlying structure in a set of data. An investigation of leisure, sport and tourism may have used a set of questions designed to measure risk, boredom or adventure using (say) 20 items (questions). On the basis of the answers given by the respondents, factor analysis can be used to examine the way in which these 'hang together' and tries to identify the minimum number of underlying factors that will do a reasonable job of explaining the variation that is being measured. For example, in this way Iso-Ahola assessed the benefits of leisure and boredom in leisure (Iso-Ahola and Weissinger, 1990).

Cluster analysis (CA) – tries to identify groups (clusters) of people/things within the set being examined. This is done on the basis of the variables identified as being of interest. For example, as part of a talent identification scheme we might

(Continued)

---

[3]Factor Analysis is derived from principal components analysis, the two are procedurally different in statistical terms but satisfy similar challenges for social scientists.

(Continued)

want to group athletes on the basis of some set of attributes, or we might want to group countries according to the characteristics of the tourism they host or generate. Some procedures start with every case separate and then successively join together those that are most similar until all cases are in the one group; other procedures work in the reverse direction, successively splitting the group. This produces a dendrogram (tree diagram) that allows you to see at what stage groups get combined/split. See, for example, Walker et al. (2005) on motivations for gambling or Aguiló Pérez and Rosselló Nadal (2005) on host perceptions of tourists.

Discriminant analysis (DA) – I was always taught that DA should be used when groups of people/things have already been defined and you want to examine whether a particular set of variables really does distinguish between the two groups. The SPSS programme conceptualises discriminant analysis in a rather different way, using it to predict which category people/things should be assigned to on the basis of the variables measured. Having read something like Bourdieu's (1984) theories of cultural capital, for example, we might come up with a proposition that distinctly different value sets are brought to bear by working-class and middle-class people in their evaluations of holidays or sports. Discriminant analysis would allow us to determine whether the measurement of these value positions does divide the overall sample in two along the lines we propose (Brown and Tinsley, 1983). Interestingly, discriminant analysis then allows an examination of those allocated to one class group who give responses closer to those expected of the other – e.g. what are the characteristics of those working-class people who think more like the middle class?

Multi-dimensional scaling (MDS) – although not often used in our area of research, MDS is used to reveal what is thought of as the 'hidden structure' in the way people think about a set of objects. Stockdale (1985) did this for leisure activities. The idea is that people use their own criteria to evaluate a set of objects (leisure activities), unconstrained by what the research team might think is important. On the basis of the statistical relationships between the judgements of all the respondents the researchers can:

> infer how many dimensions are required to account for the judgements, how important the various dimensions are, and with some additional data, what the dimensions actually mean, so that even if people are unaware of the basis on which they made the judgements we can infer this from a simple behavioural response. (Stockdale, 1985: 84)

MDS also allows the people to be grouped on the basis of the judgements they have made.

There are many variations on each of these themes and there is a lot of skill in selecting the most appropriate and then in interpreting the findings.

Confidence Limits

Most of the time you will have data/numbers gathered from a sample rather than the population from which you have selected them (remember this does not mean the entire population of the country, but might be holidaymakers visiting your resort, students at your university or elite sports men and women). Your hope should be that your sample represents that larger population (and most people are interested in that larger population rather than your sample). The sample is only an approximation for the population, and hence the statistics produced are only an approximation. So to what extent is it reasonable to generalise (make inferences) from the sample to the broader population?

It is possible to use your sample to calculate a range within which the population value is likely to fall. The values at each end of this range are the *confidence limits*. Different degrees of confidence can be used, but the most common is the 95% confidence interval (within which the corresponding population value is likely to lie 95% of the time). On his website Hopkins[4] offers a 'plain-language definition' of the confidence interval as 'the likely range of the true value'. It follows that the narrower the confidence interval the greater the precision – and greater precision is highly desirable. Other things being equal, greater precision comes with larger sample sizes (Chapter 5).

Significant Differences

Before finishing this chapter I need to return to the challenge identified earlier that relates to whether 'the difference we have recorded between two (or more) groups could easily have occurred by chance or if it is big enough to persuade us that the groups are quite distinct'. If you are working with interval data that are parametric, the most common techniques are a cluster around the t-test and analysis of variance.

Whichever test is used it is associated with a measure of significance, which, crudely put, allows you to assess the probability of that difference happening by chance. If you do the calculations for yourself using a calculator you will need a set of statistical tables to allow you to judge the significance of the figure you have calculated. If you use a computer package you might see in the output something like '$p < 0.05$'. Roughly translated this means 'the probability that this could have occurred by chance is less than 5%'. Depending upon the test, we can then be fairly confident that we have revealed a significant relationship or difference. It is this 0.05 level that is most commonly used as the cut-off for judging significance, but you may see people reporting other levels – e.g. 0.1 or 0.01.

---

[4]http://www.sportsci.org/resource/stats/generalize.html

We might, for example, want to know whether there is a difference between the amount (number of hours) of physical activity men and women do in a week. In simple terms, the t-test is a way of comparing the mean number of hours for each group. Once again there are alternatives for ordinal measures that you can use for attitudinal data (e.g. the Mann-Whitney U test). If instead of sex the independent variable was age, there might be several different groups. It would be possible to do several different calculations of 't' to test for difference between each pair of groups, one at a time, but this is where analysis of variance comes into its own. Analysis of variance takes several different forms depending upon the nature of the groups and their measurement, so you will need to check carefully that you are using the right one. Despite its name, analysis of variance is in fact based on testing the difference between means.

More often though, data from a questionnaire are nominal/categorical, so something else is necessary. In Tables 11.1a and b there appears to be a clear difference between the two groups in their response to this question, but is that just the kind of difference that might occur by chance or is there something more to it than that? The most commonly used statistic in such circumstances is Chi Square, a non-parametric statistic that can be used with nominal data like these. Your favourite computer statistics package should be able to calculate this for you and tell you whether you have a 'significant' finding (if you have to do the arithmetic with a calculator it is fairly straightforward – see virtually any conventional statistics text). Because of that I don't intend to go into any detail here, but it is useful to know the background to it. Basically what happens is that the observed values (as recorded in Table 11.1a) are compared with the values that would be expected if there were no difference between the groups. It is important to remember that Chi Square has to be calculated using absolute values and not frequencies.[5]

The thinking goes something like:

We've established that overall 47 out of 75 councillors are in favour of spending more money; if they were allocated in the same proportions to the two groups of councillors, how many councillors would we expect to find in each of the cells in the table?

For the first cell (administration/yes), the calculation is $43 \times 47/75 = 26.95$ because we know that there are 43 councillors in the party forming the administration.

The equivalent is done for each cell and then the differences between those 'expected' values and the values actually recorded (observed) in those cells provide the basis for the calculation of Chi Square.

---

[5]Chi Square becomes unreliable if there are any cells with an expected frequency of zero; or there are more than 20% cells with an expected frequency of less than five (recent versions of SPSS will alert you if these assumptions have been infringed). Most statistics texts carry this warning about small numbers, but at the other end of the scale, with much larger sample sizes using Chi Square leads to conclusions that very small differences are highly significant.

So I calculated the value of Chi Square to be 1.5 (rounded here to one decimal place), but that on its own is of little value. Is it big/little, good/bad? Some kind person has already calculated the theoretical distribution and produced a table of critical values at different levels of significance. These critical values also depend on the size of the table. What are called the 'degrees of freedom' equal the number of rows (in this instance two) minus one, times the number of columns (two) minus one. Easy! One degree of freedom, and according to the table the critical value at 0.05 level is then 3.84. The value I calculated is clearly less than that, so it is well within the bounds of chance and gives us no reason to believe that political affiliation is associated with a systematic difference in whether or not councillors think more money should be spent on leisure provision. (Before you go quoting that in your essays on the politics of leisure, these data were made up.)

Hollingshead (1949) ran a series of Chi Square tests on data gathered from high school students in Elmtown. Among other things he found that there was a statistically significant difference between different social classes for the number of extra-curricular clubs they were involved in at school, going to the cinema, going to dances and the class of people they dated. This is not particularly surprising to us in light of what we know about social divisions in participation, but I cite it here because I introduced the study earlier as an example of ethnographic work using participant observation. It has become very fashionable in recent years to write about multi-method research, but it has a long tradition.

Further Lines of Enquiry

Clearly if you are going to use one of the standard statistical packages it makes sense to get hold of an associated guide. For example, for SPSS you could try Ntoumanis (2001) *A Step-by-Step guide to SPSS for Sport and Exercise Studies*, or *SPSS Made Simple* by Kinnear and Gray (2004). Each guide relates to a particular version of the software, so what you see on the screen may not quite match what it says in the guide, but once you have a grasp of how the basics work it is normally possible to work out what is going on with the assistance of the on-screen help feature.

Those guides/manuals also provide an introduction to the statistical techniques they are dealing with. If you want more detailed information on multi-variate techniques, you could try *Using Multivariate Statistics* by Tabachnick and Fidell (2000).

Don't forget, *data analysis can be fun*. Treat it as a detective story. Some people believe it is a cold, objective process, but it involves rather a lot of subjectivity. What happens if we choose not 0.05 but some other value as the cut-off point for determining appropriate levels of significance? Beware too because different researchers may favour different statistical procedures in conducting their factor analysis, for example, and choosing the number of factors produced or interpreting the meaning of the factors themselves. Similarly, different researchers may decide on different 'solutions' that consider different numbers of groups in a cluster analysis, choosing solutions that 'make sense' to them.

The more you read what other people have done, the better informed you will be in conducting your own analysis. The more familiar you become with the different techniques as a result of your own research, the better the insight you will have into the research of others.

12

Analysing Qualitative Data

> … in my view there are usually no Brownie points awarded for successfully gathering your data. In the final assessment, everything comes down to what you do with your data. (Silverman, 2000: 239)

The analytical challenge presented to the qualitative researcher is how to move beyond simply recounting what people said to the interviewer or what the researcher saw. Although it should have been evident from the start, this is where the tension between testing theory, using theory to interpret findings, and generating new theory comes to a head. And all this without the standard formulae that quantitative researchers can follow. This chapter will address:

- the principles of data reduction, categorisation and organisation
- drawing conclusions and verification
- the move from the individual to the general
- alternative ways of organising the data
- what the computer can (or cannot) contribute.

Having done some good interviews, observations or whatever, you are likely to have large amounts of raw data (transcripts, field notes, etc.). The challenge now is to make some sense of all that material. Had you been doing quantitative research you may have known all along that the data you were collecting were going to be subjected to t-tests, for example, to examine whether there are significant differences between two groups. That degree of formality and prescription is rarely the case in qualitative research, and the computer won't know what to make of all these words. The process of analysis should already have been underway while the data were being collected (I shall be returning to this), but now it has to be formalised. The following are useful orienting questions no matter which direction your analysis heads in.

- What were the initial research challenges I set myself?
- What data have I got?
- What does it all mean?
- What is there about it that will be of interest and use to others?

Data Preparation

Perhaps it is less obvious than is the case with quantitative data, but there is still a necessary process of rendering the data into a form you can use for analysis. This might mean ordering and making sense of field notes, using forms to extract data from newspaper reports or transcribing hours of tape recordings. Take a look at the literature and you will find many alternatives for dealing with data on tapes alone. The most common being:

(a)   conducting the analysis directly from the tapes, on the basis that any transcription of the interview introduces a further loss of information and corruption of the conversation

(b)   transcribing the interview in such a way as to produce a faithful written reconstruction of what was said

(c)   producing a written summary that covers the main points and includes useful quotes

(d)   devising some sort of coding framework in advance and then extracting data from the tape to address the various headings that have been chosen.

I like to work from a full transcription that allows me to consider word for word what was said (b). Having said that, the kind of transcriptions I need are not as detailed as those required by people doing conversational analysis, who like to have the length of pauses recorded along with all the stutters, 'ums' and 'ers' and some indication of how it was said (e.g. 'laughing' or 'tapping table nervously'). How long this process takes depends on the level of accuracy and detail required as well as the skill of the person doing the transcribing and the technology available.[1] One of my colleagues claims he can transcribe an hour of tape in two hours, but I don't believe that is possible (to produce the kind of transcript I want); another claims it takes him three hours, but he doesn't do the typing himself. I

---

[1] There are specialist transcribing machines that audio typists use. These allow the speed of playback to be adjusted, have foot pedals for play and rewind, and restart just before where you stopped. However, in most work/study environments these are scarce, and sod's law says that if you find one it will not be compatible with your recording equipment. One day voice recognition software may become sufficiently sophisticated to handle this challenge, but at the moment software 'trained' to recognise your voice will be confused by your respondent.

estimate that it takes me about five hours to transcribe an hour-long interview, making sure that I have recorded what was said rather than what I thought was said as I try to listen and type at the same time.[2] This is a laborious task and it is very tempting to get someone else to do it for you (if you have the money), but on the other hand slaving over the transcription does make you very familiar with what the respondent had to say and this is an enormous help when it comes to analysis.

The Process of Analysis

Is it possible just to arrive at the truth using no more than intuition?[3] Does the analysis come through a mystical process of ideas dawning, or are there more formal procedures that we can use to help us in our analysis? Many qualitative researchers stumble into their analysis, eventually work out a process they feel comfortable with and then after the event try to find a rationalisation for what they have done, often by looking to the accounts of other researchers for justification. A common structural framework then looks something like this:

1. familiarisation with data
2. organising data
3. displaying data
4. drawing conclusions
5. verification/checking
6. linking to theory.

I am totally persuaded that the first thing to do is to read everything you have, and then read it all again, in order to *familiarise* yourself with the material. That makes it easier to *reduce* the amount of data that has to be analysed without losing any of its richness and to *organise* it into meaningful structures. The researcher may summarise and paraphrase, selecting those elements that seem to offer most insight. Usually the process of organisation involves some form of coding responses into

---

[2]Just so you do not embark on the exercise lightly, try transcribing a pilot interview for 15 minutes, then time how much of the interview you have dealt with - not a lot - so that you can calculate how long it would take you to do one lasting an hour.

[3]Some argue it is exactly like this and that knowing can only come in this way, forged by our personal experiences; others seek more formal approaches (see Chapter 15 for a consideration of the different ways people see the world of research).

different categories, breaking the data down and putting them back together again. This allows the analyst to move from specific instances (occasions or respondents) to larger patterns. As soon as a set of categories has been established the prospect of quantification opens up (counting the number in each); a prospect embraced by some, rejected by others. The process of *displaying* the data is part of the analysis in its own right. At its most simple this may be achieved by the researcher through narrative text, perhaps supported by illustrative quotes from respondents. But researchers (e.g. Miles and Huberman, 1994) often devise graphical representations using tables, matrices, charts and diagrams (Chapter 13). In *drawing conclusions* analysts look for regularities and patterns that might suggest explanations. As there may be ambiguity in this, good practice suggests that *confirmation* of those interpretations should be sought from others – research colleagues or those involved in the research. For many involved in this style of research the latter is both essential for the analysis (it is their lives and they are the experts) and an ethical requirement to avoid misrepresentation. I shall return to the link to *theory* at the end of the chapter.

What I have been saying so far is conceptually not that different from a conventional approach to quantitative research: formulate problem, gather data, analyse. However, as I have indicated already, some researchers want to break away from such procedures and adopt a more integrated, iterative approach in which data collection and analysis are interactive. It might be something like Figure 12.1. This is a bit like different styles of investigation in detective stories – following hunches and emerging lines of inquiry rather than sticking to the previously agreed and approved procedures.

Creating and Refining Categories

Assuming there are transcripts of the interviews (either notes written at the time or a typed version of the tape-recording), most people then mark their scripts and make notes in the margin. The most common procedure is to try to use people's responses to allocate them to discrete categories (e.g. on their attitudes to fashion in sport or management styles adopted at the leisure centre). So you need a set of issues and a set of categories for each issue. Some people devise a framework for this on the basis of the theory they have been basing their research on, while others try to distil key issues and categories from what the respondents themselves have said. You will need to devise rules by which you can decide which category your respondent should be allocated to. Why this one rather than that one?

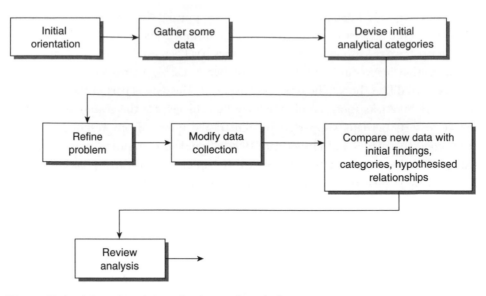

Figure 12.1   Interactive data collection and analysis

Imagine a piece of research in which part of the literature review has identified four managerial archetypes, and another part identified three routes to organisational change. Qualitative data gathered in various leisure centres could then be used to assign each manager to one of the four types. In the process it would be possible to see how well the previously defined categories match these circumstances and decide whether these need revision. Similar procedures could be used to determine what strategy had been used to respond to some external impetus for change, like the implementation of legislation requiring improved provision for disabled access. That could allow an examination of the relationships between types of manager and strategies used to introduce change, and to explore what impact those have on different indicators of success.

Other researchers object to that kind of approach insisting that it is all too easy to see what you want to see and thereby reaffirm previously suggested patterns. Much better, they suggest, to allow your categories to arise naturally from the data you have gathered, not trying to force them to match preconceptions.

Examples in the Exercise of Coding

It is all very well talking about these things in the abstract, but they can only really be understood through practical examples. To provide you with some insights into the kinds of problems encountered, I want to take a more extended look at a project about the changing significance of leisure in the period around retirement (Long and Wimbush, 1985).

The example in the box below is an extract from just one interview in the retirement study, and is there to give you some orientation. The focus of the interviews had been on issues like outlook on work and leisure, structuring time, attitudes to retirement, quality of life. One of the main areas of interest to researchers studying retirement has been the consequences of this change in status for people's social networks. Having read the various transcripts, four basic categories were identified with a view to allocating each respondent to one of them. The four categories used were:

1. a *privatised lifestyle* with few social contacts and where non-work activities were centred on the home (e.g. watching TV, household maintenance, reading)
2. a *family based* network of social contacts where non-work and non-domestic activities are orientated towards fulfilling relationships with the family (e.g. visiting, going out, day trips)
3. a *limited social* network where non-work and non-domestic activities are centred on a commitment to a club, a group or an interest (e.g. social club, bowling club, golf club, scout group)
4. a *highly socialised* network of contacts generated by a high level of activity in several fields (e.g. home, family, friends, interests, clubs).

You might be able to spot some of the difficulties in trying to implement this. For many of the respondents this was easy enough to use, but the edges of the categories are not precisely defined and it was not always easy to determine which was the most appropriate category. Indeed, even with a clear image of each category there were respondents who seemed to be able to fit in more than one, though in practice it was only the second that could be combined with one of the others. This is not something we were unaware of. We had decided that it did not matter that the categories were not mutually exclusive (try telling a scientist that), but it did make life a bit more complicated when we tried to relate respondents' social networks to other aspects of their lives. It might seem to be a very subjective process, but in this instance it was possible to cross check with other data taken from a time diary and there was a clear relationship with the average (mean) number of leisure pursuits mentioned in the interview.

Try working out what system you would use for classifying different types of social network.

Having decided your own procedure for analysis, see how easy it would be to apply it to respondents 16 and 80 below.

Mr 16 enjoys his work and is being allowed to wind down to retirement following a heart attack a few months ago. Although he is friendly with the people at work he does not seek to socialise with them beyond work hours even though there is a social club, and he tells them he is not a very sociable person. He admits to feeling lonely sometimes since the death of his wife 11 years ago and won't go on holidays on his own so does not know what to do with the five weeks holiday he is about to start (though he is planning a Nile cruise post-retirement to revisit wartime experiences). Nevertheless he does have social contact through his family, particularly sisters and daughters, and had a phone call from friends at the start of the interview. Most of his other contacts seem to be through the church. His activities are restricted because he does not have a car and his physical mobility is hampered by angina and fibrositis. He acknowledges that he has few interests, but is not unduly worried by the prospect of retirement.

In retirement Mr 16 says he misses the social contact of his work, but has not bothered with the retired persons' club run by the company. He reiterates that he is 'not a terribly social person more a loner' and 'I don't really have many friends outside the family'.

If Mr 16 completed a standard questionnaire in retirement he might be assigned to the group that, with retirement, has 'disengaged'. However, he does more than he at first reports and his activity patterns are not very different from before retirement. The interviewer noted that 'he keeps insisting that he is lazy, but in fact does more than he thinks'. This was her 'analysis'. *Was this a reasonable conclusion when it contradicts what the respondent presents as his 'analysis' of himself and his life?*

Mr 80 has a limited social network around the railway [works] club and the attached bowling club. Other social interaction has been restricted by long working hours. He sees his daughters and their families regularly, but they are not especially close (less contact than Mr 16, for example).

In retirement Mr 80 also misses the social contact provided by his work, and is not too sure about being the youngest pensioner at the railway club, where he spends more time. He now sees more of the people around 'the scheme' where he lives, and does more activities together with his wife.

Simply allocating people to categories though is only part of the challenge. What we really want to know is:

- how those in one category relate to/differ from those in another
- how the position adopted with regard to one issue affects the response to another
- what the relationships are.

Analysing Data: Complications and Challenges

This sort of coding exercise might take place at more than one level.

- For example, continuing with the example of social networks, the key components might be identified as being: (presence or absence of) partner, family, friends, workmates, others.
- For each of these our readings may identify key issues around nature of contact, activities engaged in together, reaction to the respondent's retirement, etc.
- Examining each of these we might code typical responses. For example the codes for the responses of the partner are indicated in the box below:

Q23. Wife's Attitude

1. Pleased/looking forward to it
2. She persuaded me to retire
3. About time
4. Good for my health
5. Be glad of help around the house
6. Be glad of the company
7. Doesn't want me under her feet
8. Unhappy
9. Not bothered one way or the other
10. Encourages special activity
11. Don't know/Doesn't say
12. Worried I'll have nothing to do.
13. Ambivalent – some good, some bad
14. Wants to move

- Those first level codes may then be combined into a second tier of coding, e.g.:
  - welcoming and supportive; accepting; negative
  - views it in terms of 'me'; views it in terms of 'him'; views it in terms of 'us'
- And each of those may be evidenced in terms of issues related to: finance, time, role, etc.

By now you should have worked out what you think is the most appropriate procedure for analysing the data you have been presented with from one or two respondents. But our data came not just from two people. Are the procedures you have devised robust enough to be applied to the data we had from more than 100 respondents? If 'yes', that is all well and good. If 'no' is there something wrong with your procedures, or is it just unrealistic to try to apply qualitative techniques to a sample of this size? Even in qualitative research the number of respondents clearly is important. For example, basing a theory of retirement on respondents 16 and 80 would give a far less enthusiastic picture than was suggested by the sample as a whole.

Following is an example of a fairly common approach taken from our main report (Long and Wimbush, 1985). This presentation relates to different styles of adaptation to retirement. It is a matrix that has 'collapsed' the large number of respondents into a smaller number of 'coping strategies'; I suppose this is not unlike the procedures of cluster analysis used in multivariate quantitative analysis (see the previous chapter). The strategies for coping with retirement emerged from reading and re-reading the transcripts (the value of full transcriptions is really revealed at this stage), identifying the main approaches and then having discussions between the researchers to agree the aggregations:

- Active 'leisure'
- Active 'work'
- 'Take-it-easy'
- Part-time jobbers
- 'Stuck-at-home'
- Continued employment.

We then identified how each of those groups typically addressed certain areas of adjustment required by retirement.

- Nature of activities
- Level of activities
- Sources of life satisfactions
- Attitudes to retirement
- Sources of sociability
- Status/self image.

Respondents had to be allocated to one of the styles of 'coping'. For this kind of analysis, if there are some people who do not fit too well, it does not matter (the idea is to establish archetypes), though if there are too many who do not fit there is something wrong with the categories being used. Each transcript then had to be reviewed and notes made about how they related to the areas of adjustment. Reviewing the collective experience, we then sought to crystallise what characterised that particular coping strategy and distinguished it from the others (Figure 12.2).

More generally, we had recorded quotes from respondents and other material onto index cards referenced with the code number for the respondent. Today we

Figure 12.2 Coping strategies and areas of adjustment

Coping Strategies

Adjustment Areas	Active 'leisure'	Active 'work'	'Take-it-Easy'	Part-time jobbers	'Stuck-at-home'	Continued employment
Nature of Activities	More time devoted to previous leisure interests (catching up on things not had time for while working) and may have taken on more activities.	Intensification of previous/new jobs to compensate for loss of full-time employment.	Wife and family-centred activities. Not out much – little outside domestic/family sphere.	Part-time work and more time given to previous leisure interests/activities and wife and family. Self-created gradual retirement scheme.	Activities often restricted to domestic sphere due to poor health and mobility. Lack of variety.	Work-centred activities and life. Little time for other things. Leisure interests/activities poorly developed..
Level of Activities	Busy, little spare time. Many and varied commitments.	Busy, little spare time. Time structures based on previous working day. Wary of losing work discipline.	Usually has spare time. Takes life easy, relaxed pace.	Still active, but more relaxed pace. Routines centred on part-time job.	Time hangs heavy. Gets bored. Much unstructured time.	Very busy. Little spare time.
Sources of life satisfactions	Generally transferred to 'leisure' and home.	'Work' still an important factor in life satisfaction, but satisfaction gained through non-employment activities.	Misses aspects of work (e.g. sociability, time structures, money, satisfaction) but satisfactions transferred more to wife and family life.	Work-based satisfactions still predominant. Hobbies/leisure not regarded as compensating for these.	Misses work and its satisfactions. Restricted opportunities to develop others.	Work is central source of satisfactions. Usually plans to extend these into retirement.

(Continued)

Figure 12.2 Coping strategies and areas of adjustment (*Continued*)

Adjustment Areas	Coping Strategies					
	Active 'leisure'	Active 'work'	'Take-it-Easy'	Part-time jobbers	'Stuck-at-home'	Continued employment
Attitudes to retirement	Enjoys retired life – happy to stop working. Positive outlook – 'make the most of it'.	Enjoys retired life, but would go back to job if could. Happy as long as busy.	Low expectations. Enjoys more relaxed pace of retired life. Generally happy, but some dissatisfactions.	Quite happy, but still has to face problems of how to cope with full retirement.	Not enjoying retired life very much. Largely negative attitudes.	Negative attitude to retirement. Worries about time use and coping financially. Retirement only vaguely considered.
Sources of sociability	Varied outlets for sociability.	Predominantly interest-based though quite extensive networks.	Largely family and wife-centred sociability.	Mostly family and wife-centred but some outside social contacts (through work).	Largely dependent on family and wife for social contact otherwise isolated.	Largely privatised social networks beyond work contacts.
Status/ self-image	Not concerned except want to be seen to be active, alive, fit, 'young for your age'.	Being seen to be productive/creative, a busy bee – not wanting to be an OAP.	Good family man, helping others in family, protector.	As at work, but usually lower status job.	Denuded.Cannot see replacement activity.	Same, but threatened.

would use a computer package. Armed with the outline structure we had agreed for the report, it was also now possible to reference the cards according to the section to which the comments most closely related.

Computer-Aided Analysis

Computers can be extremely helpful in analysing qualitative data, handling volumes of data that would otherwise be very unwieldy. They make retrieving and exploring data much faster. Most of these computer programs follow the same procedures as paper and pencil techniques that researchers have been using for decades (similar to those outlined above) and are particularly effective in dealing with approaches based on systems of categories. If they are to do more than search for specified words, the researcher normally has to assign codes to sections of text. Responses can then be moved around and grouped.

Apart from storing records in an organised database, most of the software packages can deliver facilities for:

- Coding – assigning bits of text to categories by attaching key words or tags just as you would do if marking hard copy with a highlighter pen or using a card index.
- Search and retrieve – finding relevant bits of texts and making them available for inspection.
- Linking data – making connections between relevant bits of data, e.g. to cluster into larger categories. This also allows an analysis of which feelings, sentiments and values are associated with particular categories.
- Memos to record thoughts and reflections as you go along – helps interpretation later.
- Content analysis – frequency of words, phrases or categories.
- Displaying data – creating 'maps', graphs and diagrams for a visual representation of findings.
- Drawing conclusions – interpretation still has to be provided by the researcher.
- Building theory and testing hypotheses – developing systematic and conceptually coherent explanations of findings.
- Feeding directly into reports.

As with other forms of research, the closer the link you can make between data collection and analysis the smoother the process.

Computers may help with the mechanistic aspects, but the analysis and interpretation still have to be supplied by the researcher. None of these packages will do the thinking for you, though they may channel your thinking in a particular way, so be careful to choose the one that most closely matches your ideal model of qualitative analysis. If you do decide to use a computer package, try not to let it distance you from the data. If the process becomes one of simply shifting blocks of words around you will have lost much of the advantage of engaging in qualitative analysis. There can be no substitute for 'knowing your data'; whatever else, you must retain that familiarity.

Sad to say, in some people's eyes, qualitative research can gain more credibility and status by using computers because of the association between computers, 'hard' data and science – an image thing. Beyond that, proponents suggest that using a computer encourages the researcher to be more exploratory/investigative, because once the initial coding has been conducted, it is easy to ask the 'what if' questions. You are not deterred by the huge amount of labour required for manual processes because the computer can do that quickly.

However, some people are not persuaded that it is quite that easy in practice. The package does not deliver all it promises or in quite the right way, or it is harder than they had been led to believe to provide the instructions, or it just takes too long to get things set up and become familiar with the package. Others consider the use of computers anathema to qualitative analysis. To them, machines and intuition are irreconcilable. This is sometimes associated with the suggestion that the software effectively structures your thought processes, establishing boundaries at the expense of creativity.

As with all software, there is a learning curve to negotiate, and unfortunately, while your university or place of work may have people around who are capable of providing support for packages for statistical analysis, support for these qualitative packages is usually harder to find. These packages are intuitively quite easy to understand but a significant investment of time spent learning and practising is necessary, though the speed of data handling then begins to pay dividends. If you are the kind of person who feels comfortable and at home on the computer it is probably worth the investment, otherwise for most small-scale research projects combining your word processing skills with pencil, paper, scissors and paste should be perfectly adequate.

Generalisation and Theory

Some people argue that the most qualitative researchers can achieve or even aspire to is to describe some aspect of the world. For me that is just not enough. If that is truly the goal I think we should leave the task to others who are better equipped – poets, novelists or even journalists.

Followers of Geertz reject the goal of generalisability – every instance must be seen as carrying its own logic, sense of order, structure and meaning. This is an extension of the work of cultural anthropology in which everything is interesting in its own right. Many have adopted that stance, but it doesn't seem to stop them generalising (Payne and Williams, 2005). It would be wrong though to mistake Geertz's (1973) term, 'thick description'. It actually offers rather more than a straightforward description as the aim is to produce a contextualised, layered account that recognises the 'story' is contingent on a range of embedding factors (family, economic position, etc.). Nonetheless, compare that kind of position with Jennifer Mason's:

> I do not think qualitative researchers should be satisfied with producing explanations which are idiosyncratic or particular to the limited empirical parameters of their study. … Qualitative research should produce explanations that are generalizable in some way, or which have a wider resonance. (1996: 6)

But qualitative researchers cannot follow the procedures of statistical inference that survey researchers rely on. So the more common goal is to work out what the data can tell us about the theories we work with rather than about the population as a whole. Bryman argues that 'the issue should be couched in terms of the generalizability of cases to theoretical propositions rather than to populations or universes' (1988: 90).

It is hard enough to say something non-trivial about the experiences of one or two people, but throw in a few more and at some stage you are almost certain to think, 'Oh ****, they don't fit – there goes another theory up in smoke'. Znaniecki (1934) developed what he called a process of 'analytic induction' to demonstrate how he sought to develop theory.

Define the phenomenon to be explained

Formulate a hypothetical explanation

Study one case to see if the hypothesis works

     YES   Carry on to next case

     NO   Reformulate the hypothesis or redefine the phenomenon to leave out the case (e.g. 'x' holds for all people except 'a')

Continue until a universal relationship is achieved

Negative cases disprove, but practical certainty comes from just a few cases

More recently in leisure, sport and tourism you are more likely to read research papers that have followed a 'grounded theory' approach, originated by Glaser and Strauss (1967), that makes use of a similar inductive process of constant comparison. This took its name from the commitment to creating theory grounded in the data that reflect the way people experience and understand their lives, and not from the minds of the researchers. Both approaches involve trying out, rejecting and refining.

In response to earlier criticisms of the microscopic approach of grounded theory, Corbin and Strauss (1990) stressed the importance of analysing the broader context represented by surrounding people, economic conditions, cultural values, etc. However, it is a challenge to make those relationships seem justified rather than extravagant assertions.

Silverman (2000) offers some clues about how this can be done by making links to theory. Recognising that this is a difficult challenge he suggests:

- looking to history – earlier data offer an insight to processes of change
- looking to context – reviewing the organisation, political climate, etc.
- comparing – examining similarities and differences between different sections of your data or a separate data set
- considering the implications of your data for broader issues
- borrowing concepts from elsewhere – introducing ideas from theories developed in different areas and then examining the relationships suggested.

At this stage researchers are often looking just to the finishing tape of completing the write-up, but it is really important to look backwards too and make sure full use is made of the ideas revealed by the literature review.

Further Lines of Enquiry

One of my favourite books for offering insights to qualitative analysis is Silverman's (2000/ 2004) *Doing Qualitative Research*. It has a companion volume *Interpreting Qualitative Data* (2nd edition, 2001) that provides more detail. *Qualitative Data Analysis* by Miles and Huberman (1994) is an excellent source of ideas about how to organise, analyse and display data.

Holt and Dunn (2004) provide an example of applying a grounded theory approach that is clearly set out, showing how they investigated what contributed to soccer success in talented athletes.

The research methods literature often refers to CAQDAS which stands for Computer Aided [or Assisted] Qualitative Data AnalysiS. Probably the most commonly available software is N-Vivo, a Windows compatible system, but there are many others around – e.g. Ethnograph, MAXqda, AnSWR, ATLASti; or HyperQual and HyperRESEARCH that operate on Apple Macs. For more about the relative merits of the different CAQDAS systems, visit Koenig's pages at: www.lboro.ac.uk/research/mmethods/research/ software/caqdas_comparison.html.

13

Data Display

Looking at displays helps us to understand what is happening and to do something – either analyze further or take action – based on that understanding. (Miles and Huberman, 1994: 11)

Displaying data is both an aid to analysis and a means of communicating thought processes and findings to other people. Like the challenges of the previous two chapters these are not independent of the way the brain works. Different people find different representations better at communicating the intended message. Following the same sequence, quantitative data appear before the qualitative as the chapter considers:

- presenting informative tables
- simple graphical representations of quantitative data
- finding ways of portraying qualitative data.

Having considered some aspects of data display in the previous two chapters as part of the analytical process, the emphasis here is on communicating research findings to others. These two aspects of the research process may need different forms of graphic representation. For example, pie charts are a popular way of presenting simple messages to a readership, but few researchers would use them as an aid to analysis. Commonly that analytical role of data display might involve patterns of distribution, reviewing the appropriateness of alternative summary measures (from means to regression lines) and relationships between variables. Statistical techniques can be very seductive but they are an abstraction and may lead to unwarranted conclusions; getting a visual 'fix' on the data is a useful reminder of what is really going on. That is why there are also graphical representations produced by computer packages as part of the output from many of the multi-variate statistical techniques. This is to allow researchers to visualise the findings of something that is mathematically complex.

Most analytical packages on the computer have some facility for displaying data. If you have been doing qualitative analysis, you are likely to be restricted to the program you used for the analysis, but quantitative data are more transferable. For example, many researchers who choose SPSS for its analytical power use Excel as a more flexible way of displaying data. There are also separate packages that allow very sophisticated representations of the data, especially if you develop an interest in geographical mapping systems.

I was originally going to use good looking graphic representations that I cut and pasted from the web, but then I decided that you could easily do that; better to use, for the most part, examples that I had worked through myself. There is nothing particularly refined about any of the figures in this chapter; following the principles of the rest of the book they are there to demonstrate ways of thinking rather than technical sophistication.

There is a rather overworked Chinese saying that a picture is worth a thousand words. Well it rather depends on the picture and the words. Maybe it is because of the different ways people have been trained or perhaps it is because of something more fundamental in the way different brains work, but people respond differently to the various forms in which data are presented to them. I am quite happy working with the raw numbers in a table for example. I like the detail that provides. Before you get the idea that I am just weird, let me reassure you I am not alone. For example I recently took a look at a report for Sport England (Leisure Industries Research Centre, 2003) on volunteering in sport, which has 44 tables (plus four in an Appendix), only a single diagram and not a graph or chart in sight. However, many do prefer more graphic representations.

There are a number of considerations to be taken into account when deciding the most appropriate form of data display:

- Quantitative or qualitative (*input*) – What kind of data are involved?
- Analysis or communication (*purpose*) – Is it to clarify the process or present the findings?
- Summary or detail (*amount*) – Is it to contain the main points or as much detail as possible?
- Impact or information (*visual*) – Is it about the image or the information to be conveyed?

In general it is easier to summarise categorical variables, and so quantitative variables are often converted to categorical ones for descriptive purposes.
www.bmj.com/statsbk/1.dtl

Displaying Quantitative Data

Tables

Let me start with the humble table as this is so often overlooked or taken for granted. Tables may be used to summarise one, two, or sometimes three or more variables. For illustrative purposes here I shall consider a two-way table (two variables), and to provide a focus for discussion I have included below a simple table taken from one of our studies (Table 13.1).

For readers to be able to interpret a table accurately it should contain the following information:

- Title – should offer a clear indication of what the data represent, and include a sequentially assigned number to allow identification of the table in the text and in the list of tables that appears at the beginning of the report/dissertation.
- Base – surveys commonly relate only to those over a certain age or living in a particular administrative area (for example I have to be careful with the government data I deal with and check if it relates to the whole of the UK (including Northern Ireland), Great Britain or England). This should be specified, if not in the table then in the accompanying text.
- Labels – clear identification of each of the variables involved (here, *sex of respondent* and *improvement proposed*) and each of the values assumed by those variables (e.g. *better equipment*).
- Values in the cells of the table – conventionally computer packages handling survey data will calculate the absolute values (preferable for small sample sizes), percentage of the total sample, percentage of whatever is represented in the column (probably the most common form), or percentage of whatever is represented in the row. In other kinds of research your table may contain any number of different representations: some measure of finance, accidents on holiday, etc.
- Form – data may have been weighted to represent the population rather than just the sample, or standardised relative to some norm (e.g. prices in 2000).
- Sample size – commonly shown as n =.
- Source – if the report draws on data from more than one data set, the source(s) should be identified, normally at the foot of the table (if it is a report of a single survey this is superfluous).
- Notes – about the question asked, variations between different years of the survey, missing data, why total percentages do not sum to 100, etc. may also appear at the foot of the table.

Table 13.1   Improvements to Mansfield parks proposed by local schoolchildren

| | Sex of respondent | | |
	Male	Female	All
Improvement proposed		percentage of respondents	
Better equipment	40	42	41
Clean it up	12	21	16
Safety (security staff, cameras, gates)	13	15	14
New/better sports facilities	12	4	8
Repair equipment, facilities, etc.	7	7	7
Dogs (ban, separate, fine owners)	5	1	3
Improve environmentally	5	4	5
Other	8	6	7

Source: Mansfield Schools Survey (Centre for Leisure and Sport Research, 2001) (n = 717)

Table 13.1 comes from data gathered from schoolchildren in Mansfield (UK). Those who had visited a park in Mansfield during the summer holidays were asked what they would do to make it better if they were in charge. This was an open-ended question with the responses eventually coded into one of eight categories

If these are responses to options presented to respondents you may want to keep them in the same order as they originally appeared in the questionnaire; if they are responses to open questions that have been categorised you may want to group like with like; or you may want to present them in rank order according to frequency of response.

Exercise

Table 13.1 is certainly not presented as a perfect example. You can judge it for yourself against the considerations above.

Consider the difference between the data represented here which show, for example, that 21% of the girls wanted better cleanliness and the alternative formulation that says that of those that wanted better cleanliness 62% were girls.

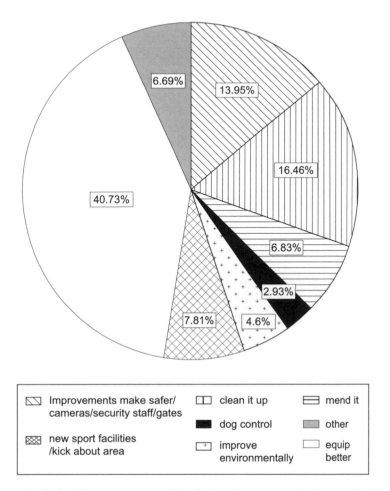

Figure 13.1   Pie chart of improvements to Mansfield parks proposed by local school children
Source: Mansfield Schools Survey (Centre for Leisure and Sport Research, 2001) (n = 717)

The same sorts of principle apply to other forms of graphical representation like those discussed below. Details like spacing, the use of lines, bold text or italics will depend on the house style of your employer, university or publisher.

Pie charts

Pie charts are those familiar circles divided into slices, each slice in proportion to the size of the respective response or whatever other category is being examined. The example in Figure 13.1 shows the same responses as in Table 13.1.

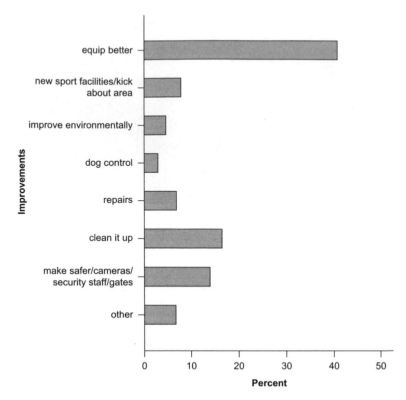

Figure 13.2   Bar chart of improvements to Mansfield parks proposed by local schoolchildren
Source: Mansfield Schools Survey (Centre for Leisure and Sport Research, 2001) (n = 717)

Some people seem besotted with pie charts and use them at every opportunity. From my use of language you may gather that I do not share that enthusiasm. They may help to emphasise either that one or two groups dominate or that all groups are more or less the same size. However, most people can get that much of a message from the raw numbers anyway, and pie charts may obscure more subtle variations. It is true that you can put the respective numbers in the pie chart as well, but I prefer some form (and there are many) of bar chart.

Bar charts

A bar chart like Figure 13.2 contains the same data. I find it much easier to assess/ interpret this kind of representation even without the labels providing the number of responses – of course these can be added if you wish. It is more straightforward to compare the lengths of different bars than the angle (or area) of the segments of a circle.

Bar charts can get more complex. Using them it is possible to represent more than one variable at a time. Figure 13.3a/b simply shows whether or not boys and girls had visited a play area during the summer. This time vertical bars have been shown with actual numbers in the sample rather than percentages. Whereas Figure 13.3a presents the bars side-by-side, Figure 13.3b stacks them. Figure 13.3b shows that there are almost exactly the same number of boys and girls in the sample and that it is the girls who are slightly more likely to have visited a play area in the school summer holidays. Part of the reason for this can be seen in Figure 13.4a/b which reveals how they were more likely to have been taken there by their family or to have gone with friends. Whereas 13.4a gives a better impression of who accompanied children to the play areas, 13.4b gives a better idea of the difference between boys and girls. Alternatively, of course, it is possible to combine who accompanied the children in each of the male and female columns.

Questionnaires often contain some form of attitude scale (Chapter 6). I have often seen the output presented as a graph of the median responses to each statement. Alternatively the net positive or negative ratings may be used, as in Figure 13.5, which comes from park users' assessments of different aspects of the park – the number who gave a rating of (very) satisfied minus those who gave a (very) dissatisfied rating.

If you have a continuous variable (e.g. age) rather than a discrete variable (separate categories, e.g. type of holiday), the corresponding representation is a **histogram**. The key issue then is to make sure that the width of the boxes is in proportion to the variable being measured (e.g. years). Just think about this for a moment. What is normally of interest is the underlying distribution, not something created by the categories of the researcher. Imagine that on the basis of questionnaire data people attending a music festival have been assigned to an age group. Imagine too that three of these age groups are 20–24, 25–29 and 30–39. Clearly the last of these covers twice the span of years, so it is not surprising that there are more people in this category. As represented in Figure 13.6a it looks as though attendance at this music festival was more popular with the 30–39 age group than with the other two. A more accurate impression is conveyed by Figure 13.6b. In a histogram the number of people is represented by the area of the respective boxes rather than the height of the box. Working from raw data the computer will normally offer you equal intervals, which gets over that problem, but you may be working from data that have already been grouped, either by you at the design stage or by previous researchers.

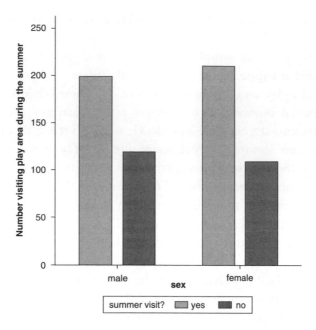

Figure 13.3a Boys and girls visiting a play area during the summer holidays
Source: Mansfield Schools Survey (Centre for Leisure and Sport Reseach, 2001) (n = 717)

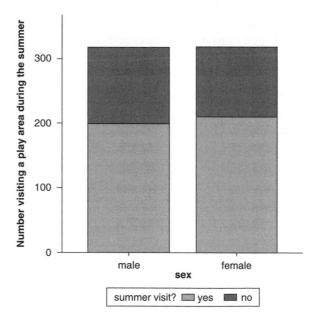

Figure 13.3b Boys and girls visiting a play area during the summer holidays
Source: Mansfield Schools Survey (Centre for Leisure and Sport Research, 2001) (n = 717)

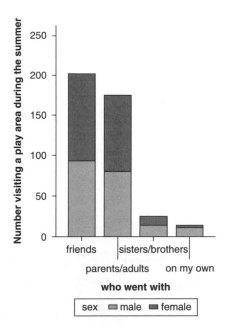

Figure 13.4a   Who accompanied boys and girls to the play area
Source: Mansfield Schools Survey (Centre for Leisure and Sport Research, 2001) (n = 717)

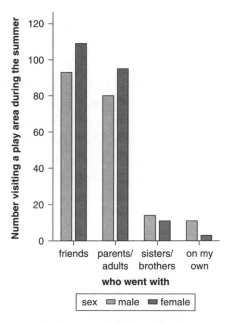

Figure 13.4b   Who accompanied boys and girls to the play area
Source: Mansfield Schools Survey (Centre for Leisure and Sport Research, 2001) (n = 717)

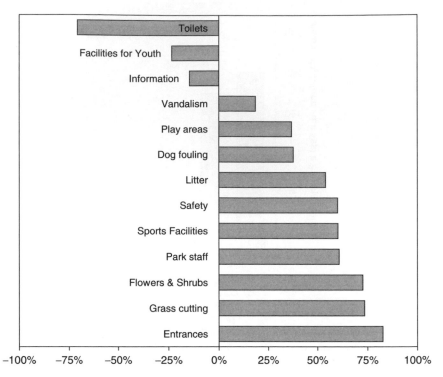

Figure 13.5   Net postitive and negative reactions to aspects of the parks
Source: Mansfield Park Users Survey (Centre for Leisure and Sport Research, 2001) (n = 717)

Sometimes in more scientific journals you may see strange aerials sticking out of the top of the bars showing the mean scores of each group. These represent the standard error associated with each group. A variation on this is the 'box plot' which is one of the standard options offered by SPSS, for example, which shows the median and the interquartile range (i.e. the middle half of the distribution). These offer an alternative representation of the two key elements of a distribution (Chapter 11), a measure of central tendency and a measure of spread.

Line graphs

Graphs are typically used to examine changes over time, e.g. in the number of students taking the geography of tourism elective each year (Figure 13.7). In that case, university managers may be interested in examining trends. As usual, it is important to know the context. For example, was the big increase in 2001 because of a sudden rise in popularity in this subject, a change of tutor, an easier assessment regime, or simply a bigger intake to the course as a whole that produced larger numbers for all electives?

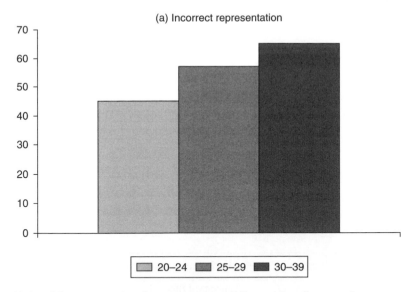

Figure 13.6   Histograms showing age groups of those attending event

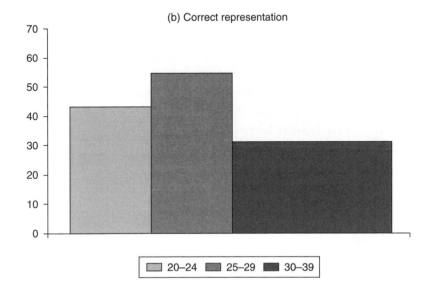

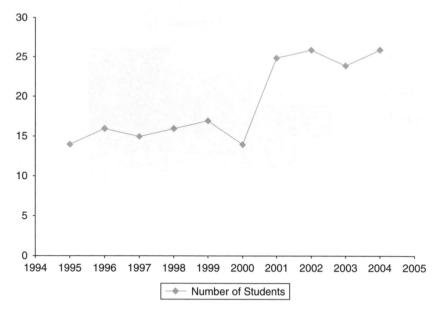

Figure 13.7   Number of students enrolling on geography of tourism module

Cumulative frequencies (ogives)

Quite often we might want to show not just the numbers in various categories, but the numbers or proportion who are 'at least' or 'up to' particular values: e.g., those with incomes less than £20k, those with at least brown belt standing in a martial art or those who have travelled from within a particular range to get to the event. Figure 13.8 is an example of this last kind of challenge – establishing catchment areas. What we see here is not that 12% travelled 6–6.99 kilometres to get to the centre (though we can work that out), but that four out of five (81%) came from within a seven kilometre radius.

When represented by a curve rather than a series of bars this is referred to as an ogive.

Scatterplots

Also known as scattergrams, these plot the values recorded for two variables (interval or ratio) at the same time, to provide a visual representation of the

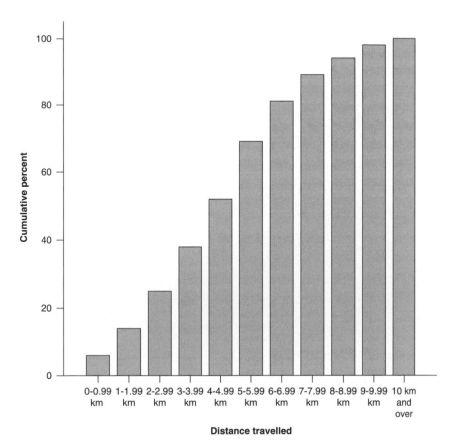

Figure 13.8   Distance travelled to the cinema

relationship between them. Kinnear and Gray give an example based on tennis skills:

> The principal of a tennis coaching school thinks that tennis proficiency depends upon the possession of a degree of general hand–eye coordination. To confirm this hunch, she measures the hand–eye coordination of some pupils who are beginning the course and their proficiency in tennis at the end of the course. (2004: 155–6)

Using SPSS it is easy to get a scatterplot [Graphs, Scatter] like the one in Figure 13.9a, which suggests that there probably is a relationship. Indeed, performing Pearson's correlation confirms that.

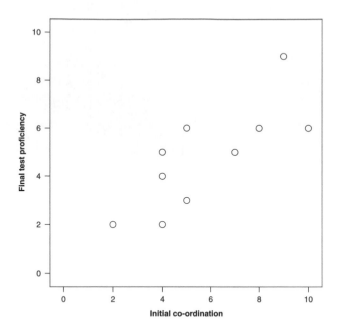

Figure 13.9a   Example of a scattergram

It is relatively simple to add to this scatterplot a line that best fits the distribution of points in the scatter.[1] As in Figure 13.9b this is most commonly a simple linear regression (you may see this referred to as 'least squares') which minimises the distances between the various points and the line (alternatives are available).

> Once you've got the hang of it, it is fairly straightforward to produce a lot of visual images of the data. Just because you can do it, however, does not mean that you should do it for every variable or combination of variables, and certainly does not mean you should overload the report with graphs/images. For example, a pie chart adds little if anything to the statement that 46% of respondents were female and 54% male.

Displaying Qualitative Data

When it comes to presenting qualitative data the pictures come less easily, and less attention is paid to alternative forms of presentations. Some forms appear in most reports of qualitative research and so go unrecognised.

---

[1] Although I say it is relatively simple, the way I have been shown to do it is not intuitively obvious. In SPSS (Version 12 for Windows) double click on the scatterplot to open the chart editor; choose 'Edit'; choose 'Select chart'; right click on one of the data points; choose 'fit line'.

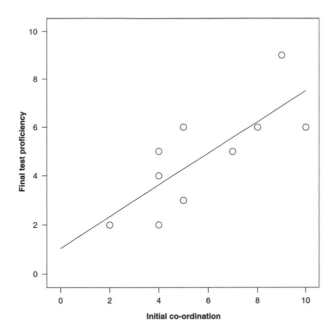

Figure 13.9b   Example of a scattergram with line of best fit

1. Paraphrasing – putting into your own words what was said to you during your data collection allows the information to be summarised, but the challenge then is to remain faithful to the original.
2. Selecting illustrative quotes – the difficulty here is to decide what is illustrative. A quote selected because it is typical may be so unexceptional as to prompt readers to ask why it should have special attention drawn to it. On the other hand picking the 'good quotes', those that seem to be particularly perceptive, runs the risk of giving undue emphasis to the more articulate respondents and sidelining others, thereby distorting the general picture.[2] When using these it is all too easy to assume that they 'speak for themselves'. That may sometimes be the case, but it is usually necessary to set them in context and offer some interpretation, e.g.: Who said it (not the name, but their characteristics/position)? What prompted the comment? What is meant by it? What are the implications? How does it relate to what other respondents said or what has been drawn from the literature?

---

[2]The same issue arises if selecting photographs, with a need to balance the quality of the photograph with the usefulness of the content.

In this context it is useful to be mindful of van Maanen's (1988) distinction between different forms of representation.

Realist – a detailed, matter-of-fact representation. Although the researcher is 'invisible' they control the representation and alternatives are excluded.

Confessional – a frank account clearly written from the perspective of the researcher, but may emphasise the researcher at the expense of what happened.

Impressionist – a personalised account telling the story in a way that allows the reader to relive the experience, but may suggest more coherence than was evident at the time.

Each of these different accounts may have its advantages, but it is important to recognise the limitations too.

Some extremely simple forms of presentation can be surprisingly revealing. For example, just setting out in a simple sequence the key events during the implementation of some organisational change can be extremely helpful to the reader in showing how events unfolded.

Matrixes galore

The sheer volume of data that qualitative research typically produces means that it is important to find effective ways of organising and packaging it. Miles and Huberman (1994) offer a host of ideas on using different forms of matrixes to help synthesise qualitative data, e.g.:

Checklist matrix – can be used to show the possession of attributes (e.g. to assess sporting aptitude or compliance with legislation about access for people with disabilities) or the occurrence of certain events. These may be done in the field – e.g. through (participant) observation at the venue or in the classroom – or constructed after the event from recorded/transcribed interviews or field notes.

Role matrix – respondents appear on one dimension and themes along the other. Respondents may then be grouped according to their roles (relatively easy to do if computerised). For example, in our work on racism in sport, we might be interested to know how people assess the extent of racism in their sport, who the main perpetrators are and what the impact of campaigning has been. If responses are ordered according to role it is easy to see, for example, if managers see things similarly to other managers and differently from coaches, players and referees.

Effects matrix – records a change observed in a particular domain (e.g. introduction of new training methods, change of manager, or children leaving home), then the effect of that change is recorded alongside it. The matrix can be made more complex by, for example, recording direct and indirect effects. If this is done initially for each organisation or participant, the next step might be to work out a more generalised representation for different types of organisation/participant.

Explanatory effects matrix – producing an effects matrix in this way is relatively simple, but invites further questions for consideration in the analytical process, most obviously, why those effects should have occurred. This may be represented by the respondents own accounts or by your analytical interpretation.

These normally produce huge matrixes (matrices if you prefer). The challenge is then to collapse them to a manageable size. One example of what a display matrix might look like is provided by Figure 12.2 in the previous chapter in which different areas of adaptation were considered in the context of different styles of 'retirement'.

Organisational charts

Those interested in management studies will often come across organisational charts that show who (which section) in the organisation is responsible for what, and to whom they are answerable. These may be clearer and easier to take in, and less tedious, than a formal written account. These are not just helpful to explain the structure to outsiders (e.g. finding out who is responsible for children's play in the Council), but can be useful to the organisation itself if it identifies gaps, confusion, overlap or a lack of 'fit'.

Other forms of organisational chart are used to show processes, e.g. how the restructuring of organisational change is introduced, negotiated and implemented. These can be extended to present a model of decision-making, as in Figure 13.10, which is an attempt to show how families make their holiday choices. These might be constructed for each case/respondent/family and then combined to produce a general model of the process. This is a fairly basic model. It is not hard to see how it could become more complex: adding stages and influences; building in feedback loops and iterations (going round part of the system again); or incorporating decisions with alternative branches for 'yes', 'no', 'don't know'. This illustrates one of the key dilemmas of representation: deciding the optimal balance between showing sufficient detail to do justice to the process and keeping it simple enough for an easily understood, generalised model. These are a form of flow chart. They may also be used to explore sequencing in order to give a clue to causation.

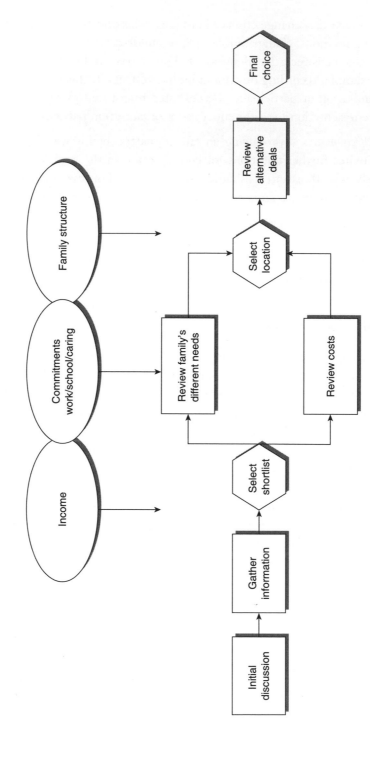

Figure 13.10   Flow chart for family holiday decision-making

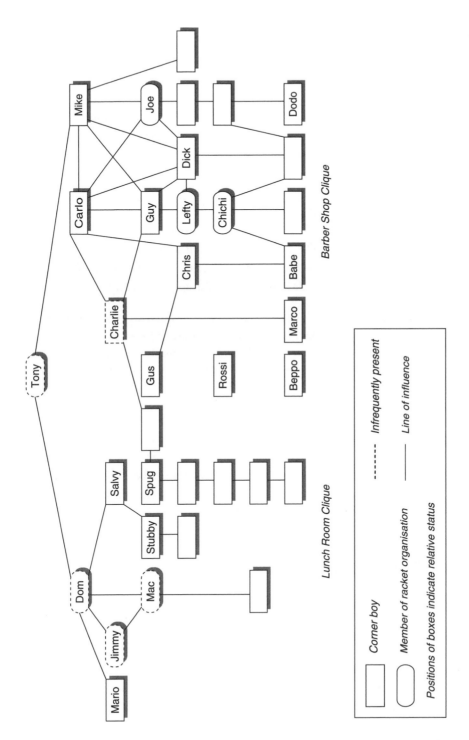

Figure 13.11 Informal organisation of the Cornerville S & A Club: early September 1939 (from Whyte, 1955: 156)

Social networks

Imagine that you are interested in the relationships that underpin people's leisure relations, whether in your sports club or the community centre or the social relations of work colleagues. Then whether you are drawing on Goffman's (1961, 1963) ideas of encounters and gatherings, or network theory, or more recent interest in social capital, you might need some way of representing interactions between people. In the previously mentioned study of *Street Corner Society*, Whyte (1943)[3] became interested in how groups hung together, what the relationships were and who was able to exercise power in a social hierarchy. When he first joined one of the local social clubs he looked for '*the* leader', but couldn't find him. His participant observation revealed that was because there were two distinct cliques. Whyte's mapping of who talked and hung-out with whom allowed him to record patterns of influence and how they changed over time, and hence to see how some things came to be and others did not. In describing Figure 13.11 he says:

> The accompanying chart presents a picture of the informal organization of the club at this time. The names of members who do not figure in the story have been omitted. While it is not necessary for the reader to keep in mind all the names that appear here, comparison of this chart with the two which follow may help him [sic] to visualize the evolution of personal relations within the club. (Whyte, 1955: 155)

These charts were not casual doodlings, but the result of a long series of mappings of spatial arrangements of people in the club over several months.

The idea of data display is to find a way of portraying simply a lot of material with a view to helping your readers see what you are talking about. However, it can also be an important part of the analytical process, helping you see the shape of the wood rather than the form of the individual trees.

Further Lines of Enquiry

The best thing to do is to identify what works for you when you are reading accounts of other people's research in newspapers, on the web or in academic journals. You should find it easy to locate material on the presentation of quantitative data, but there are fewer sources for qualitative data. Miles and Huberman (1994) are very keen on using maps, charts and matrixes to help organise and synthesise qualitative data. See also Jones (1985) writing about the analysis of depth interviews for her take on various 'mapping' or charting procedures.

---

[3]The copy I have is in fact the 1955 2nd edition.

14

The Responsibilities
of the Researcher

How is our 'right to know' balanced against the participants' right to privacy, dignity and self-determination? (Robson, 1993: 29)

Growing attention is being paid to the ethical and responsible conduct of research. However, many still find it difficult to appreciate the ethical considerations beyond the narrow confines of medical or dangerous 'scientific' research. These are issues all social scientists have to address in their research. As well as practical exercises, the chapter contains a series of challenges to convey the message that it applies to you not just to others. The key components are:

- responsibilities to respondents
- responsibilities to self
- responsibilities to the research community, the client and society
- advice on completing an ethics form.

Ethical issues may, of course, be the focus of the research investigation, for example: ethical tourism; fair play and the 'professional foul'; risk in outdoor adventure; legal liability; recreational drug-taking; or relationships between youth leaders and the young people in their care. However, my concern here is with the ethics associated with conducting research.

Despite some people's protestations to the contrary, I find it difficult to imagine research in the social sciences that does not have ethical implications. Even if there is no direct interaction with others, our research is about people and it involves revealing things, making judgements and creating new knowledge, all of which will have consequences for others. Quite often these ethical considerations will be of little consequence, but they should be reviewed carefully. Not being a philosopher I find it easier to tackle these issues from the perspective of the responsibilities of the researcher rather than wrestle with the niceties of the distinction between ethics and morals. In providing a good insight into ethical considerations in research Robson suggests:

> While both are concerned with what is good or bad, right or wrong, ethics are usually taken as referring to general principles of what one ought to do. Morals are usually taken as concerned with whether or not a *specific* act is consistent with accepted notions of right or wrong. (1993: 30)

See what I mean? Fortunately, most of the professional associations have developed codes of conduct and ethical guidelines that they expect their members to abide by, and these are now available on their websites. I tend to take my lead from an organisation I have been a member of since it started, the Social Research Association.[1] The SRA considers these issues in terms of responsibilities to society, respondents/participants, client/funder, the research community, and self.

I have chosen to discuss these issues towards the end of the book but in practice, of course, this has to be addressed at the outset and reviewed throughout the project. You may well be required to seek ethical approval for your research before you are allowed to start. Increasingly, universities are adopting their own ethics procedures for research. In the UK if you are doing a piece of sports science research involving some form of intervention or otherwise tackling issues of wellbeing, you may also need formal approval from the NHS Research Ethics Committee.

Sometimes discussions of ethical issues can seem a bit abstract, so at various stages of the chapter I have presented you with ethical dilemmas in my version of the party game, Scruples. Although these are scattered through the chapter they do not relate only to the section in which they appear. What initially appears a simple issue may have many ramifications. If at first it appears that there is no dilemma, try to work out why for some people there might be. You should also be making the links to the research you are planning.

Dilemma 1

Design a research project that will allow you to examine whether/how violence on television affects children.

---

[1] I certainly do not want to suggest that the SRA were in any way pioneers. For example, the European Society for Opinion & Market Research has had a code of conduct since it was founded in 1948, as has the Market Research Society since 1954.

Responsibilities to Respondents

One of the general principles is that the researcher should avoid undue intrusion into the lives of the people being researched. Always ask yourself whether it is possible to use information that already exists rather than imposing on people. Certainly we should not make people feel they have been treated as objects of measurement without respect for their individual values and sense of privacy.

We need to consider the impact our research may have on people's lives. They are not the same after we go away (or maybe researchers just have an inflated impression of the impact they have). At the very least the people involved are likely to think more about the subject of the research – e.g. retirement, 'race', risk, recreational conflict, redundancy or relationships – which may be unsettling or cause friction. For example, in our work on retirement I was concerned that we might be forcing people to think about something that some would find unpleasant, but on the other hand, being within six months of retirement that confrontation was going to happen sooner rather than later anyway. I am sure you can think of other research that may address, or stray into, areas that are far more sensitive.

Although it is often overlooked, whether the judgements associated with the analysis of the data are made on the basis of the researcher's value set or that of the participants is also an important ethical issue, particularly when the participants have been constructed as an 'other' in terms of 'race', class or gender.

In confidence?

Researchers typically reassure people that whatever they say will be treated in confidence, but what do we mean by that? Strictly interpreted it would mean that nobody else would find out what had been said. Well there would be limited value in that kind of research (keeping it to ourselves). Quantitative and qualitative researchers face rather different issues here.

In quantitative studies we typically deal with aggregate data, so the views/behaviours of any individual are concealed. But at what point does that separation of the data from the individual occur? For complete confidentiality the name or identifier [2] should never be collected, but there are all sorts of good reasons, why it might be necessary to do so. Names might be needed to allow reminders to be issued to non-respondents in a postal questionnaire, or if people are eligible for a prize draw, or if a

---

[2] Just removing the name may not ensure confidentiality if, for example, we observe that someone aged 63 scored particularly highly on some scale when there is only one person aged 63 in the firm.

sub-sample are to be selected for further involvement, or if it is a longitudinal study that requires data from different stages to be combined, or if there might be some need to check back to clarify responses. In these circumstances, careful design and effort can limit leakages if it is particularly important that people should not be identified. Remember though that even when there is no identification on the questionnaire or test sheet, if a third person (e.g. a teacher) is collecting them in they can easily peek.

In qualitative studies the emphasis tends to be more on the whole person and it is the detail of their lives that is vital. By 'in confidence' researchers might mean that individuals will not be quoted and that only the general findings will be reported, but research accounts frequently use direct quotes. Maybe then, what should be offered is anonymity, but this is more easily promised than delivered. Even the use of pseudonyms may not conceal the identity of respondents from those around them. Moreover, even if individuals cannot be identified their lives may be laid bare or their group (e.g. sports fans) denigrated. This is why it is important that respondents are given the chance to say whether or not they approve of how you plan to use the data. In some projects the findings are negotiated with the respondents, but others disapprove of this approach on the basis that it is handing control to people who may find it difficult to be objective.

Having said that, most people who have agreed to an interview are happy for their views to be made public. Indeed, they may feel it is owed to them that their observations are fairly attributed to them. This, of course, implies that they are clear about what they have agreed to.

Informed consent

There is an expectation that people should know what they are letting themselves in for when they get involved in a research project. In some research environments people are asked to sign a kind of affidavit making a declaration that they have been fully informed and consent to their involvement; indeed it seems to be the dominant expectation where I work. While this may be necessary in some circumstances for legal reasons, if you ask people to do this when you are asking about their last holiday or what they do out of school they may start wondering what on earth is going on. Advocates of getting signed consent maintain that it is reassuring to the participant; my feeling is that the reverse is likely to be the case and that in fact it is likely to challenge the building of trust and lead to self-censored, pat responses. Many of the people I want to interview are wary of anything that smacks of the legal system, and don't forget it is they who are asked to sign.

Whichever side you come down on, the general principle is that it is important to be open and above board, explaining what is entailed in the research and how information will be treated. There are of course circumstances in which it would just be impractical to seek informed consent, signed or not. For example, the researcher is unlikely to have sought informed consent to use material gathered through hearing conversations at a sporting occasion or in a club (always assuming it is possible to hear anything above the music). In such circumstances there are still different ways of seeing the admissibility of this evidence.

Individuals are unlikely to be identified, so no harm will accrue.	But … damage may be done to a collective – e.g. a club's supporters, or fans more generally, or some cultural/class group.
If material is gathered in the public realm it has been put there by people aware that others are present.	But … there is an important difference between having others around and being scrutinised as part of a research project.

Researchers sometimes insist that some form of deception is necessary to get people to say what they really think rather than what they think they ought to say, or to behave as they would 'naturally' behave. Some of these issues were discussed in Chapter 8 in relation to observation, but the same principles may apply in other circumstances. People typically try to decide the balance between the damage that might be done to those involved in the research and the benefit that may be derived from the knowledge gained.

Dilemma 2

You have a target for the number of respondents you want. However, you find it difficult to reach this number because when you tell people how much work is involved, they refuse.

What do you do? Map out the options and identify the ethical issues involved with each.

There has been growing concern about the exploitation and abuse of vulnerable people, and steps have been taken to try to make sure that the risk of this happening is reduced. In the UK, anyone working with vulnerable people (e.g. children, frail older people or people with mental health problems) is expected to subject themselves to a police check, which is handled by the Criminal Records Bureau (www.crb.gov.uk).

Think about how you would like to be treated, but remember, some people may be more sensitive than you.

Responsibilities to Self

This dimension often gets overlooked. Probably the main issues here are: personal risk; the danger of compromising your own value set; and gaining appropriate attribution for your work.

The Social Research Association has been keen to address the risks that researchers face because of the situations they may be put in, or put themselves in. For example, if you are at a sporting venue interviewing fans about crowd behaviour or racism, it does not take a vivid imagination to recognise that some people may take exception to what you are doing and threaten you. Similar risks may be encountered when conducting a park survey, doing a home interview or any number of other forms of research. Fortunately the risks you might imagine very rarely materialise, but there are things that you can do to reduce any threat:

- if there are club stewards, police or other officials around, make sure they know what you are doing and stay within sight of them
- if possible, work in pairs
- carry a mobile phone
- let other people know where you will be.

At various times in this book points have been raised about value-neutral research. However, at the same time as it is wrong to impose your values on those involved in the research, you should not compromise your own values and belief in what is right for you. In the study of *Street Corner Society* that I have already mentioned, Whyte (1943) spent some time exploring political processes in the community. Because he was doing participant observation he did what others around him in the political machine did, and this got him involved in repeat voting – i.e. assuming other people's identity to vote several times – even though he thought this was 'wrong'. Maybe because he got arrested he decided in future to remain true to himself and his values. Equally, if you are opposed to tobacco/alcohol/gambling, you should not be afraid to stand on principle and refuse to do research in their interest. Remember, your own reputation is at stake and ought to be worth something to you.

If your work is good enough to be used by others, then, just as you are expected to give proper attribution to the work of others, you should expect to get appropriate credit for the work you have done. For example, I agree with the advice given by the British Sociological Association that students should normally be the first-named author on any multi-authored article based on their dissertation. If you work for a private company, a public agency or research centre, it may be standard practice for all reports to be issued under the collective identity. That was the case at the research centre at which I worked for a number of years, but our reports carefully documented the contributions of each person involved in the study.

Dilemma 3

While conducting your interview, your respondent makes a pass at you. What do you do?

1. pretend you didn't hear and avoid dealing with it
2. laugh it off
3. accept
4. decline gracefully
5. other.

How does this affect the interview and the research?

Responsibilities to the Research Community

Our fellow researchers have a right to expect that we should engage in good quality research that produces findings that can be trusted. In line with this, objectivity came to be seen as a vital characteristic of scientific research – the idea that people would conduct research free of values and personal limitations, such that a common approach would produce findings that all could agree on. As will be discussed in the next chapter, there are many researchers who question whether it is possible to be objective. Indeed, it is sometimes suggested that those who argue in favour of objectivity are the ones least likely to recognise their own 'biases', operating within an unthinking acceptance of the dominant value systems of their society. Some researchers make no bones about subscribing to a set of values that commit them to doing research designed to promote change (e.g. those subscribing to Critical Theory or radical feminism). Whatever your theoretical or political position I believe that your interests are best served by sound, rigorous research that will allow you to engage in debate with others. Hence, there is an expectation that researchers should uphold professional integrity.

If any one researcher does not subscribe to high professional standards they may contribute to researchers generally getting a bad name in much the same way as all politicians can become 'tarred with the same brush' as a result of a scandal that may have been nothing to do with them personally. If people have bad experiences of research they are less likely to agree to be involved in the future, thereby threatening not just response rates but the very viability of some projects. More immediately, you have a responsibility to uphold the good name of your employer or host institution. For example, the actions of students do not just reflect upon their university, but affect the reception that subsequent students will get when they try to conduct research in the future.

You also owe it to other researchers who may be reading your research to present clearly the research methods that have been adopted so that it is possible for them to assess the techniques and findings. They need to be able to appreciate how the findings were derived if they are to use them as part of their own argument.

It is essential to give appropriate credit for the work of others, whether in the form of published work or the contribution other people have made to the research you are reporting.

Responsibilities to the Client

Although some researchers are fortunate enough to do research for their own interest, most are funded by somebody else. While there may be a responsibility to produce findings that will be useful to the client, researchers have to resist any pressure to produce 'desirable' findings. Despite what clients might think, convenient results may not be in their best interests – far from it if they lead to the implementation or perpetuation of ineffective practices. Despite the belief that the customer is always right, as the experts in research, researchers may have to offer advice and guidance on what represent appropriate research questions, design and methods. Although they own the findings, clients should not direct the research to produce particular findings.

People reading this may not have a client in a formal sense, though they may still experience similar tensions. For example, the research for a dissertation or other course project may have been conducted through the good offices of a local business or organisation, in return for which they might reasonably expect a report at the end. However, what they need is likely to be very different from what has to be produced as a requirement for the course. If you are in this situation make sure you know exactly what you have to produce for both parties.

It is also important that you recognise what implications the source of funding may have had for the research you read about. You may be alert to how the interests of the client can affect research on whether meat, butter or alcohol is good for you, but exactly the same applies to research on how sport is good for you or on the benefits produced by tourism.

The client may provide information (e.g. pricing and cost structures related to competitive tenders) that would not otherwise be available to you. There is then an obligation to treat this in confidence in the same way as for information provided by respondents. At the same time, clients need to appreciate the responsibility researchers have to others when reporting. For example, this means making the methodology open to others, not treating it as confidential. One of the biggest sources of tension between funders and researchers is over what can be published from the research. Research conducted for commercial purposes may never go further than the people commissioning it (and the price normally reflects that), whereas widespread dissemination would more normally be expected of research conducted in the public arena. The debate here is over who owns the knowledge and ideas – the people who generated them or the people who paid for them. It is a bit glib to say that these matters should be sorted out before the research begins; circumstances change.

Dilemma 4

You are doing research supported by a charitable foundation into the leisure lives of children whose parents have separated. You have the approval of the child and the mother, but the mother does not want you to approach the father. The child still sees both parents. What should you do?

Responsibilities to Society

Much research is undertaken in the belief that widening knowledge will eventually benefit society. Let's be honest, the small-scale research we are talking about here is unlikely to pose questions on a par with whether it was right or wrong for scientific researchers to develop the atomic bomb or for a revolutionary AIDS treatment with startling effects to be withheld until sufficient randomised control trials have been completed. However, the ripples may spread out beyond those directly involved in the research; if the research is to inform policy it will have implications for a wider group and their interests should also be considered. For example, in competition for scarce resources the outcome of the research may deny provision to some areas/people.

Clearly in such circumstances we should not be party to work likely to misinform or mislead rather than advance knowledge. Just as we hope that the government will use the best measures of inflation, unemployment or educational effectiveness, we have a responsibility to use the best tools available.

We have a responsibility to tell the truth, not lie, not make things up. But do we have a right to tell the truth? Might it sometimes be right to be secret about the findings? This is at the heart of some struggles over publication, when, for example, a government department tries to suppress research findings and the researchers 'leak' the report. We need also to be aware of how the research findings may be used by others. However, knowing that some people may try to use the findings to the advantage of some and disadvantage of others should not necessarily be a reason for not collecting the data in the first place. Their presentation though must be as accurate as possible with statistics and other findings qualified with suitable caveats. It is important to remember this because sponsors (and other readers) rarely want to see this in reports, preferring a straightforward, unequivocal message.

Despite my initial observations about the import of the impact, I decided to keep this dimension in the chapter because it is not unusual for researchers to invoke 'the greater good', that wider interest, as a reason for what might be questionable actions relating to individuals involved in the research. This might only be implicit, as in, 'We did not tell them about _____ because it was important that we identified their "true" beliefs/actions, which might otherwise have been concealed'.

Dilemma 5

Your council believes that providing leisure opportunities for 12–16 year olds during the summer holidays will reduce crime and vandalism. However, to provide convincing evidence you need a comparative study that compares areas with the leisure programme with those without. Is it right to withhold provision? Are there alternative approaches?

Dilemma 6

During the course of your interviewing or observation at the club, you get access to privileged information about an incident that put a member of the police force in hospital. Should you overlook it, treat it as information for your research or inform the police? Would it make any difference if it was about someone dealing heroin? Or if someone was supplying/consuming performance enhancing drugs in 'your' sport, would you inform the national governing body?

Advice on Completing an Ethics Form

Many organisations require researchers to apply formally for ethical approval before they embark on their research. What is required may vary depending upon whether the organisation is motivated by a concern for research ethics or legal liability. However, you might typically be asked to provide information on the following.

Project design:

- the project's aims
- research design
- methods of data collection and analysis
- whether you have sought advice on statistics/methodology from suitable experts.

The intention here is to make sure that resources will only be devoted to good quality research, and the efforts of researchers and participants will not be wasted on research of little value.

Relationships with participants:

- the number and type of participants
- how participants will be selected and recruited
- whether or not participants will be paid
- whether informed consent will be gained (and what will happen if participants are unable to give informed consent)
- what information will be provided to participants
- what will happen to the participants
- whether they or the researchers will be subject to any risks (and how potential risks will be dealt with)
- whether they will have the right to withdraw.

This relates to the previous set of concerns about research design and should provide reassurance that the participants are appropriate to address the research challenge. However, importantly, it is about how participants will be treated.

Confidentiality and data protection:

- what precautions will be taken to ensure confidentiality and anonymity
- how the data will be stored.

This is now the subject of international legislation (data protection acts). The committee will probably seek assurance that research data will be stored securely. Where possible, anonymity should be preserved by removing identifiers, using pseudonyms and making sure there is no direct link between identifiable individuals and the data you hold on them. There is a particular concern regarding data held on computers. So, for example, you are not supposed to have names and addresses associated with your questionnaires or interviews. If that information is not needed do not store it. If it is needed (e.g. for longitudinal research), the identifiers and data should be kept separately.

Relationships with the commissioners of the research:

- who is funding the research, whether they will impose any restraints on the conduct of the project and whether there will be any limitations on publication of the findings.

This arises from the concern that researchers should produce findings without fear or favour, and there should be no pressure on them, however indirect, to lean one way or the other. The committee may also be concerned that your own rights are protected.

Most of these considerations would, of course, be covered in the research proposal anyway. So rather than having to provide extra information it is more a case of presenting it for a different purpose. Make sure you answer all the questions and complete all the sections on the form, otherwise people on the committee may worry about what is missing. The reviewing panel will want to be reassured that you are:

- open and not trying to hide anything
- aware of the ethical issues associated with the kind of research you are proposing
- reflective and thoughtful
- proposing worthwhile research
- technically competent.

Further Lines of Enquiry

As an example, the ethical guidelines of the Social Research Association can be found at www.the-sra.org.uk/ethical.htm. The SRA has also produced a code of safety associated with risk assessment to try and ensure the wellbeing of researchers. The recently produced RESPECT (not the political party) guidelines are intended to form the basis of a voluntary code of practice covering the conduct of socio-economic research in Europe (at www.respectproject.org). RESPECT also covers a range of related issues like data protection.

The Market Research Society gives useful advice on appropriate procedures for involving children and young people: www.mrs.org.uk/standards/children.htm.

Funding organisations may well have their own expectations, like the (UK) Economic and Social Research Council: www.esrc.ac.uk/ESRCInfoCentreImages/ESRC_Re_Ethics_Frame_tcm6-11291.pdf.

Oliver's (2003) *The Student's Guide to Research Ethics* helps to identify ethical issues that researchers may encounter and offers ways to resolve them.

15

Ways of Seeing, Ways of Thinking

> What a man sees depends both upon what he looks at and also upon what his previous visual-conceptual experience has taught him to see. (Kuhn, 1970: 113)

The way we see the world and what we believe about the way it operates has a fundamental effect on the way we research it. This extends beyond a choice between quantitative and qualitative techniques, to the selection of what are useful data, to the theories we use to explain the data and even to the questions asked in the first place. Not only do different kinds of researcher have different ideas on these matters, but which set of ideas is dominant changes over time. The chapter covers:

- the cycle of the research process – deductive and inductive reasoning
- normal science and scientific revolutions
- paradigms in leisure, sport and tourism.

I suggested in the opening chapter that we should not be hidebound in our approach to research and that we should choose from the range of different research techniques the one best suited to the particular task. Reading the different chapters you may have started to feel that it might be a bit more complicated than that. Perhaps for you some techniques just did not seem right. This may be because you have an aversion to mathematics or because you are not keen on talking to people, but it may be more fundamental than that. Different people see the world in different ways.

Relationships Between Data and Theory

One of the things that concerns scientific researchers (I include social scientists here) is the relationship between data and theory in this process. The distinction is

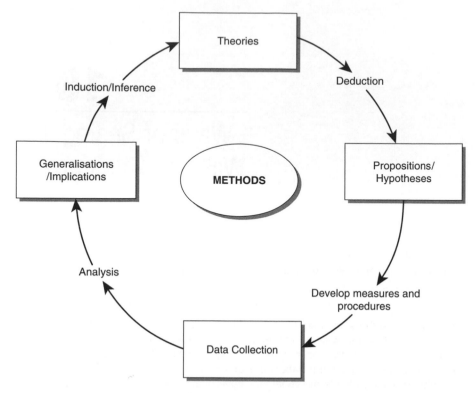

Figure 15.1   A cycle of generating and testing theory

commonly made between inductive and deductive approaches (Figure 15.1).[1] This is conventionally represented as a circle to indicate that the research process can begin in more than one place. Crudely speaking, inductive approaches start at the bottom of this cycle and deductive approaches start at the top. Induction involves reasoning from a set of data to try to produce explanations of what has been recorded in an effort to arrive at a set of rules/laws/theories that can be more generally applied. Deduction starts from a set of theoretical propositions and then gathers data to test whether the theory works. These are often described as theory generating/building and theory testing, respectively. Some see these as fundamentally different approaches, others see them as parts of the same whole, a continuing cycle.

---

[1]Before you accuse me of plagiarism, I am well aware that this figure is not original, but versions of it appear in so many books it is difficult to know who to attribute it to.

In practice there is rarely a 'clean' start in generating knowledge. It is difficult to imagine theory in the absence of observed data, as it would be hard to devise the building blocks. Equally, if you have no theory you have no way of deciding what you should be recording and then understanding and interpreting what you see. Even when we think we are starting with a clean sheet we hold in our heads a model of how we think the world works.

People often associate qualitative research with induction, and quantitative research with deduction. Like so many generalisations it does often work out like this, but it is not necessarily so. Certainly, many qualitative researchers argue that it is wrong to bring predetermined theories to bear as that may rule out perfectly good explanations and that instead it is better to allow understandings to arise directly from the data we gather. However, there is no necessary reason why qualitative researchers should not use a deductive approach, and quantitative researchers typically use surveys inductively, gathering data to examine whether there are relationships between any number of variables, albeit usually with pre-defined categories.

Induction

Collect data

Order these into different classifications/categories

Look for relationships between variables (regular association may suggest an empirical law).

It is likely that some data will not fit into these sets or patterns. Are these 'just' exceptions or is a better set of categories needed?

Deduction

Start from a set of initial conditions

Apply a set of appropriate laws

Leads logically to a particular outcome.

This reasoning can be checked against empirical data. However, just because the link has been confirmed on one occasion does not mean it will do so on future occasions. How many times would it need to happen to persuade us that it constitutes a 'rule' – how much evidence is enough?

So which comes first, the theories or the data collection, the chicken or the egg? The answer is a different kind of egg, or is it chicken? In other words, rather than a circle we have a spiral, which at the end of the cycle comes back to a slightly different place, a modified understanding (theory) or gathering data in a different way or interpreting it differently. We still have to make a decision though about where in this process our own research is going to start. It depends on what we think constitutes knowledge (what makes convincing evidence) and how we can know the world (which investigative approaches get us close to the real thing). That debate gets even more complicated when people start asking whether there is a single, tangible, 'hard', 'real' world out there for us to know, or whether it is better to think about how we construct it in our heads.

Exercise

Figure 15.1 might be the big picture of the development of knowledge, but individual researchers do tend to put the emphasis on different arcs of the circle. Maybe it does not matter which route we select, but the heat generated between researchers discussing this suggests that it is rather more significant than whether you say 'tomarto' and I say 'tomayto'. Think carefully here about what is happening in your own research project, whether you are starting with deduction or induction (and whether you are completing the cycle), and try to use the discussion in this chapter to work out why someone might argue you should adopt the other approach.

Falsification

I have always been mystified by the argumentative riposte in the face of contradictory evidence: 'Well that's the exception that proves the rule'. I cannot see how. All it has done is proved that there are at least some exceptions that do not comply with the general rule. Following Popper's line of reasoning, it only takes one black swan to disprove the general law that all swans are white (I think that came from Karl Popper, but it may have been Bryan Magee). Presumably the implication to be drawn from the popular riposte is that if people can recognise it as an exception it throws into sharper relief the more general pattern.

So, one line of argument goes, if in the social sciences it is difficult to 'prove' something, we should instead look to see how easily we can disprove alternative propositions – this approach tests the robustness of our explanations. There are parallels in both quantitative and qualitative research. In the former it is common not to demonstrate that two groups are different, but to demonstrate that it is highly unlikely that they are drawn from the same population (the process of rejecting the null hypothesis that there is no difference between the two groups and accepting the alternative hypothesis that there is). In the latter it is more of an argumentative, interrogative approach that prods and questions an emerging explanation. We look to establish plausible accounts that remain credible when subjected to close scrutiny.

There is a question of what might be referred to as scale, scope or compass here. On the basis of centuries of observation we accept that the sun will rise again tomorrow. With better measuring equipment we now know that there are very, very small deviations from the previously calculated 24 hour/365 day cycle; and greater knowledge of the universe tells us that the sun will not continue in this form forever. However, for the purposes of running my daily life, I am prepared to operate on the assumption that the sun will rise above the horizon again tomorrow morning, even if it is obscured by clouds where I live.

We have come to accept in the social sciences that there are likely to be exceptions to any proposed rule or law. Most of the time we are looking for broad patterns based on what mathematicians might refer to as 'fuzzy sets', collectives of like things without clear boundaries. We are looking for approximations that will be 'good enough' to allow us to get a reasonabe understanding of how different people interpret the world, to predict roughly what will happen if …, or to formulate suitable policies.

Normal Science

Like many other researchers, when I try to work out how knowledge develops, I make use of ideas set out by Thomas Kuhn in *The Structure of Scientific Revolutions* (originally published in 1962, but with a 2nd edition in 1970 and a 3rd in 1996) and adapt those to the social sciences. While I was writing this I heard someone on the radio suggest that 'disagreement is the process of science'. The speaker was referring to someone putting forward an argument, someone else contesting it and new knowledge being produced as a result of that disputation (a sort of dialectic process). Kuhn saw things rather differently as a result of examining the big picture and considering how science developed over the centuries. He suggested that the 'normal science' most researchers engage in operates in an environment of broad agreement: agreement about what is worth studying, about common concepts and categories, and over which methods to use.

Normal science is typically concerned with a search for greater precision and accuracy, deriving laws, designing ways of operationalising and testing theories in nature and exploring possible alternatives offered by a theory. This allows the determination of significant 'facts', matching those facts with theory, and developing theory further. I have put 'facts' within what are called scare quotes as a reminder that there are many researchers who dispute that there is such a thing as a fact on the basis that what we believe we know is a social construction – just one example of how different researchers see the world in different ways.

In the process of normal science existing theory can be used to make predictions, directed to new applications and to tidying-up explanations of how things work. This, Kuhn likened to puzzle solving, working within a given framework to fill in some of the gaps (fitting pieces in the jigsaw). Many problems are ruled out as being too abstract to be amenable to objective research, the concern of another discipline or just too difficult. While this may appear blinkered and unlikely to make the major breakthrough (it is just tinkering at the margin), only those problems that can reasonably be expected to get solved are addressed and one study builds on another. Progress is made easier by being able to take some things as given and not having to go back to first principles each time someone starts a project.

Paradigms

Sooner or later in reading about research methods you will almost certainly come across the term 'paradigm'. At its most basic a paradigm can be seen as a worldview. It can also be seen as the framework of beliefs shared by a (research) community; sharing through practice and writing produces common models of the world and how things work.

In another programme I heard on the radio, a paradigm was referred to as 'the assumptions we forget to articulate'. This is a helpful reminder of how the paradigm we adopt underpins everything we do, with all the advantages and disadvantages that entails. Patton's description of a paradigm is instructional here:

> a general perspective, a way of breaking down the complexity of the real world. As such, paradigms are deeply embedded in the socialization of adherents and practitioners: paradigms tell us what is important, legitimate and reasonable. Paradigms are also normative telling the practitioner what to do without the necessity of long existential or epistemological consideration. But it is this aspect of paradigms that constitutes both their strength and weakness – their strength in that it makes action possible, their weakness in that the very reason for action is hidden in the unquestioned assumptions of the paradigm. (1978: 203)

It is easy to see from that how paradigms inform 'normal science' in its problem solving.

As indicated by the quote at the beginning of this chapter, Kuhn suggests that a paradigm is a prerequisite of perception itself; what you see depends upon what you look at, your previous visual/conceptual experience (the way you have been taught to think), and how you look. In the absence of a paradigm all the facts that could possibly be relevant to the development of knowledge appear equally relevant. Without a standard set of methods to use or phenomena to be explained, each researcher is free to choose supporting observation and method. While this may be liberating and encourage creativity among individuals, it is hard to make progress across the field of study.

The paradigm debate is often reduced to whether quantitative techniques are preferable to qualitative ones, but there is rather more to it than that. The crucial questions that people debate in comparing paradigms are of the kind:

1. What is real? (ontology)
2. How can we know anything? (epistemology)
3. What methods can we use to find things out? (methodology)

These then have consequences for the techniques used. Surprise, surprise, different scholars 'read' the literature differently to reveal slightly different sets of paradigms – e.g. compare Guba (1990) and Sparkes (1992). Please forgive the crude characterisations in what I say next. These are not meant to provide definitive statements on what different paradigms are, but to help you recognise that there are different ways of seeing the world and to question how those are represented in your own research.

Central to the first of these questions is the debate about whether or not there is a single, objective, knowable reality, driven by a consistent set of laws. For those who have not thought about this before it may seem a bizarre question: surely if it is 'there' it is real? However, on reflection most would acknowledge that different people experience what appears to be the same thing differently, whether it is a holiday resort, the ice in the bath after a training session, or a concert/gig. 'Constructivists', for example, take this even further and argue that there is no reality other than what we put together in our heads, and that this is based on our social experiences, making it historically and spatially specific. This is referred to as a relativist perspective as opposed to the realist perspective of the positivist approach that acknowledges only an objective reality.

The second question returns to the issues of subjectivity and objectivity that were discussed in Chapter 2. Should we only believe what we can observe and measure, or what we can interpret from people reporting to us, or only trust our own direct experiences? The 'positivist' tradition insists that in order to be confident in what we observe we must set our personal values aside and be objective. The researcher must avoid personal bias and remain separate from the research if it is to be possible for different people to do the same research and get the same answers. 'Post-positivists' might question whether it is possible to achieve true objectivity, but would still strive towards that as their research ideal, whereas other approaches, like those of 'critical theory' and 'constructivism', celebrate the subjective. They argue that we cannot escape our values and biographies, and these necessarily mediate our enquiry so that we have to understand ourselves if we are to understand society. The researcher and researched are interlinked so that findings are the result of their interaction.

Let me fairly freely paraphrase Guba (1990) to introduce how people operating within different paradigms might view the third of the questions above, on methodology.

(a) Positivists prefer an experimental approach in which hypotheses are formulated to be tested empirically under controlled conditions.

(b) Post-positivists modify this by conducting their inquiries in more natural settings and make use of qualitative methods as well. In doing so they may acknowledge a role for grounded theory (Chapter 12) and discovery.

(c) Critical Theorists insist that the purpose of research is not just to understand the world, but to change it. They argue that it is essential to remove 'false consciousness' that has been instilled by the ideology of the dominant powers in society, and use research to bring about 'transformational change'. This is the key challenge set for research endeavours by Marxists, neo-Marxists, radical feminists and critical race theorists, for example, so it is not hard to see how they would come into conflict with positivists who argue that the researcher's personal perspectives should be kept out of research.

(d) Constructivists try to draw-out individual constructions of the world that are then compared and contrasted, sometimes to try to arrive at consensual constructions.

These three types of question often slide together when people start arguing about research. For example, is it possible to measure something like talent, creativity or sporting ability? Some might be quite confident in asserting 'yes, we can'; others might admit that it cannot be done accurately, but they know how to estimate it; others would insist that it is an impossible mission; and others would suggest that maybe it is the wrong question and it would be more informative to address another. In the context of that range of answers different researchers would react differently: look for a surrogate (alternative) measure; break the central concept down into more manageable, constituent parts; or explore what techniques people have used to develop their talents.

Is it possible to measure quantitatively something like people's views on the extent of racism in sport? Some people insist that unless we can do that we have no basis for comparing one sport with another or assessing change over time; it is the only way that the social sciences can come close to emulating the sciences. Others insist that any measurement or scale has to be flawed as that is just not the way people's brains work, and it is much more revealing to encourage people to tell their stories. Those inclined towards quantitative research might argue that they are concerned to deal with fact rather than what they see as 'opinion'. Consequently they may use as an indicator of whether racism has increased or decreased in the sport the number of incidents of racism reported to the league. Other things being equal, this might be a good measure, but other things are rarely equal. For example, there may be more racial incidents recorded now than ten years ago, not because racism has increased, but because players from minority ethnic groups think that there is now more chance that the league will take action on their complaints.

Exercise

The nature of people's research depends upon their beliefs about the world and how best to conduct investigations, what they can reasonably be expected to find out, their favoured theories, the policy context and, sometimes, who is paying for the research.

Consider a kind of investigation that has attracted a lot of research interest: the benefits that accrue to a city as a result of staging some cultural event. For a long time the concern was almost exclusively with economic benefits, but that has gradually broadened. How would your worldview interact with those of others to shape the research?

Even working out how much people spend on such an event is difficult enough. Are people good at recording how much they spend on something? If they are interviewed at the event they may spend more after the interview; if they are interviewed later, back at home, they may forget some of their spending. And there is other related expenditure too – on travel, food, accommodation, retail, etc. What would they have spent the money on if they had not spent it on going to the event? Maybe local businesses would still have benefited.

Further questions to consider:

How was that spending converted into jobs? Of what kind? For how long?

What are the related costs, not just the direct costs of provision, but those associated with things like policing, littering, increased traffic congestion, other provision that has been sacrificed to let this event happen?

Are there other benefits like favourable media coverage and a boost to the city's image that could attract future business?

What contributed to a successful event and what detracted from it? What makes it a success and in whose eyes?

How does the satisfaction that people get from the event relate to what they have paid to attend? Who benefits and who bears the costs? Did the event perpetuate the existing order or help to promote change?

Would it have been better to stage an alternative event or invest in something entirely different, like building more houses or employing more teachers?

What is the legacy? What are people stimulated to do next?

Progress?

At various times world events or new research will expose failings in the paradigm. Alternative models might then be proposed, but it is difficult for these new explanations to win acceptance because their proponents may literally be talking a different scientific language. People become entrenched in their own view of the world. I recently did an online course run by Bob Dick of Southern Cross University who suggested that researchers tend to judge their own paradigm by its exemplars (i.e. best practice). As he observed, this is probably fair enough as it is the exemplars that define the ideals of the approach. On the other hand, he notes, 'other' paradigms are often judged by their poorest examples (i.e. those easiest to criticise). This makes movement less likely.

If paradigms are so resistant to change, how can new paradigms become accepted?

1. The new paradigm offers explanation in an area the old one has previously failed to reconcile.
2. It may prove able to explain a problem not previously recognised.
3. The new paradigm offers neater, simpler explanations.
4. It may not explain everything but researchers put faith in its potential.
5. Not explaining everything is a bonus. If open-ended it leaves problems for others to solve, thereby offering career prospects.

In the social sciences it is much easier for a state of affairs to exist in which there are competing paradigms rather than the single dominant one expected in 'mature' sciences. Nonetheless there are still ebbs and flows, struggles for dominance that can be charted. In our own field of leisure, sport and tourism this is complicated by the fragmentation that has occurred, creating more distinct areas of study.

When interest in leisure, sport and tourism really started to take off among academics and policymakers in the 1960s there was an empiricist emphasis on gathering data to learn how many were doing this or that.[2] The dominant disciplines in UK leisure studies at that time were geography and planning and after a while this data gathering became allied to multi-variate statistical modelling in an attempt to explain relationships and predict behaviour. Towards the end of the 1970s and through the 1980s more critical perspectives, inspired by neo-Marxist and, later, feminist writers, politicised the field as sociology took over as the dominant discipline. At about this time tourism studies became increasingly separated. A decade later and those structuralist perspectives were being challenged by postmodernists who questioned what they saw as the overly

---

[2]I'm basing my comments here on the UK. If you are based elsewhere you can work out how patterns differ there.

deterministic grand theories of previous decades, choosing to emphasise instead difference and choice. By now the distinction between sport and leisure research in the social sciences had become more marked, though following similar trajectories.

This 'story' is told from the perspective of the communities of researchers I see around me. If I was concerned with the study of elite sport rather than sport as a social phenomenon, for example, I would construct a different history of the development of sport research. Equally, despite international journals, our fields have tended to develop slightly differently in different countries. So while sociology might have become established as the dominant discipline in leisure research in the United Kingdom, in the United States it has been psychology and resource planning. Coalter (1997) has suggested that the more scientific approach to research in the United States has allowed more purposeful, incremental progress in a generally agreed direction.

One paragraph can hardly do justice to so much research and if your reading of the literature in leisure, sport and tourism suggests a different historical development, that is fine. The purpose here is to draw attention to what are referred to as different 'moments' or 'turns' in the development of a field of study. What is important is that you should reflect on how the way you view the world will affect the nature of your research and the findings it produces.

Within the field of leisure studies it is arguable (I would argue) that there is no dominant paradigm, indeed there has never been one. Writing some time ago, Rojek (1985) chose to see it as multi-paradigmatic because of the free borrowing from other disciplines. Although Henderson (1991) follows Kuhn (1962) in arguing that it is not possible to inhabit more than one paradigm, I have found it rewarding to explore what I call inter-paradigmatic space. Perhaps it is not surprising then that the idea of attempted triangulation comes naturally. Perhaps because of this in-between world, the multi-method approach (see, for example, Layder, 1993) comes fairly naturally to many leisure researchers.

Further Lines of Enquiry

In reading about your subject you are likely to come across several calls for a new paradigm or papers charting a paradigm shift. Some of the discussions of paradigms can seem very abstract, so you may find it easier to follow the review of the paradigms debate by Andy Sparkes (1992) which he sets in the context of physical education. Karla Henderson (1991) offered her take on paradigms in leisure, while Goodson and Phillimore (2004) do something similar for tourism.

16

Ways of Writing and Communicating

André Previn [exasperated]: You're playing all the wrong notes.

Eric Morecambe [pained]: No, I'm playing all the right notes, but not necessarily in the right order.

It should go without saying that there is little point in doing outstanding research if the findings are not communicated effectively to others. Indeed, without this skill the research may not even get underway, because it may be necessary to get ethical approval or, more generally, to get a research proposal accepted. Most of this chapter is about writing research, but there are other forms of communication in which researchers may engage. The chapter covers:

- identifying your audience and styles of writing
- putting together a proposal
- distinguishing between writing dissertations and reports
- wider dissemination of research findings.

Writing Style

The way the research story is written may determine whether or not anybody pays attention to it. At its most simple, a well written piece is easier for the reader to follow. In any field, writing tends to accord with generally accepted styles and conventions. Partly because of those established conventions, academic writing can seem very formal and put a barrier between the researcher and the reader, but alternative styles may suggest that the research does not deserve to be taken seriously. This book is written in quite a personalised style, which may equally alienate people because it can sound opinionated. After all, who is Jonathan Long to be telling us this?

Basically, writing effectively takes a lot of effort and a lot of practice. When writers talk about 'finding their voice' they are referring to trying to develop their own style of writing. You need to find a style that you feel comfortable with, but that will also appeal to your intended audience. The general public, those with a particular interest in your topic, your boss/tutor may all be keen to know about the research, but expect to read something of different length and at different levels of detail and complexity. And,[1] of course, styles vary according to the medium – proposal, dissertation, report, article for a professional magazine or academic journal, etc. You might be lucky and have a tutor/boss who is prepared to accept a dissertation/report written entirely in the style of text messaging, but as I write this I suspect they are few and far between even in an exciting area like leisure, sport and tourism. For better or worse there are conventions that people are expected to observe, but within those there is still plenty of scope for variation in expression. The obvious thing to do is to study how other people do it. That may identify good practice, or make you more aware of what you want to avoid.

> Never take as gospel what people writing in a book say you should do (even this one). Think about who you are writing for, and if possible check with them to see what they expect.

Let me start with some general points.

Keep it simple – People writing about their research can easily fall into the trap of believing that using big words and complex modes of expression will give their research greater credibility. 'At the commencement of the research …' What is that about? There is nothing wrong with the simpler 'start' or 'beginning'. Some people seem to keep a thesaurus beside them so that they can fit in as many big words as possible. It may work, but it is more likely to sound pretentious. The simpler alternative is usually preferable unless there is a real distinction that you are trying to draw attention to by the use of more complex language. People also use a thesaurus to avoid the repeated use of the same word. I am not persuaded of the merit of that either. This can get very confusing for the reader – better to find the word that best fits and stick with it. Why swap it for something that is second best? It is also better to write short sentences that address one main idea.

---

[1] Of course you cannot start a sentence with 'and'.

Avoid jargon – I think we have all been told this at one time or another – easier said than done. What has become accepted as everyday terminology by one group may be obscure to most others. Consider carefully whether your readers will understand what you mean by sustainable development, ethical tourism, intrinsic motivation, social capital, globalisation, Key Stage 3, etc. These problems are aggravated by the use of acronyms – e.g. KPIs for key performance indicators. Having read parts of this book, it may seem a bit rich that I suggest people should cut jargon from their writing. We could all try harder. Just because some other writer (even if it is me) does not always match the standards of plain speaking, it should not be taken as a sign that jargon improves communication. One of the common criticisms of researchers is that the theory they bang on about obscures the meaning by using grand sounding expressions. This is sometimes a fair criticism, but good theory, properly communicated, should make clear things that previously went unrecognised.

Using the first person – Some people insist that it is wrong to write in the first person (i.e. to use 'I' or 'we'). This comes from the scientific tradition which insisted that the personal should be kept out of research in order to remain objective and that to achieve that the researcher had to remain separate from the research. A rather different view is put forward by those who argue that we can only know and understand through awareness of ourselves. As such they place the personal researcher at the heart of the research endeavour and encourage the use of 'I' to make that clear. In my own writing the use of this pronoun varies depending upon the type of output (more common here than in a journal article, for example). I certainly do not subscribe to the 'never use I' position; on the other hand, excessive use of 'I' does appear to detract from the value of the research. Contrivances like the use of 'the researcher' to refer to yourself strike me as faintly ridiculous. Especially when reporting what you did, it seems to me perfectly sensible to use 'I' – it helps to remind people that the research findings were generated by a living, breathing human being, not some mechanical process. However, there are other ways of reducing the use of 'I'. For example, 'When I was interviewing I had to …' can be replaced by 'During the interviews it was important to …' So my general advice is to limit the use of 'I' but not at the expense of sounding unnatural.

Consider the tense you write in – Some consistency is helpful, but people often deviate from strict convention. For example, although it seems obvious to use the past tense when writing about findings/ideas from published literature or your own investigations, writers often deliberately use the present tense to make it seem more immediate. Moreover, on different occasions the tense may change for what appears to be the same thing. For example, while in your research proposal you should be using the future tense in your methodology section to explain what you plan to do, in the dissertation itself this should be written in the past tense reporting what you have done.

Provide structure – This can be helped by appropriate use of paragraphs and sub-headings. Try and make sure the reader knows where the argument is taking them by clustering like ideas together, arranging them in a logical sequence and explaining what is going on.

Avoid sexism and racism – Most of the professional associations expect members to adopt a non-sexist, non-racist style of writing and one that is not disparaging of people of other religions, with disabilities or different sexual orientation. This is in line with the ethical issues of respect for others discussed in Chapter 14. Some associations offer advice on what constitutes good practice, e.g. from the British Sociological Association on its website www.britsoc.co.uk. Some individuals may disagree with some of the suggestions, but reviewing them will make sure that unconscious errors are not made. Equally, different people will adopt different ways of avoiding inappropriate language. For example, it is clearly inappropriate to refer to an unspecified researcher, respondent, policymaker, child or basketball player as being 'he'. It may have been acceptable in the past to refer to all as 'he', but the thought is now considered bizarre. So people variously alternate he and she, or use he/she or (s)he.[2] Some writers prefer to use 'one', but nowadays this may be regarded as slightly pretentious. An alternative is to write in the plural, or even use 'they' as a singular substitute for either he or she.

Substantiate your arguments – You should not assume that assertions will satisfy your reader so give them enough supporting evidence for them to be persuaded that what you are saying is at least plausible.

Edit ruthlessly – It is hard to edit your own work and remove material that may have taken a long time to write, but is important to get rid of the waffle that was put there when you were worried how on earth you would have enough to write about. Cutting that out will give you the space to provide the kind of detail that readers need, for example, to understand how your findings were generated.

Individual foibles

We all have our pet hates. One of mine is the style of writing that strings together several nouns – e.g. 'organisation crisis management planning procedures'. Maybe I should remain calm, but I get upset when:

---

[2] Some feminist writers deliberately use 'she' throughout to draw attention to the way in which so many other authors have used 'he' unthinkingly.

- nouns substitute for verbs – e.g. I hope to read that 'the working group was given the task of _____ ' rather than 'was tasked with _____ '.
- nouns substitute for adjectives – e.g. team game (I deliberately chose one there that has become accepted into common parlance to show that things do change).
- adjectives becoming nouns – e.g. 'overweight' as in 'the modern disease of obesity and overweight'.

Others tell me that I am being unnecessarily pedantic and that in a few years what I find objectionable will be accepted as part of normal-speak [sic].[3] I also like to read something that at least approximates good grammar and I get irritated by the incorrect use of apostrophes. In standard writing they are used to denote possessives (belonging) and in writing speech they are used to mark missing letters (e.g. can't) – they do not represent plurals.

Reporting speech

As implied by the last sentence formal writing normally avoids the casual expressions we use in speech – hence 'cannot' instead of 'can't'. Speech is normally marked by being enclosed between inverted commas. Whether single or double inverted commas are used may depend on the publisher's house style, your personal preference or some convenience like using single inverted commas when quoting published sources and double inverted commas for reporting what your respondents have said. You may have to consider how faithfully you report what respondents have said. At first sight it may seem strange to do anything other than report exactly what was said, but it is not quite as straightforward as might initially appear.

- People typically do not speak in grammatically correct, coherent sentences, so you might decide to do a bit of tidying up.
- Some people speak with very broad accents or in strong dialect. Should you remain faithful to their original or represent what they have said in a way that is a bit closer to standard English? The answer may depend on your anticipated audience and how easy they will find it to follow what is being said.
- Some people use obscene and offensive language that you may be wary of repeating in its raw form.

---

[3]You will often see 'sic' used in academic papers. It comes from Latin, meaning 'thus'. Basically it is used to draw attention to something that doesn't appear right. This is done to indicate either: 'I know, I know, I've done it deliberately' if it is in the author's own writing; or, 'it may be a mistake, but that's what it said in the original' if referring to someone else's. Here it would have been more correct to say 'be accepted as the norm'.

Rules is rules

Any language is held together by grammatical rules. These are not just arbitrary; they allow us to follow more easily what has been written. Writers need to have a reasonable grasp of them, not just to be able to comply with them, but to know when it is acceptable to do something else (like splitting infinitives).

> A man approached the bus stop and asked the person standing there, 'What time's the next bus due at?' When the person he had asked pointed out to him that he should not end a sentence with a preposition, the immediate rejoinder was, 'OK then, what time's the next bus due at, you smug *&%^*! [expletive deleted]?' thereby complying with the rule.

'Rules' in grammatical terms are for guidance and the important thing is that what we write should be 'fit for purpose' (an expression that is itself grammatically suspect).[4] And in terms of the earlier discussion of sexist language, it could, of course, have been a woman approaching the bus stop, probably with a buggy and a shopping bag because in this sexist world it is women who have to …

It makes sense to use the checks for spelling and grammar that your word processing package offers, but unless it is better than mine, 'the computer' is not always right, and if you are unsure what the correct formulation should be it is of limited assistance.

Positive and Negative Inferences (values)

Even in the reporting of statistics the language used can make an enormous difference to people's understanding of the data. In Chapter 6 I mentioned a question we used in more than one survey that got a fairly consistent response:

> Most players at one time or another will receive abusive remarks from both players and spectators, but sometimes players get abuse because of the colour of their skin.
>
> Do you think this is:
>
> Acceptable/part of the game ☐
>
> Sometimes acceptable when they play badly ☐
>
> Never acceptable ☐

---

[4]Please don't go through this book and identify all the grammatical failings. It will keep you busy for far too long while you should be doing your research.

Approximately 87% thought it never acceptable. So:

- 'Only 13% thought it acceptable or sometimes acceptable that players should be abused because of the colour of their skin.'
- 'As many as 13% thought it acceptable or sometimes acceptable that players should be abused because of the colour of their skin.'

Is this a cause for celebration or regret?

> **IF IN DOUBT, DON'T OVER-ELABORATE**
>
> **KEEP IT SIMPLE**

Writing a Research Proposal

It is difficult to give standard advice about writing a research proposal because people do so in different circumstances. It may be as part of a tender in response to a brief issued by an organisation for a piece of contract research, or for a research council/trust, or for a committee/board, or for a dissertation/thesis. Whatever the circumstances, make sure you respond to the criteria provided by the people to whom the proposal will be presented.

A dissertation is only a small-scale piece of research, so rather than trying to arrive at definitive findings you should be designing a project that will allow you to demonstrate that you have acquired research skills and conducted a competent piece of work (other research may still be small-scale, but have more ambitious goals and perhaps be expected to inform decision-making). If the proposal is for a dissertation you need to formulate a research problem in theoretical terms that can be examined through empirical investigation (or an extended critique). More generally, a proposal should demonstrate to the assessor that you: know what you are doing, where you are headed and why; have some appreciation of what others have done and how that might help you; have thought through what you will actually do.

So whatever the scale of the research and its purpose, at its core the proposal should contain:

(a) the background to your chosen field and an explanation of why it is important and worthy of study (if it is for a dissertation this should also demonstrate its relevance to the course being studied).

(b) a precise statement of what your research problem is (including aims and objectives) – give the assessor confidence that the research is purposeful rather than drifting, and that it is achievable (Chapter 2).

(c) a thematic review of existing work in the field – clearly this cannot be a definitive literature review, but should demonstrate concisely that you are at least alert to the major contributions in the field (Chapter 3).

(d) your proposed methodology – you should demonstrate that you are aware of the methodological issues in the area you have chosen, and that your proposal represents a rigorous and viable approach. (It should specify precisely what information you need to address the challenge you have set yourself, where you will get that information, what instruments you will need to collect it and how you will analyse it. Project yourself forward so you can specify what you will actually be doing. You should also identify any ethical considerations or health and safety issues, though you may also have to complete a separate ethical release form.)

(e) a properly referenced bibliography (Chapter 3) – this should include only those publications to which you have referred in your proposal. (Any publications which you have identified as being likely to be useful to you, but which you have not yet been able to consult, may be included in a separate note.)

(f) a timetable (if required), setting out the various stages of your proposed project, and details of the research instruments you intend to use (draft questionnaire, interview checklist, observation schedule, time diary, etc.).

This is not necessarily a lengthy document, but it needs to be precise, explaining exactly *what* you are going to do and, very importantly, *why*. It should demonstrate clearly that you have got to grips with the issues in your chosen area and the practicalities of research. Of course the details may change once the research is underway, but having done the necessary groundwork you should be in a position to direct your project so that you make best use of your time at your desk and in the field.

One of my former mentors used to explain how he became suspicious when he read proposals that spent more time considering previous research than explaining what the proposed research would do. Before it revised its website, the Economic and Social Research Council made a similar observation about why applications for funding were unsuccessful:

> many applications are unsuccessful not because they lack interesting or important research ideas but because they fail to communicate adequately how these research ideas will be explored and translated into an achievable plan of action. Many applications devote too much space to explaining why the research is important and too little to detailing the research it is actually planned to conduct.

CAN YOU SEE THIS IN YOUR PROPOSAL?

Coherent argument

focus

clear definitions

thoughtful

precision

practical relevance

logical

link
to
theory

plan of action

responsible/ethical researcher

familiarity with the literature

methodological rigour

Some of the most common shortcomings
of research proposals:

- too grand in scope and not achievable – need to narrow the focus
- lack of clear and precise aims and objectives – alternatively they have already been achieved by previous research
- access to the people/environments needed is unlikely
- inadequate awareness of existing research – little evidence of reading.

Exercise

In the associated file on research methods resources at www.leedsmet.ac.uk/carnegie/default/jalong.htm you will find an outline proposal for 'Movers and Shakers'. Obviously it is not a 'real' proposal; it is intended to demonstrate the kinds of thing that should be addressed in a proposal. Does it comply with the advice offered here?

It will help your writing if you do a mock-up like this before you progress to the full proposal.

Writing a Dissertation

Always check what is expected on your course.

The abstract – These differ in size and construction depending upon circumstances, but the general form is: this is what I wanted to find out about (you might want to add in 'why'); this is what I did; and this is what I found out.

The introduction – should be based on the original proposal, explaining the basic research challenge and its significance.

The literature review (Chapter 3) – needs to distil the main ideas and provide a stepping-off point for your own investigation. One of the key features of a dissertation should be that the ideas identified as being important in this review recur elsewhere and are shown to be integrated into your research. One of the clearest indications that the literature review has been ripped-off from somewhere else is when it sits in splendid isolation, unconnected with the rest of the dissertation.

The methodology – contains an element of literature review too. However, few readers want to see yet another standard account of, for example, the difference between quantitative and qualitative techniques. Instead they want you to demonstrate that you are aware of the key methodological issues and have been able not only to identify good practice but to implement it. So in those circumstances I think it is better to use that literature to explain why you chose to conduct your research in the way you did. Remember to provide enough detail about how the research was carried out for the reader to be able to understand where the data have come from. Have you provided enough information to allow someone else to conduct a parallel study (same sampling procedure, research implements, administration, coding, etc.)?

Reporting findings – following the traditional scientific route, a simple, straightforward description of findings precedes and is kept separate from a discussion of their significance (you will find this model commonly adopted in some journals). Alternatively, in the social sciences it is not unusual to see the discussion integrated with the findings. Part of the trick is to convey the idea that the research was meticulous and rigorous (people need to feel that they can 'trust' it), while making it an interesting read. Few readers want an account that runs mechanistically question by question from 1 to 31 of your questionnaire. Similarly, few people want to read a straightforward recounting of the Director, Ms Clarke, saying this, this and this. You started out with some question(s) that interested you, so construct this section in a way that lets people see how the issues are beginning to be resolved. Think about alternative ways of presenting the data (Chapter 13)

Conclusions – Some people just provide a summary, but for a dissertation there ought to be something more. Although no new data should be appearing at this stage, you should be reflecting on the significance of what you have found out from the different elements of your research. Sometimes there may be an expectation that formal recommendations will be provided, but even if not it is important to work out the implications of your new knowledge, considering 'what it all means'. This section should 'close the circle' by linking back to the original research questions and the key ideas that emerged from the literature. The conclusions should not just be bright ideas that you have had, but should emerge naturally from the research.

There should be a clear thread from the initial idea through the specification of the research problem and the review of previous literature to the identification and conduct of appropriate methods, then the consideration of findings to the eventual conclusions.

Writing a Research Report

Make sure you comply with your organisation's house style.

Although the research that has been conducted may be very similar to what would be done for a dissertation, the output typically has to serve a different purpose and is directed to a different audience. This different audience may be quite varied. Whereas with a dissertation you know your primary audience is one or two lecturers on your course, a research report may have to be written for highly informed professionals, committee members responsible for decision-making, practitioners 'on the ground', or the wider public. These might all want a slightly different style and content.

The different audience may suggest the use of a different vocabulary, but beyond that some of the most common ways a research report might differ from a dissertation are:

- The emphasis tends to be more on practical application, and less emphasis is usually put on the literature review and methodology. The latter may be dealt with only cursorily or relegated to an appendix.
- Information is often presented in chunks rather than the smoother flowing text of a dissertation.
- Paragraphs are often numbered to help people refer to sections when the report is discussed by a committee or working party.
- Knowing that few have the time or inclination to read a lengthy research report, most such documents are now accompanied by a much shorter 'executive summary'.

It is sensible to clarify whether the people you are reporting to expect you to make recommendations or they see that as the business of their committee/working group. If they are to carry credibility, recommendations must be seen to come directly from the data, and obviously they need to represent measures that can realistically be put into practice.

Things can get difficult when whoever has commissioned the research feels they should be able to control what is in the report. It is important to recognise that what you write may put them in an awkward position, but what was the point in asking you to produce the report if the findings are to be adjusted for the sake of convenience?

At the end of the day

I enjoy writing about my research, but it is like decorating, always taking longer than expected. It is only fun if you have enough time to do a good job. Whatever else you do, make sure you leave time to proofread your proposal, report or dissertation and make the necessary corrections. After all it would be a terrible waste if slipshod work at this stage led to the product of all that 'blood, sweat and tears' being undervalued by your audience.

Alternative Presentations

Academics are often criticised for being bad at disseminating the results of their research. In light of the time and effort invested in the research, its findings should be brought to the attention of as many people as possible. As I have already mentioned, it is now common to provide an executive summary to get the main points across to people who do not have the time, commitment or stamina to read the full report. This may be anything from two to maybe a dozen pages depending upon the scale of the research being reported.

There are researchers who are concerned that the conventional ways of writing about research necessarily fail to capture the essence of the lives we are studying. Ethnographers in particular may look for more representational styles that reflect the lifeworld rather than the research laboratory (e.g. van Maanen, 1988). This might mean writing in a style that would be more familiar to the subjects of the research than to academics. In conjunction with this you may come across writers exhorting us to cut away from the restrictions of formal texts and to experiment with alternatives like poetry (see, for example, Sparkes, 1996). I recognise the power of poetry, but feel that researchers are probably not the best poets and we might better leave it to those who are. A wider audience might also be reached via video, an exhibition, illustrated web pages, articles for academic journals or professional magazines, and conference presentations – the latter sometimes take the form of a poster.

Oral presentations

If you get the chance to go along to present your findings to the people who commissioned the research, or other potential users, take it. It is now common for people to use PowerPoint slides as the basis of a presentation. I normally do, but

I have to say that I find it refreshing when people do not feel the need to do that. As you will know from being in the audience, the use of fancy PowerPoint slides no more guarantees a quality presentation than sophisticated statistical analysis or complex theory. More important are a confident and engaging style, persuasive data clearly presented and the identification of a few key issues for policy or practice. The standard advice if you are using slides is to limit the amount of information on any one slide and use a correspondingly large font size. It is a good idea to leave your audience with something tangible to remember the presentation by. Even if most bin it, it will act as a useful reminder for those who are interested.

You may also have the opportunity to present a paper at an academic or professional conference. The nature of these has changed substantially over the years. Speakers are more likely to be given 20 minutes than an hour and are more likely to present rather than read a paper. I feel like strangling those speakers who proceed to waste 10% of their session complaining that they have insufficient time to put forward their ideas. Better to be realistic about how much can be covered and content yourself with presenting that well rather than trying to cram in ever more information. First time speakers often worry about the questions they may be asked. Far worse is not to be asked any, so it might be worth priming the person chairing the session with a suitable question to avoid that awkward silence.

Video

There are many people who just do not want to read yet another report, and if you want to reach 'the public', a substantial proportion are unable to do so. Although it is still not common, researchers occasionally produce a video to communicate their findings. If this is the intention from the outset the video may evolve organically, but the final product will still need to be carefully constructed. If the video is a bit of an afterthought it is important to avoid people doing little more than speaking a cut down version of the text of the report. Just as it is easy to think anyone can write a questionnaire, most of us think we can make a video. Apart from the technical skills of handling the equipment, which are not trivial if it has to be of broadcast standard, writing an effective script is very different from writing the dissertations and reports discussed above. If it is going to end up like a report, it is easier just to write the report. Think about what video allows you to do differently. It can convey the environment in which people perform their leisure lives, the buzz of the club scene, the rush from extreme sports, or the sweat of the gym.

Dealing with the media

If one of the goals is to disseminate the research findings to the widest possible audience it is necessary to attract the interest of the mass media. This normally involves issuing a press release. A few points to note:

- Getting the timing right – Consider whether it is better to coincide with a big event or when they have nothing else to write about. For example, if you have been doing research on ethical holidays or ethics in sport, do you want the release to coincide with the main holiday season or the Olympics? That might give the reporters 'something to hang it on', but on the other hand they will not be short of things to write about. It might be better to wait until they are more hungry for a story, but by then the viewers/readers may no longer be interested in the subject.
- Start the press release with one or two findings to grab attention, then fill in details.
- This is one occasion when one or two sentence paragraphs are a good idea.
- Quotable quotes – Select quotes from someone in the research team, from a representative of the funding agency or someone who might be expected to use the research findings, and 'a name'.
- It may sound obvious, but always make sure people reading the release know how to get more information from you or your team.

If it is an important enough piece of research the press release may be accompanied by a press conference.

In a media interview you may find that the reporter/interviewer or producer has their own agenda. This can be awkward as they may then want you to talk about their idea of the key issues rather than what the research was really about. If the piece is being prepared for later it is possible to work together on material that will do justice to the research and also 'make a good story'. If the piece is going out live that comfort zone does not exist. Several years ago I was advised to note down a few key points and give that to the reporter/interviewer at the outset and make it quite clear that had to be the ground covered in the interview. It made me less nervous in advance, but like many good ideas it only worked on some occasions. The issue of style discussed at the beginning of this chapter becomes accentuated for radio and TV. Is it better to try to retain some gravitas to lend credibility to the findings or to be familiar to try to break down barriers?

Further Lines of Enquiry

In their book, on *Reading, Writing and Reasoning* Fairbairn and Winch (1996) manage to offer good advice without being dogmatic. Also helpful is Bell's (1999) book, *Doing Your Research Project*. Robson (1993) and Silverman (2000) offer useful advice on writing research proposals.

The online writing workshop from The University of New South Wales has been recommended to me: www.writingworkshop.edtec.unsw.edu.au/index.html.

There is a commendable Campaign for Plain English, whose website (www.plainenglish.co.uk) describes 'Plain English' as 'language that the intended audience can understand and act upon from a single reading'. Thomas and Nelson (2001) draw on Day's (1983) work to help their jargon-busting efforts.

A Few Reminders

- write for your audience
- keep it simple and effective – avoid sounding pompous
- cut out the unnecessary
- construct reasoned arguments rather than assert beliefs
- ensure a coherent thread through clearly structured sections
- leave time for checking, editing and redrafting
- avoid plagiarism like the plague.

Appendix: Glossary

Rather than being definitive this glossary is intended to provide an idea of the terms being used so that reading the book is not disrupted too much. As you read more widely you will arrive at more refined definitions of these terms.

Case study – examination of a particular individual/group/project.

Concept – a unity of thought representing an idea like 'power' or 'patriarchy' derived from a particular model of the world.

Construct – model devised on the basis of observation to relate the observed to a theoretical framework.

Critical approach – challenging presumptions about the nature or given order of the world, i.e. 'not taking things for granted'.

Cross-sectional – representative of different types/groups of people at a moment in time.

Discourse analysis – an interdisciplinary approach to the analysis of communication. It examines how speech/language is constructed to do a job in different circumstances.

Discrete – separate and distinct – when applied to variables it is usually counterposed with 'continuous' where the number of points on the scale is constrained only by the sophistication of the measuring equipment. So someone's height or income might be considered a continuous variable, whereas the number of 'leisure goods' they bought in the past week is a discrete variable. As the number of values on a discrete scale increases the distinction becomes of little consequence.

Ecological validity – rooted in the 'reality' of people's experiences rather than the contrived circumstances of the laboratory or questionnaire.

Emic – generated by the participant/respondent (**etic** – generated by the researcher).

Empathy – the process of putting yourself into other people's shoes in order to understand them better.

Empirical – based on (measurement derived from) observation and experiment.

Epistemology – on 'knowing', the relationship between the knower and the knowable; theory of knowledge; method – e.g. concerned with such problems as distinguishing spurious from genuine knowledge.

Ethnography – detailed description and analysis of cultural and social practices based on direct observation of activities.

Functionalism – that social events can best be explained in terms of the functions they perform for the continuation of society as an organic whole.

Generalisability – being able to make general statements about the population at large on the basis of particular cases/investigations.

Hermeneutics – process of interpretation, particularly of human behaviour and social institutions (+ discussions of the purpose of life).

Heuristic – helping to learn/discover/investigate.

Histogram – data display format that allows the representation of continuous (rather than discrete) variables.

Hypothesis – a suggestion about the state of affairs that is put forward as a basis for testing (i.e. subjected to verification/falsification) through subsequent investigation.

Inductive – moving from a set of observations/experiences to a conclusion beyond that information (**deductive** – proceding by logic from a set of premises to a conclusion such that if the premises are correct the conclusion must be correct).

Iterative – process of repetition to refine thoughts/process/etc.

Likert scale – a set of items to which respondents indicate the extent to which they agree/disagree.

Longitudinal – change over the course of time.

Member checking – allowing interviewees/participants to approve interview transcripts or analysis of data collected.

Meta analysis – comparison of the results of a series of previous studies to determine common trends and/or new insights.

Metaphysics – theory of concepts and their development.

Methodology – on how to discover 'knowledge'.

Mixed method – use of different research techniques in combination.

Non-parametric – statistics independent of assumptions about data being normally distributed from a random sample.

Normal distribution – when physically displayed, data exhibit the classic bell curve.

Objectivity – free from the values of the researcher, without bias or prejudice.

Ogive – cumulative frequency curve.

Ontology – nature of being, 'reality', the knowable; set of entities presupposed by a theory.

Paradigm – set of beliefs which influence what should be studied.

Parametric statistics – based on assumptions about the parameters of the population, most commonly that it is normally distributed and/or that each of the groups being examined has the same variance. When such assumptions are not justified a non-parametric alternative is needed.

Phenomenology – based on people's own experiences of the world and the constructs they use to make it understandable to them.

Population – all of the people within the category being investigated.

Positivism – holds that there is a world independent of the researcher and participants that can be objectively measured to establish social facts through the application of the scientific method to all forms of knowledge (observe and measure to test hypotheses).

Recursive – notion that we create the structures that create us and monitor our performances within those structures, and are monitored by others.

Reductionist – attempt to account for a range of phenomena in terms of a single determining factor.

Reflexivity – awareness of the impact of the researcher's own background and experience upon the work conducted (self-reflection and self-referral).

Relativism – position that holds phenomena can only be understood from within the culture and value systems that produce them; all knowledge is socially produced so there are no independent standards of truth; theory cannot provide criteria of truth independent of itself.

Reliability – degree to which the same methods used by different researchers and/or at different times produce the same results – consistency when repeated.

Sample – a sub-set selected from all items, units or people of interest to the investigation.

Sampling error – differences between measurements from the sample as opposed to the total population it represents.

Sampling frame – an exhaustive list of all items/people in the population from which the sampling is to be conducted.

Semantic differential – a scale based on bi-polar adjectives (e.g. cheap/expensive).

Semiotics – the study and interpretation of signs and symbols.

Structuralism – seeking to explain social phenomena by reference to the underlying structures of the mode of production (e.g. Althusser).

Surrogate – a measure used as a substitute for the one that is of central interest, because for one reason or another that is unavailable or unable to be measured.

Theory – rules linking a set of concepts, assumptions and procedures used for explanation/prediction.

Triangulation – a process by which different perspectives are brought to the research (e.g. through different sources of data or research methods and techniques).

Validity (external) – degree to which specific findings can be seen to be more generally applicable.

Validity (internal) – degree to which we are measuring what we say we are measuring.

Variable – something that can assume more than one value and can therefore be measured (e.g. income or motivations for choosing holiday destinations). The **independent variable** affects the **dependent variable** – e.g. age (IV) affects participation in leisure (DV).

Verstehen – to understand

Further Lines of Enquiry

If you want more sophisticated definitions, there are several disciplinary or research-based dictionaries available, e.g.: Schwandt, T. (1997) *Qualitative Inquiry: A Dictionary of Terms*. Thousand Oaks, CA: Sage; Vogt, W. P. (2005) *Dictionary of Statistics and Methodology: A Non-Technical Guide for the Social Sciences*, 3rd edn. Thousand Oaks, CA: Sage; and Miller, R. L. (2003) *The A-Z of Social Research: A Dictionary of Key Social Science Research Concepts*. Thousand Oaks, CA: Sage.

There are now also several aids online. For example, the US Environmental Protection Agency offers a glossary of terms used in evaluation: www.epa.gov/evaluate/glossary.htm.

References

Aguiló Pérez, E. and Rosselló Nadal, J. (2005) 'Host Community Perceptions: A Cluster Analysis', *Annals of Tourism Research*, 32(4): 925–41.

Becker, H. (1958) 'Problems of Inference and Proof in Participant Observation', *American Sociological Review*, 23(6): 652–60.

Becker, H. (1998) *Tricks of the Trade: How to Think about your Research While You're Doing it*. Chicago: University of Chicago Press.

Bell, J. (1999) *Doing Your Research Project*, 3rd edn. Buckingham: Open University Press. Originally published 1987.

Berger, J. (1972) *Ways of Seeing*. Harmondsworth: BBC/Penguin.

Blackshaw, T. (2003) *Leisure Life: Myth, Masculinity and Modernity*. London: Routledge.

Boelen, W.A.M. (1992) 'Street Corner Society: Cornerville Revisited', *Journal of Contemporary Ethnography*, 2(1): 11–51.

Bourdieu, P. (1984) *Distinction: A Social Critique Of The Judgement Of Taste*. London: RKP.

Brown, M. and Tinsley, H. (1983) 'Discriminant Analysis', *Journal of Leisure Research*, 15(4): 290–310.

Bryman, A. (1988) *Quantity and Quality in Social Research*. London: Unwin Hyman.

Bulmer, M (1977) 'Introduction: Problems, Theories and Methods in Sociology – (How) do they Interrelate?', in M. Bulmer (ed.), *Sociological Research Methods: An Introduction*. London: Macmillan Education. pp. 1–33.

Bulmer, M., Sturgis, P. and Allum, N. (2006) *The Secondary Analysis of Survey Data*. London: Sage.

Burgess, R. (ed.) (1982) *Field Research: A Sourcebook and Field Manual*. London: George Allen and Unwin.

Burgess, R. (1984) *In the Field: An Introduction to Field Research*. London: George Allen and Unwin.

Butler-Paisley, M. and Paisley-Butler, W.J. (1974) *Sexism in the Media: Frameworks for Research*. Paper presented to the annual meeting of the Association for Education and Journalism, San Diego.

Centre for Leisure and Sport Research (2001) *Community Views of Parks Services*. Unpublished report from CLSR. Leeds: Leeds Metropolitan University.

Chadwick, B., Bahr, H. and Albrecht, S. (1984) *Social Science Research Methods*. Englewood Cliffs, NJ: Prentice-Hall.

Clarke, A. (1993) 'Everybody Loves Somebody: Significant Signs in Leisure and Tourism', in C. Brackenridge (ed.), *Body Matters: Leisure Images and Lifestyles*, LSA Publication No. 47. Eastbourne: Leisure Studies Association. pp. 218–24.

Coalter, F. (1997) 'Leisure Sciences and Leisure Studies: Different Concept Same Crisis?', *Leisure Sciences*, 19(4): 255–68.

Coalter, F. (2002) *Sport and Community Development: A Manual*. Edinburgh: sportscotland.

Cohen, A.P. (1985) *The Symbolic Construction of Community*. London: Tavistock.

Cohen, J. (1977) *Statistical Power Analysis for the Behavioral Sciences*. New York: Academic.

Coleman, P. (1991) 'Ageing and Life History: The Meaning of Reminiscence in Later Life', in S. Dex (ed.), *Life and Work History Analyses: Qualitative and Quantitative Developments*. London: Routledge. pp. 120–43.

Corbin, J. and Strauss, A. (1990) 'Grounded Theory Research: Procedures, Canons, and Evaluative Criteria', *Qualitative Sociology*, 13(1): 3–21.

Dale, A., Arber, S. and Procter, M. (1988) *Doing Secondary Analysis*. London: Unwin Hyman.

Day, R. (1983) *How to Write and Publish a Scientific Paper*. Philadelphia, PA: ISI Press.

Denzin, N. (1970) *The Research Act*. Chicago, IL: Aldine.

Denzin, N. (1978) *Sociological Methods: A Source Book*, 2nd edn. New York: McGraw Hill.

de Vaus, D. (1991) *Surveys in Social Research*, 3rd edition. London: Allen and Unwin.

de Vaus, D. (2001) *Research Design in Social Research*. London: Sage.

de Vaus, D. (2002) *Surveys in Social Research*, 5th edition. London: Routledge.

Duffield, B., Long, J., with Dowers, S. and Vaughan, D.R. (1987) *Tourism and the Economy of Scotland*. Edinburgh: Scottish Tourist Board.

Fairbairn, G. and Winch, C. (1996) *Reading, Writing and Reasoning: A Guide for Students*. Buckingham: Open University Press.

Fink, A. (1995) *How to Ask Survey Questions*. Thousand Oaks, CA: Sage.

Frankenburg, R. (1982) 'Participant observers', in R.G. Burgess (ed.), *Field Research: A Sourcebook and Field Manual*. London: Allen & Unwin. pp. 50–2.

Gans, H. (1962) *The Urban Villagers*. Free Press: New York.

Geertz. C. (1973) *The Interpretation of Cultures*. New York: Basic Books.

Glancy, M. (1986) 'Participant Observation in the Recreation Setting', *Journal of Leisure Research*, 18(2): 59–80.

Glaser, B.G. and Strauss, A.L. (1967) *The Discovery of Grounded Theory: Strategies For Qualitative Research*. Chicago, IL: Aldine.

Goffman, E. (1961) *Encounters: Two Studies in the Sociology of Interaction*. Indianapolis: Bobbs-Merrill.

Goffman, E. (1963) *Behaviour in Public Places: Notes on the Social Organization of Gatherings*. New York: Free Press.

Gold, R. (1969) 'Roles in Sociological Field Observation', in G. McCall and J. Simmons (eds), *Issues in Participant Observation*. Reading, MA: Addison-Wesley. pp. 30–9. (Re-published in Bryman, A. (ed.) (2001) *Ethnography. Volume 2: Ethnography Fieldwork Practice*. London: Sage.)

Goodson, L. and Phillimore, J. (2004) 'The Inquiry Paradigm in Qualitative Tourism Research', in L. Goodson and J. Phillimore (eds), *Qualitative Research in Tourism: Ontologies, Epistemologies and Methodologies*. London: Routledge. pp. 30–45.

Grusky, O. (1963) 'Managerial Succession and Organisational Effectiveness', *American Journal of Sociology*, 69(1): 21–31.

Guba, E. (1990) *The Paradigm Dialog*. Newbury Park, CA: Sage.

Hakim, C. (1982) *Secondary Analysis of Social Research*. London: George Allen & Unwin.

Hedges, B. (1986) *Personal Leisure Histories*. London: Sports Council/ESRC.

Henderson, K. (1991) *Dimensions of Choice*. State College, PA: Venture.

Higgs, C., Weiller, K. and Martin, S. (2003) 'Gender Bias in the 1996 Olympic Games: A Comparative Analysis', *Journal of Sport and Social Issues*, 27(1): 52–64.

Hoinville, G., Jowell, R. and associates (1977) *Survey Research Practice*. London: Heinemann.

Hollingshead, A. (1949) *Elmtown's Youth: The Impact of Social Classes on Adolescents*. New York: Wiley.

Holt, N. and Dunn, J. (2004) 'Toward a Grounded Theory of the Psychosocial Competencies and Environmental Conditions Associated with Soccer Success', *Journal of Applied Sport Psychology*, 16(2): 199–214.

Holt, N. and Sparkes, A. (2001) 'An Ethnographic Study of Cohesiveness in a College Soccer Team over a Season', *The Sport Psychologist*, 15(3): 237–59.

Iso-Ahola, S.E. (1980) *The Social Psychology of Leisure and Recreation*. Dubuque, IA: William C. Brown.

Iso-Ahola, S. and Weissinger, E. (1990) 'Perceptions of Boredom in Leisure: Conceptualization, Reliability and Validity of the Leisure Boredom Scale', *Journal of Leisure Research,* 22(1): 1–17.

Jones, S. (1985) 'The Analysis of Depth Interviews', in R. Walker (ed.), *Applied Qualitative Research*. Aldershot: Gower.

Kinnear, P. and Gray, C. (2004) *SPSS 12 Made Simple*. Hove: Psychology.

Kish, L. (1949) 'A Procedure for Objective Respondent Selection within a Household', *Journal of the American Statistical Association*, 44: 380–7.

Kuhn, T. (1962) *The Structure of Scientific Revolutions*. Chicago: University of Chicago Press.

Kuhn, T. (1970) *The Structure of Scientific Revolutions*, 2nd edn. Chicago: University of Chicago Press.

Layder, D. (1993) *New Strategies in Social Research*. Cambridge: Polity.

Leisure Industries Research Centre (2003) *Sports Volunteering in England, 2002*. London: Sport England.

Long, J. and Wimbush, E.J. (1985) *Continuity and Change: Leisure Around Retirement*. London: Sports Council/ESRC.

Long, J. and Wray, S. (2003) 'It Depends Who You Are: On Asking Difficult Questions in Leisure Research', *Loisir et Société*, 26(1): 169–82.

Long, J., Wimbush, E. and Duffield, B. (1988) *Craigroyston and Community Schooling*. Edinburgh: Centre for Leisure Research/Lothian Regional Council.

Long, J., Hylton, K., Welch, M. and Dart, J. (2000) *Part of the Game: An Examination of Racism in Grass Roots Football*. London: Kick It Out.

Long, J., Nesti, M., Carrington, B. and Gilson, N. (1997) *Crossing the Boundary: A Study of the Nature and Extent of Racism in Local League Cricket.* Leeds: Leeds Metropolitan University.

Long, J., Welch, M., Bramham, P., Hylton, K., Butterfield, J. and Lloyd, E. (2002) 'Count Me In: The Dimensions of Social Inclusion through Culture and Sport'. Report to the Department for Culture Media and Sport. www.lmu.ac.uk/ces/lss/research/countmein.pdf.

McCall, G.J. and Simmons, J.L. (eds) (1969) *Issues in Participant Observation.* Reading, MA: Addison-Wesley.

Manning, P. (1987) *Semiotics and Fieldwork,* Sage University Paper series on Qualitative Research Methods, 7. Newbury Park, CA: Sage.

Marsh, C. (1982) *The Survey Method.* London: George Allen and Unwin.

Marsh, C. (1988) *Exploring Data.* Cambridge: Polity.

Mason, J. (1996) *Qualitative Researching.* London: Sage.

Mass Observation (1987) *The Pub and the People*, 2nd edn. London: The Cresset Library.

May, T. (2001) *Social Research.* Buckingham: Open University Press.

Messner, M., Duncan, M. and Cooky, C. (2003) 'Silence, Sports Bras, and Wrestling Porn: The Treatment of Women in Televised Sports News and Highlights', *Journal of Sport and Social Issues*, 27(1): 38–51.

Miles, M.B. and Huberman, A.M. (1994) *Qualitative Data Analysis: A Sourcebook of New Methods*, 2nd edn. London: Sage.

Miller, R.L. (2003) *The A-Z of Social Research: A Dictionary of Key Social Science Research Concepts.* Thousand Oaks, CA: Sage.

Mills, C.W. (1959) *The Sociological Imagination.* New York: Oxford University Press.

Nichols, G. (2005) 'Reflections on Researching the Ability of Sports Interventions to Reduce Youth Crime: The Hope of Scientific Realism', in K. Hylton, J. Long and A. Flintoff (eds), *Evaluating Sport and Active Leisure for Young People.* Eastbourne: Leisure Studies Association. pp. 23–44.

Nichols, G. and Taylor, P. (1996) *West Yorkshire Sports Counselling – Final Evaluation Report.* Sheffield: Leisure Management Unit, University of Sheffield.

Norman Chester Centre, Sir (1999) *The FA Premier League National Fan Survey, 1999.* Leicester: the Centre.

Northedge, A. (1990) *The Good Study Guide.* Milton Keynes: The Open University.

Ntoumanis, N. (2001) *A Step-by-Step Guide to SPSS for Sport and Exercise Studies.* London: Routledge.

Oliver, P. (2003) *The Student's Guide to Research Ethics.* Maidenhead: Open University Press.

Oppenheim, A.N. (1992) *Questionnaire Design, Interviewing and Attitude Measurement*, 2nd edn. London: Pinter.

Patrick, J. (1973) *A Glasgow Gang Observed.* London: Eyre Methuen.

Patton, M. (1978) *Utilization-focused Evaluation.* Beverly Hills, CA: Sage.

Patton, M. (1990) *Qualitative Research and Evaluation Methods*, 2nd edn. Thousand Oaks, CA: Sage.

Patton, M. (2002) *Qualitative Research and Evaluation Methods*, 3rd edn. Thousand Oaks, CA: Sage.

Pawson, R. and Tilley, N. (1997) *Realistic Evaluation.* London: Sage.

Payne, G. and Williams, M. (2005) 'Generalization in Qualitative Research', *Sociology*, 39(2): 295–314.

Policy Action Team 10 (1999) *Arts & Sport: A Report To The Social Exclusion Unit*. London: Department for Culture, Media and Sport.

Popper, K. (1959) *The Logic of Scientific Discovery*. London: Hutchinson.

Pritchard, A. (2001) 'Tourism and Representation: A Scale for Measuring Gendered Portrayals', *Leisure Studies*, 20(2): 79–94.

Putnam, R.D. (2000) *Bowling Alone: The Collapse and Revival of American Community*. New York: Simon & Schuster (Touchstone).

Robson, C. (1993) *Real World Research*. Oxford: Blackwell.

Robson, C. (2000) *Small Scale Evaluations*. London: Sage.

Rojek, C. (1985) *Capitalism and Leisure Theory*. London: Tavistock.

Ryan, C. and Martin, A. (2001) 'Tourists and Strippers: Liminal Theatre', *Annals of Tourism Research*, 28(1): 140–63.

Sabo, D., Jansen, S., Tate, D., Duncan, M. and Leggett, S. (1996) 'Televising International Sport: Race, Ethnicity and Nationalistic Bias', *Journal of Sport and Social Issues*, 20(1): 7–21.

Saipe, R. (1995) 'An Ethnographic Study of a Night Club: A Researcher's Experience', in J. Long (ed.), *Nightmares and Successes: Doing Small Scale Research in Leisure*. Leeds: Leeds Metropolitan University. pp. 49–55.

Sapsford, R. and Jupp, V. (eds) (1996) *Data Collection and Analysis*. London: Sage.

Schwandt, T. (1997) *Qualitative Inquiry: A Dictionary of Terms*. Thousand Oaks, CA: Sage.

Scott, J. (1990) *A Matter of Record: Documentary Sources in Social Research*. Cambridge: Polity.

Silverman, D. (2000) *Doing Qualitative Research: A Practical Handbook*. London: Sage.

Silverman, D. (2001) *Interpreting Qualitative Data: Methods for Analysing Talk, Text and Interaction*, 2nd edn. London: Sage.

Silverman, D. (2004) *Doing Qualitative Research: A Practical Handbook*, 2nd edn. London: Sage.

Sirakaya, E. and Sonmez, S. (2000) 'Gender Images in State Tourism Brochures: An Overlooked Area in Socially Responsible Tourism Marketing', *Journal of Travel Research*, 38(4): 353–62.

Sparkes, A. (1992) 'The Paradigms Debate: An Extended Review and a Celebration of Difference', in A. Sparkes (ed.), *Research in Physical Education: Exploring Alternative Visions*. London: Falmer Press. pp. 9–60.

Sparkes, A. (1996) 'The Fatal Flaw: A Narrative of the Fragile Body-Self', *Qualitative Inquiry*, 2(4): 463–494.

Sport England (2001) *Performance Measurement for the Development of Sport – A Good Practice Guide for Local Authorities. Main report*. London: Sport England.

Spradley, J. (1980) *Participant Observation*. New York: Holt, Rinehart and Winston.

Stockdale, J. (1985) *What is Leisure? An Empirical Analysis of the Concept of Leisure and the Role of Leisure in People's Lives*. London: Sports Council and Economic & Social Research Council.

Strategy Unit and Department for Culture, Media and Sport (2002) *Game Plan: A Strategy for Delivering Government's Sport and Physical Activity Objectives*. London: Strategy Unit.

Strauss, A. and Corbin, J. (1990) *Basics of Qualitative Research: Grounded Theory Procedures and Techniques*. Newbury Park, CA: Sage.

Tabachnick, B. and Fidell, L (2000) *Using Multivariate Statistics*. Needham Heights, MA: Allyn and Bacon.

Thomas, J. and Nelson, J. (1990) *Research Methods in Physical Activity*, 2nd edn. Champaign, IL: Human Kinetics.

Thomas, J. and Nelson J. (2001) *Research Methods in Physical Activity*, 4th edn. Champaign, IL: Human Kinetics.

Tomlinson, A. (1989) 'Whose Side Are They On? Leisure Studies and Cultural studies in Britain', *Leisure Studies*, 8(2): 97–106.

US Department of Health and Human Service (2002) *Physical Activity Evaluation Handbook*. Atlanta, GA: US Department of Health & Human Services, Centres for Disease Control and Prevention.

van Maanen, J. (1979) 'The Fact of Fiction in Organizational Ethnography', *Adminstrative Science Quarterly*, 24: 539–611.

van Maanen, J. (1988) *Tales of the Field: On Writing Ethnography*. Chicago: University of Chicago Press.

Vaughan, D.R. and Long, J. (1982) 'Tourism as a Generator of Employment: A Preliminary Appraisal of the Position in Britain', *Journal of Travel Research*, 11(2): 27–31.

Vogt, W.P. (2005) *Dictionary of Statistics and Methodology: A Non-Technical Guide for the Social Sciences*, 3rd edn. Thousand Oaks, CA: Sage.

Wacquant, L. (1992) 'The Social Logic of Boxing in Black Chicago: Toward a Sociology of Pugilism', *Sociology of Sport*, 9: 221–54.

Wacquant, L. (1995) 'The Pugilistic Point of View: How Boxers Think and Feel about their Trade', *Theory and Society*, 24: 489–535.

Wacquant, L. (2003) *Body and Soul: Notebooks of an Apprentice Boxer*. Oxford: Oxford University Press.

Walker, G., Hinch, T. and Weighill, J. (2005) 'Inter- and Intra-Gender Similarities and Differences in Motivations for Casino Gambling', *Leisure Sciences*, 27(2): 111–30.

Wegner, L., Fisher, A. and Muller, M. (2002) 'Reliability of the Leisure Boredom Scale for Use with High School Learners in Cape Town, SA', *Journal of Leisure Research*, 34(3): 340–50.

Weiss, C. (1998) *Evaluation: Methods for Studying Programs and Policies*, 2nd edn. West Jersey: Prentice Hall.

Wheaton, B. (2000) '"Just do it": Consumption, Commitment and Identity in the Windsurfing Subculture', *Sociology of Sport Journal,* 17(3): 254–74.

Wheaton, B. (2003) *Lifestyle Sport: Consumption, Identity and Difference*. London: Routledge.

Whyte, W.F. (1943) *Street Corner Society*. Chicago: Chicago University Press.

Whyte, W.F. (1955) *Street Corner Society*, 2nd edn. Chicago: Chicago University Press.

Whyte, W.F. (1982) 'Interviewing in field research', in R.G. Burgess (ed.), *Field Research: A Sourcebook and Field Manual*. London: Allen & Unwin. pp. 111–22.

Whyte, W.F. (1984) *Learning from the Field*. Newbury Park, CA: Sage.

Wolcott, H.F. (1995) *The Art of Fieldwork*. Walnut Creek, CA: AltaMira Press.

Znaniecki, F. (1934) *The Method of Sociology*. New York: Farrer & Rinehart.

Index

Please note that page references to non-textual information such as Figures or Tables are in *italic* print. Titles of publications beginning with 'A' or 'The' will be filed under the first significant word. Numbers (e.g. 20) are filed as if spelled out (e.g. twenty).